GENEVIEVE BOAST

·········· **TOUGH** ··········

BLISS

RESTORYING LIFE

"You must tell the story that unites."

Copyright © Genevieve Boast, 2018

The right of Genevieve Boast to be identified as the author of this work has been asserted by her in accordance with the Copyright, Designs and Patents Act 1988.

All rights reserved. No part of this publication may be reproduced, stored in a retrieval system or transmitted in any form or by any means (electronic, mechanical, photocopying, recording or otherwise), without the prior written permission of the author.

ISBN: 978-1-979726-25-2

This book is dedicated
to the boundless adventure
of being human

GRATITUDES

It's clichéd, but completely honest, to express gratitude for each and every person and experience in my life that has helped to create my story as you read it here. Without every one of them, I would not be who I am and this book wouldn't have been written. That being said, I have some specific gratitudes to express:

To my friend, Mike Smith, who was the spark that ignited the flame of this book and who spent many hours editing the text.

To my sister, Kelsey, without whose eagle eyes for grammar, the story wouldn't have made sense.

To Simone Muller for challenging me to push the edges of my comfort zone.

To my rainforest friend, Kira, whose exquisite artwork graces the cover and chapters.

To my friend and teacher, Brooke Medicine Eagle, for writing a Foreword that inspires us to bridge our past and future human stories.

To Lawrence, Rosa, Barbara and Giles, for taking the time to read and write beautiful recommendations that encouraged me to keep going.

To my elder sister, Tanah, for inspiring and guiding me to the truth of universal law.

To Ant and Tash for helping me to tell my story from the place of power beyond words.

To the incredible team at The Write Factor who helped me to publish this story and bring it to the world.

To my mother, father and sisters, who chose to walk beside me through my darkness and my light.

Most importantly to Euan and my two partners in crime, Alex and Liv. Without them, I would never have grown up or felt safe enough to do my real work.

My eternal gratitude to the ancestors and future ones who have, and always will, play a part in our unfolding human story, and to my earth and star family who have been there to guide and support me in eternity.

Thank you.
All of you.
From the depths of my soul.

RECOMMENDATIONS

Reading *Tough Bliss* is the literary equivalent of taking a long, hard look in the mirror and then learning to love what you see.

—Rosa Martin,
Co-Founder of Liquid School

Tough Bliss is a gift to humanity. Gen Boast shares her sacred, expansive life journey with raw honesty and deep self-awareness to reassure us to trust life.

—Barbara Savage,
Founder, Tribal Trust Foundation

Genevieve Boast's extraordinary book, *Tough Bliss*, is a combination of searingly honest autobiographical narrative, philosophical treatise and 'how-to' self-help manual, that combines the practical with the sacred and mystical. It touches on meditation, Christian mysticism, Native American wisdom and shamanism. The combination simply shouldn't work – yet amazingly it does, engaging the reader in a rollercoaster ride that switches from sad to glad and profoundly moving. She tells the disruptive story of her personal journey from Colorado to Cambridge, UK; from police arrest to whistle-blower; from loss to love and ultimate triumph on her spiritual quest. Be ready to be changed by reading this profound and thoughtful book.

—Michael Smith,
author of The Sound of Silence,
The Fullness of Life and Great Company

To have a friend is not necessarily to truly know a friend with all their vulnerabilities and bliss. And, if to know a friend is really to have a true friend, then Genevieve Boast will have more true friends than anyone on earth! The vulnerability she demonstrates in *Tough Bliss* is nothing less than awesome.

She achieves this heroism on each page. *Tough Bliss* is truly a handbook on how to become a full human. Using herself as a laboratory, Gen is able, like that famous beer, to reach the parts that other autobiographies and manuals just cannot reach. This is not a mere oil change or 50,000-mile service. This is a total engine change.

—Lawrence Bloom,
Secretary General, Be Earth Foundation

Welcome to a swirling rollercoaster of a read; with profundity and breathtaking flare in equal measure and at every turn – this is a book overflowing with magic and drama. Scintillating stuff!

—Giles Hutchins,
Thought Leader, Author and Speaker

CONTENTS

Gratitudes	vii
Recommendations	ix
Foreword – by Brooke Medicine Eagle	xiii
Beginning	**1**
The Spark	**15**
Who am I? Who am I really?	17
The Tests	**41**
What does my suffering teach me?	43
The Clues	**73**
How is my life giving me the answers I seek?	75
Metamorphosis	**125**
Are we prepared to let old parts of us die so that we can be reborn?	127
The Gifts	**181**
How can I give and receive the gifts of life?	183
Unity	**243**
How am I interconnected with the universe?	245
Epilogue	303
Dibliography	309
Notes	315
Index	317

FOREWORD

My wonderful friend Angeles Arrien and I once gathered a retreat group in the Bahamas, focused around the telling of our stories, and what happened was remarkable. Participants were able to be truly heard regarding their past and then move forward into sharing the visionary tale of their futures. People came alive, connected and gave voice to a deeper level of themselves than I'd ever seen in such a short time together. Our personal stories didn't separate us so much as unite us – the common story of our human foibles and challenges – and then the inspiring tale of our highest dreams was shared by all.

That powerful process awaits you here and I know no better guide than Genevieve. Her deep and broad intelligence and her 'heart-full' awareness will be marvelous guides for you.

We are, indeed, at a time of challenge and crisis in the world today. The word 'crisis' has its roots in 'cross-road' and surely we stand at a point where the choices we make will be critical. Will we be able to imagine, tell and live into a new story of connection, caring and cooperation on earth – to carry ourselves forward, leaving behind the old tales of destruction, degradation and dis-ease that lead to death? If we are to do that, we must awaken and do it consciously, so that the story is truly a new and radiant one, yet based in the ancient and magical perception of our connectedness to All Things.

This is a choice and a process, leading to transfiguration of ourselves as well as empowerment of our actions to make a difference with this one precious life we are given. AND IT MUST BE DONE WITH HEART!

Let me tell you a story of an amazing being who walked across the water into central America a few thousand years ago, bringing a teaching of love from the heart and oneness with each other and the great Creator. He was called Quetzalcoatl, Feathered Serpent, Lord of Wind and Water – among many other names. Another name he was known by was Dawn Star, for he prayed to the dawn star, Venus, every morning with his group of disciples and was himself seen as the dawning star of a whole new day on earth, where love and brother/sisterhood would create a golden time. And a radiant time ensued as people followed his way, using their resources in positive and empowering ways for the good of the people rather than in judgment and warring. This 'new day' on earth is seen by the Apache people as the time of the 8-pointed star – Venus, Star of the Heart – and perhaps is the same as the Piscean Age acknowledged in esoteric circles, a 2,160-year period in which our charge as humans is to learn to 'walk the path with heart'. We will then be able to move into the time of the 9-pointed star, represented by the throat chakra, which symbolizes our creating a golden time of abundance and harmony on earth.

So, Dawn Star moved among the people sharing his Flower Song teachings and eventually made his way back to his central temple in Golden Tula. There, he offered his final words before leaving. It's said that people from many lands gathered and formed a circle 20 miles deep and that when Dawn Star spoke, people of every culture and at the farthest distance heard and understood his powerful words.

He said, "*We have come to a critical time, a crossroads. We have created a very beautiful time, and IF you continue these ways of unity and love, your lives and the earth will grow in beauty into a golden time and the feats you accomplish will be even more powerful than mine.*" Yet, with some sadness, he continued with these words, knowing that the people were not ready and able to keep the practice and ways strong. "*If you do not keep these ways of love and unity, if you separate and divide and judge and fight, you will fall so far that standing here in Golden Tula on this radiant day, it seems inconceivable.*" And the people could not keep those ways, so what ensued on the American continent was genocide – native tribes warred and joined with incoming foreigners to attempt domination over others and everyone lost. It was a nightmare beyond imagining.

So, here we are again in our time, facing a crossroads. It is a critical time for us to make positive choices, to choose a story of love and cooperation, caring and sharing and reconnection with all life, so that we can manifest a golden time for earth, rather than the destruction and neglect that now holds sway. Now, more than ever, we must find our own story of empowerment and joyful service. And this book offers a way forward.

First, we must find our unique purpose for living – and Dawn Star reminded us that our purpose is set in our heart. We can find the spark that ignites it and live our lives through its wisdom and guidance. Then, rather than look at our challenges and tests as negative and defeating, we must see these as quests on our hero or heroine's journey to empowerment and wisdom. It is not easy for a butterfly to emerge from her cocoon, but the transformation strengthens her muscles and enables her to fly. Similarly, we must build the 'muscles' and intent to move forward in a good way, seeing our challenges in a more positive light, and encountering them with courage and even humor helps us move forward, discovering and awakening our gifts and talents. We look for answers, more often finding clues rather than solutions, and must stay awake to see and follow them. Clarifying what we seek, we learn through the journey – the journey that is our life. Finding that the essence lies within us, we then can pour that knowing through our hearts into the larger world, healing ourselves and our world.

OUR PURPOSE IS SET IN OUR HEART.

Yet, before the full awakening to our divine plan, we must dissolve and leave behind that which does not work, which does not serve us. That process is frightening – it is a leap into the unknown. Our core values will be our guide through 'the night of unknowing' where true transformation takes place, and thus, the turning outward to offer ourselves is made easier and more powerful as we have done our homework in the first stages of growth. We have matured into making our own unique offering in the world, strengthened and tempered in the fires of our challenges. We listen to the call of life and answer it with joy and power – and life gifts us with support in return. Our real beauty begins to blossom as we learn to give away our most radiant essence in concert with others.

Now, we come into the practice and power of unity. White Buffalo Calf Pipe Woman, who brought the sacred pipe (*chanupa*) and its teaching of wholeness, holiness and unity, gave me an interesting message in a recent meditation. I was asking about when we would actually be coming into this prophesied golden time and she said, *"Whenever you are caring, cooperating, sharing, loving, unifying, you ARE in the new time. And whenever you are judging, separating, damaging or fighting, you are in the old time, and the old time is passing. Choose well your ways of living!"*

More and more we understand her message through the awakening in science to the unified field – that we are, in fact, all connected. *"Whatever you do to any other being or thing in the circle of life, you do to yourself, for you are One,"* White Buffalo Woman reminds us. And she, along with other high teachers, reminds us that when we work together, we have tremendous power. That power is needed to make a positive difference in our lives and our world.

So, I commend you to the process and the guidance provided here to restory your life and the life of earth. As Black Elk,[1] the Lakota holy man, prayed: *"May the hoop of life be mended, the tree of life blossom in its center and birds sing in its branches."*

Mitakuye oyasin, for All My Relations.

—BROOKE MEDICINE EAGLE,
AUTHOR AND TEACHER, ANISE, FRANCE

BEGINNING

My mouth is dry and my heart is beating fast, sounding like the pounding waves of a turbulent ocean in my ears. I see a vast sea of faces looking expectantly back at me. They are encouraging, seeking and inviting me to speak. A thought flickers through my mind that brings with it panic. '*I can't believe you are going to tell them this,*' the voice inside me whispers. I have told no more than a handful of people this story in my lifetime. For a moment, I almost lose my ability to speak, my tongue drying against the roof of my mouth, but then a deeper feeling takes over. It is a sense of being guided by a force greater than my mind: an impulse greater than my human persona. A current of energy starts to flow through the cells of my lived experiences to my mouth and outwards, towards the awaiting ears and hearts of the audience: "*I was 17 when a police cell changed the course of my life...*"

I see a young man in the back row look up from his cell phone and lean forward. His eyes tell me he is engaged and I now know why this story wants to speak.

"*That was amazing!*" I said looking at my friend and colleague. I had just spent an evening listening to the groundbreaking sustainability projects that his organization had been leading across the globe. "*How can I help you in your work?*" I asked, humbled to be offering my services and energy to such causes.

He paused and then turned his broken office chair in order to face me directly. Slowly, he placed both his hands on my shoulders and, looking me deeply in the eyes, he said, "*You must share your *stories, Gen. The world needs to hear them. That is how you can best help me and everyone else."*

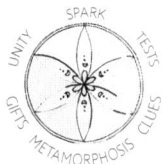

Somewhere in the back of my awareness I notice the rain lashing and splattering against the windows of our bedroom. Sighing in resignation at the late summer weather, I languidly pick up a book that I have recently purchased at the suggestion of a friend. Flicking through its pages, my thumb stops on a section close to the end. Interested to see whether synchronicity or coincidence holds a message for me, I open the page and see one small paragraph against an otherwise empty expanse of blankness. It reads: 'When one woman has the courage to tell her story, the whole world will change.'

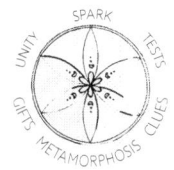

Moving beyond our human stories

Our human world is made of stories. They flow through the veins of our societies like blood; unseen and yet vital to the course of our lives. They are our primary way of making sense of our experiences and the direction we are headed, personally and collectively.

The problem is that most of us are deeply unsatisfied with the stories that we tell. We are living our lives swimming in the waters of narratives that don't feel true anymore. We exist confined within the fairy tales of what we are told will make us happy, fulfilled or successful. Most of what we have been told and sold is a lie: or at least a partial truth. Deep down, the myth of 'me' (the more power, material possessions, financial wealth I personally have, the happier I will be) is no longer working for the vast majority of people on the planet. This story is making us and our planet sick. It is the story of separation, superiority and hierarchical social success yet it ignores our basic human need for connection, meaning and belonging to something larger than ourselves.

To be clear, there are many nuances to the stories of 'me' and 'we' that will be explored as we journey through this book together. I am not advocating that we return to a narrative of communism or the archaic mythic consciousness of ancient cultures. What I am suggesting is that when we dive deeply and honestly into our unique human story – when, during that process, we ask important questions such as *'Who am I?'* and *'What is the purpose of me being here?'* – we are led back to a deep and ancient gnosis of our inherent interconnection and unity with the ecosystem of life itself. This is the story of 'we' in its biggest sense.

Our modern myths need a re-examination and redesign in the face of the problems they have caused to our human and planetary systems. From birth, we are submerged in the murky depths of our society's cultural narrative and trained to conform to this story, just like actors learn their lines in a play. Yet, for most of us, it is not the real story we yearn to bring alive through our lives. The mask we learn to wear hides our true mythic face that, if ignored for long enough, leads us into dis-ease and despair. Why do you think so many people are in a constant state of stress and suffering?

This hunger for a new, more authentic story appears in that nagging feeling in the middle of the night when you awake with your heart full of an unexplained and unexamined anxiety. It is the ever present mild tension that we try to ignore or numb with the busyness of life/addiction/escapism. It is the part of us that we have learned to block out; the memories we have tried to leave behind; the things we were told as children were not 'good enough'. These subtle but insistent voices are parts of our unique human story that whisper to us, calling us forward out of our (dis)comfort zones towards the adventure of an authentic life lived fully, vitally and beautifully.

When we can no longer ignore the voice of our discontent, we find our way to the initiation of our 'unmasking' where, by one means or another, we are given the tools that allow us to know ourselves, beneath the cloak of our socialization, often for the first time. This process of acknowledging our true self, values and dreams renders us able to transform the narratives that have guided our lives thus far and harness the wealth of gifts that we have gained along our life journey. We enter into the catharsis of releasing old stories that we have buried, hidden and ignored and as a result, we can restore and reinvent our identity, reimagining ourselves into a new story of reconnection and responsibility. As Maria Popova,[2] the Founder of the online blog Brainpickings says, *"The best of our stories are those that transform and redeem us, ones that both ground us in ourselves by reminding us what it means to be human and elevate us by furnishing an instrument of self-transcendence."*

This book is designed to be a facilitator of such an initiation of self-transcendence, offering you a set of tools to 'restore and restory' your life – if you so choose.

> THE BEST OF OUR STORIES ARE THOSE
> THAT TRANSFORM AND REDEEM US.

The only thing that stops us from living our authentic story in the world are the fears we carry inside us about what might happen if we actually DO IT. When we begin our journey that fear can remain, but from experience we get braver and increasingly tenacious, looking it in the eyes and jumping off more of our metaphorical cliffs. Falling down teaches us to stand back up. Experience breeds compassion and confidence. To face our fears, we must face our vulnerability, which is the path to our strengths.

Vanity and vulnerability are inextricably linked. Vanity would have us focus on our 'story of me' at the expense of everything else and is a dangerous undercurrent of our dominant human mythology, fueling our patterns of denial, abuse and fear. Vulnerability, on the other hand, is the essence of being human and the ultimate way to crack open life and all its magic. One of my favorite authors, Danielle LaPorte[3] says, "*Vulnerability is the prerequisite for communion and connection with life.*" If we remain closed in vanity, then we prevent ourselves from stepping onto the path of our greatest adventure. All we have to do is recognize our choice and say yes to its invitation. Every life story is a work of art created and molded by our beliefs, thoughts, feelings and actions. So, what kind of art are you creating? Are you being vulnerably human or robotically vain?

Our journey begins with the inner adventure to find the voice of our soul. What do I mean when I say 'soul'? Regardless of personal spiritual beliefs, I mean the essence and spark of genius that we are all born with and that remains as energy in the universe beyond our physical human life. This has been described in many ways over the millennia of human mythology, from the ideas of reincarnation to quantum physics. The common narrative thread here being that physical life forms are created from non-physical universal energy. This energy cannot be destroyed. It is simply recycled into different forms. This energetic spark holds within it the greatest potential story that we are capable of manifesting in our lives. I mean, our destiny. Yes, I do believe in destiny, but as a concept that entails free will and free choice to weave our story in whatever way we wish. Destiny, for me, means aligning ourselves to the highest will of life for the good of all. This choice brings with it complete and utter self-responsibility. The personal initiation into our authentic story leads us into a greater understanding of its individual context within our communal, geographical and ancestral narratives. From this expanded temporal and spatial view, we have the opportunity to consciously engage in, and influence, the evolving modern human mythology that both transcends and includes our more local and specific stories and narratives.

This initiation process invites you to remember who you really are underneath the various masks of socialization you have been taught to wear. All your life, you have been surrounded by moments, experiences and lessons that hold the potential to lead you deeply into the truth at the core of your real soul story. If you take the time to listen to and contemplate these clues, you will reawaken your mythic potential.

I am a strong advocate of action-based learning and story-making as the result of storytelling. Therefore, this is a book about my ongoing process to 're-story' my life. It is a journey of re-membering, re-awakening and re-connecting to my authentic spark and essence as a way of living in the world. Note my use of 're' here (which derives from the Latin for 'again'). In the journey to restory our lives, we are not discovering things for the first time but instead, remembering that which has lain inside us forever. Humanity has reached a stage in its journey where we are feeling the need to restory our purpose and role on the planet. This process must start with our own personal journey before it can ripple outward into new social models of change.

As a result, this is a human journey and not a hero's journey. Of course, the two are intimately linked and inspire each other, but I believe that the hero's narrative creates many problems in our world. Our obsession with celebrities, saviors and leaders carries with it an underlying outward focus of persona, obsessing over what others think of us as opposed to an inner adventure towards authentic strength. I work with far too many glorious human beings who are hampered by their inner story of, '*I'm not good enough when compared to my heroes or heroines.*' This disables self-esteem and our ability to recognize the sacredness and vast potential of our gifts.

Stories are subjective and emergent

This is a story of my younger years and as such it is raw, rough and partial. That's okay for me; the story of the self is not a fixed structure but an emerging process that is always in motion. One of my friends, Art Giser,[4] once said that he only ever taught his 'beliefs du jour' (thoughts of the day) and would be deeply disappointed if he revisited them in years to come and found that they had not changed. This book represents my stories, beliefs and 'work du jour' of which there is no fixed position, just a process of constant emergence where my beliefs change as I consistently challenge myself to travel beyond them. I am not asking you to accept my truth, just to consider its impact on your current story and reflect on the meaning for you.

When I began writing, I told myself, *'It will be very hard, almost impossible, to write an objective account of my memories.'* Then I hit on the counterargument – storytelling isn't objective. Carl Jung[5] wrote that the memories we retain as we grow, hold special emotional keys that show us how our character and unique gifts have been formed and can become our offerings to the world. This book is a collection of my memories, reflections, meanings and visions. A recollection of the moments in my life when my unique story spoke from a numinous place beyond the day-to-day world, and showed me a different way of being and seeing to the one I was living at the time. I offer these with an invitation that you explore your own story through examining the memories that emerge for you as you read.

Stories are not static: they emerge, evolve and change as we work within them. Therefore, I ask that you imagine – in the tradition of storytellers – that as you read, I am sitting there beside you. That you can hear my voice and that I am looking into your mind's eye, speaking and gesturing, weaving the story into life. I invite you to be an active participant in the listening. It is here that my story joins your story and together we make it our story.

How to use this book

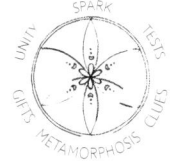

The structure of this book is seven-fold. There are six parts, divided into the 'Restory Cycle' that I have been using for over a decade. It is inspired by master mythologist Joseph Campbell's[6] classic 'hero's journey' and is adapted to move us from a story of 'me' the hero, to a story of 'we'; humanity living in a complex and interconnected universe. The cycle itself presents us with a pathway for re-initiation back into the essence of our real story and a modern mythology of inter-being.

The six stages are reflective of the six petals of the geometric pattern of the seed of life as illustrated on the cover of the book. There is much historic indigenous wisdom that points to the seed of life being the fundamental energetic building block of creation. The six petals of the seed fit within a seventh circle. When multiplied these become the ancient pattern of the flower of life. The seven circles reflect our seven chakras, the seven colors in the rainbow spectrum, and the seven stages of creation that are spoken of in the practice of alchemy. In terms of this book, you are the seventh cycle. Your own journey as you read and participate with the story-making practices becomes the seventh circle that surrounds the six stages of our journey. At the seventh stage, we transcend our previous story completely and move into an entirely new stage of our personal and collective myth.

The Restory Cycle is a framework for our journey, and yet by the very nature of 'models' it can be limiting, due to the level of generalization that is employed to simplify the complex process of change. In my experience, we can be at different stages of this cycle in different aspects of our lives concurrently, just as living systems are in constant change and emergence. The final section of Unity, by its very nature, transcends the model completely. It's a divine paradox. Thus, the structure is helpful and yet partial. I invite you to forge your own pathway through this and take what is useful to you as we journey.

I share elements of my own human story through the stages of: Spark, Tests, Clues, Metamorphosis, Gifts and Unity. Throughout each section, I offer pauses for your reflection and contemplation. The tone of the story shifts from one of monologue to dialogue and I invite you to enter into the act of story-making through 'comfort zone challenges' and exercises that will assist you in transforming your own narrative. The extent to which you engage with this invitation is entirely up to you. However, the exercises are based on years of coaching with people from across the world. They will profoundly change your life if you do them. Of course, you can choose to skip these sections, but my caveat is that *transformation only occurs when we combine awareness with action*. Change happens when we both tell a new story and dance it into being by walking our talk. This is a journey of self-responsibility, ultimately leading to communal responsibility as we are reintegrated within the family of life on earth. Are you ready to move beyond being a voyeur in your life and into being the writer and creator of your story? This choice is yours alone.

IT IS THROUGH EXPERIENCE THAT WE ARE FOREVER CHANGED.

If you find yourself continually tempted to skip the journeying exercises then ask yourself whether you have fallen prey to one of the most prevalent narratives of our human societies: The '*I don't have enough time*' story, that hides in its depths the fairy tale of the silver bullet. We have become victims of these two interlocked narratives so much in our modern world that we rarely stop long enough to reflect on the things that really matter. The seeds of our discontent lie deep underneath the numbing distractions of our societies and we are continually tempted to skip past the keys to our healing because of our addiction to 'the next big thing'. If you intend to use this book as a silver bullet or magic pill, it will disappoint you. If, however, you are ready to take responsibility for your unique story then I invite you to engage with the ideas, exercises and journeys in an experiential way. It is through experience that we are forever changed.

You can use this book in many ways dependent on your inclination and how you absorb information. The six stages of the Restory Cycle work in a cyclical fashion. However, they often overlap and dance forwards and backwards through our lives simultaneously when we become aware of them. You may wish to initially follow the cycle stage by stage – in fact, I suggest you do so initially, to get a sense of the bigger mythological patterns in your life. If you are choosing to move through the Restory Cycle in a linear fashion then there are a few additional practices that can enhance your journey. I suggest that you buy a journal and some art supplies if you don't already have these available. You don't have to be good at art but the act of creation, in whatever form, unlocks a deeper and often unconscious way of knowing your story that lies outside the realm of the rational thinking mind. You may also wish to treat this adventure as a personal retreat and create a space and environment where you can read, reflect and restory at regular intervals as you move through the material presented in this book. The time you take to journey through the cycle is self-determined and different for everyone. You will be your own guide and teacher in this respect. Can you focus and tune into the most important voice you will ever hear: your own?

Story also has an ability to work hologramatically, where each part holds an element of the whole. Therefore, the Restory Cycle can be entered at any point, creating inner transformation. Each story and memory shared here can stand alone and offer guidance in its own way. You may choose to use this book more like an oracle, flicking it open intuitively to obtain the guidance you need on any given day. Having used this practice myself for years, I have come to know its power. How you listen, engage and become the living story is up to you. Of course, any story that acknowledges its own limitations is full of paradox. I am simultaneously sharing my stories with you, whilst asking you to step beyond the confines of yours. Every story holds a grain of truth and yet is partial.

> CAN YOU FOCUS AND TUNE IN TO THE MOST IMPORTANT VOICE YOU WILL EVER HEAR: YOUR OWN?

Our call to adventure

In creating this book, I entered deeply into my own process of narrative alchemy as my story was gradually refined, restored and redefined to its essential mythic qualities. My first draft of the book evolved into a personal journey towards healing my past and becoming more whole within the darkness and light of my own story. Yet it is worth remembering that my way will not be your way, nor another's way. We must each find our own path through the forest. In the sharing of our stories, we may come to find that we hold a magical ability to remind each other of just the right thing at the right time when we most need to hear it. Some call this synchronicity, others magic. I hope that the stories I share within this book may serve as reminders to you in the same way. I believe that we are all interconnected and our stories weave together like threads in the human tapestry; that in walking by my side through my tragedies and transformations, you will be reminded of your own.

The world at large is entering into a process of restorying itself. Individuals, communities and whole cultures are discovering that their old meaning-making narratives no longer work in our globalized society. We are being asked to allow the old stories to dissolve so that we can plant the seeds of a new modern mythology in their fertile soil. The legends of the past can fuel the mythology of the future if we are able to fully jump beyond the confines of our old narrative comfort zones. We are being given the chance to be reborn.

OUR STORIES WEAVE TOGETHER LIKE THREADS
IN THE HUMAN TAPESTRY.

I believe that it is a great honor to be human at this time on earth and that the process of claiming back our personal and collective power is one of the answers to our current challenges. In the human journey, the supernatural power of the inner hero is found in the natural everyday occurrences of living amongst the jungles and deserts of our chaotic world. The modern hero narrative, favored by the global media, separates us from others in a time when I believe we need to unite in our common humanity – we are all special and we are all human. The trick is to individuate in a way that unites you back into your community and the web of life on earth, taking full responsibility for the story you personally came here to create.

The initiation of restorying our life is one that separates us from the prevalent narrative of our times yet subsequently reunites us with our human, earthly and cosmic family. We release the myth of human superiority in favor of one of interconnection. We re-member, re-store and re-connect to the vast web of life in the universe and know ourselves simultaneously as both unique and unified.

Are you ready?

Then let's begin.

THE SPARK

WHO AM I?
WHO AM I REALLY?

"Nothing in this world is fixed, even though it might seem to be so, stood here with my roots firmly embracing the earth. I stand solid as the seasons pass, as the birds migrate, as the stars swing across the sky above my branches, and yet every moment is different, every breath a transition to a new way of observing the world around me. Every silence is full of movement, no one moment the same as the one before it. Each one leaves us forever changed.

Within each of our hearts lies a longing. This is the essence of what moves us into being and becoming. It is a core desire to know more, to become more, to love more. It is the 'Earth Spark'. All our relatives on this planet share it. We can try and ignore our spark, we can try and stay still and deny our movement. I have seen many who have tried and failed. All they do is stagnate and stunt their growth. Our spark calls us into connection with new experiences, lands and peoples of all kinds. It calls us to know ourselves as an intimate part of our family here on earth. It calls us forward into life itself.

And we are all, always connected. That is the true nature of the Earth Spark. To remind us that we are all one."

This story was told to me by one of my oldest friends: a large grandmother spruce tree[7] who speaks to me in the quiet moments when my heart is wide open. She witnessed my beginning and perhaps she will also see my end. She recognized the spark that lay within my soul and has continued to gently feed its flames all the years of my human life. When I am at peace, I hear her voice.

I believe that we all come into this world with an inner spark that we carry across galaxies and lifetimes. It is this inner light that guides us when we are lost. One of the core purposes of our lives, I believe, is to activate and embody our spark of personal genius, pursuing its trail without distraction as we grow and evolve. And yes, I believe that we all have the ability to embody genius.

As children, we keenly sense our flame, our catalyzing purpose for living. It manifests in our imaginings, in the mirror of the natural world around us, and the early stories we construct to make sense of our childhood experiences. It is the quiet whisper in the music of the trees and the inner call of our curiosity to explore the world around us in our own unique way. It is the longing within our hearts that pulls us into new experiences, new places and new adventures; the impulse to grow and expand in connection with our world. Through our spark, we learn to open our 'heart's eyes' and participate in our life through its wisdom. We directly access the magic of our deeper human story in action beyond concepts of right and wrong, into an interconnected mythic realm of synchronicity and flow. Things make sense from a larger perspective. We feel at home in the world and connected to its inhabitants. We trust that we are exactly where we need to be at that moment.

WE ALL HAVE THE ABILITY TO EMBODY GENIUS.

Without listening to our spark, we become listless and stagnant. Depression and lethargy are by-products of shutting down its urges. We start to wonder what the point of all of this is anyway. When we forget to listen to its voice, we forget who we are. In a way, we start to die a little bit every day. We try and numb ourselves to the pain of our forgetting this fundamental part of our spirit.

I begin the Restory Cycle with this as our primary essence: the first segment in the seed of life. It is similar to 'the call to adventure' in Joseph Campbell's[8] classic hero's journey and yet different in that I believe our spark travels with us throughout the whole cycle of life, constantly drawing us forwards towards living our biggest story in the world. It is this spark that holds the essence of our inherent gifts and our emergent lessons to come.

I invite you to enter into your own story, just as I have done here with my early memories. We can learn much by traveling backwards down the spiral of our life and noticing where our current beliefs and narratives began. I would like to journey with you down your song lines, back into your beginnings where the spark of your genius emerged in human form.

If you wish to play with me, find a quiet space where you can retreat from the noise of your everyday life whilst you read or listen. This will be sufficient to begin. Let us become like children once more. Let us dance and sing awake the inner spark of our soul's story. Let us listen to its voice on the wind once more.

Threads of destiny

> Softly, the trees whisper to us of many things
> The life-giving intensity of the sunshine
> The stories of the stars as they pass overhead
> And yet if you listen carefully to them
> They also will tell you of your destiny here on earth

"Honey, I have something to tell you..."

Even on the telephone, the voice of my mother had a soft, mythical tone to it, as it did when she encountered something otherworldly and was trying to find the right words to describe it.

She began to tell me a story. She has told me many stories over the years we have known each other. Stories that often come at just the right time in my life to point me in a new direction or teach me a lesson. This particular story was being told at a moment when I found myself at a crossroads. One path would likely lead me towards social success, cultural acceptance and a profitable career. The other, into the deep unknown wilderness of my heart's longing and desire. I was hovering between the two trails, wondering which way to go, when my mother called me unexpectedly on this particular late-summer afternoon.

The story she told was set in one of my favorite places in the whole world; a natural cathedral amongst towering spruce, resting quietly on a Colorado mountainside: the humble, wooden All Faiths' Chapel built by Laurel Elizabeth Keyes[9] (I will come back to her later), where seekers come to find their true selves amongst the silent trees and sparkling earth.

At the time of the story, I was three months old. It is what we call a 'true story' and this is what my mother said.

"It was a bright Colorado day in September. One where the sunlight is of such intensity that it feels to the beholder that the light particles themselves dance and spin through us to the invisible song of the universe. You were just an infant, Genevieve, wrapped tightly in the old white lace christening dress that has been passed down through your father's family for almost a century. As I carried you up the warm, red earth path towards the spruce tree chapel, Laurel came down to meet us, also in a flowing white dress and smiling broadly, delighting in the day and the occasion. It was she who was going to conduct your christening ceremony amongst an audience of family and trees.

Before the ceremony began, she asked me softly, 'May I speak with Genevieve alone?'

I was surprised and yet trusted the wisdom that her deep, smiling eyes carried, so I nodded and gently handed you over to the woman in white who took you in her arms and carried you up the sun-dappled slope towards the chapel.

You were gone for only 20 minutes, but it was long enough for me to wonder what was taking so long and I wanted to find out. I started to rise from my chair in the kitchen of the old cabin adjoining the chapel, but your grandfather, sensing my concern, laid a strong hand on my arm and said, 'Julie, it will be alright.'

As if she too could sense my anxiety, at that moment Laurel came walking through the trees with you cradled safely against her breast. Coming in through the back door, she appeared angelic and ethereal, carrying an aura of gentle grace. Smiling, she approached me, handing you back to me and silently acknowledging how difficult it had been for me to entrust my baby to another. After a moment's pause, she began to speak in a hushed voice.

'Genevieve and I have spoken,' she said with a sparkle in her eyes. 'This baby comes from the stars. She is here to be a great teacher and will help many people in her lifetime. You don't need to do anything special, but know she will be a little different. You are very blessed that she has chosen you as her mother.'"

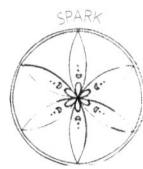

Interestingly, my mother had forgotten all about this story until much later in my life. I was 34 years old when she called me that Sunday afternoon to tell it for the first time since it had occurred. By the time it was finally spoken, I had already traveled along many different roads in search of who I was and why I was here. This story came to me at just the right moment and in just the way I needed to hear it. Listening over the phone, in quiet knowing and subtle awe of my mother's story, a shiver ran down my spine as I was reminded that we all carry a deeper story than the one we are taught to live. It is in moments like these that we are given a chance to remember.

> WE ALL CARRY A DEEPER STORY
> THAN THE ONE WE ARE TAUGHT TO LIVE.

Suffice it to say, this reminder from my mother set off a chain of choices and events in my life that ultimately led me to write this book and step fully onto the path of a storyteller and story-maker. The best stories are the ones that catalyze us into transformation.

FAMILY STORIES

WHAT HAVE YOU FORGOTTEN?

Me – Take some time to reflect on memories from your childhood that still stand out for you today. What makes them special to you? What emotions permeate your memories? How have these experiences influenced who you are today? In reliving these memories, do any others come to mind that have drifted into your unconscious?

We – Reach out to members of your family or friends who knew you when you were young. Ask them to give you their top three memories about you as a young child. What did you love and what did you hate? What brought you alive? What were the catalyzing moments in your young life (that you may have forgotten)?

Our memories are the keys that unlock our forgotten gifts, talents and genius, yet we rarely stop long enough to contemplate them. In doing so, you may remember some of the unique magic that you were born to bring to this world.

Rocks and stars

> Three stars in the night sky
> My seeking heart breathes a sigh of relief
> I know where I am when you shine
> I know I am in the arms of my family

For many years, before and after I was born, my grandparents lived up on a red rock mesa, nestled in the foothills of Colorado's Rocky Mountains. This magical place has ingrained itself deeply within my psyche and my soul. It has stayed with me long after my grandparents moved away and the house I loved so much in my youth was knocked down and preserved forever only in memory. Its fire-red canyons captured my childhood imagination and provided an endless playground for my stories and myths to be enacted within. Day after day I would run wild on the land around my grandparents' house, speaking with the yucca and playing with my friends the rocks.

The dark brown wooden house designed by my papa sat on the flat top of Deer Creek, staring out at the large sandstone giant that we nicknamed 'Ribbon Rock' because of the colored sedimentary layers that ran across its broad face in vibrant hues of orange, red and pink. Often, I would wake up before dawn and stare out of the kitchen window in the guest apartment, waiting patiently for the first rays of the golden mountain sun to brush across the face of my beribboned friend; lighting him up in an array of fiery stone flames.

Embracing the house from behind was a beautiful green mountain, covered in short Gambel oaks, Ponderosa pines, juniper, wild cherry and spiky yucca plants. The mountain watched over me as I grew up, and spoke silently when I was quiet enough to listen.

In the valley below the house sprawled ridge after ridge of red sandstone mesa rock outcroppings. They reminded me of the pictures of ancient prehistoric landscapes that my father (who was a budding archaeologist at the time) would show me in books at night before bed. This valley became my African savanna, my Jurassic grassland, my Star Wars Tatooine. The rocks were my most trusted friends, each with their own face, features and soft earthy voice. This sacred place was my home. My playground. The temple of my soul. Closer to me than any lover or friend, it has planted its seed of magic in my heart forever.

When my grandparents lived here, there were very few houses. At night, due to the lack of electric lights and the clear mountain skies, the stars would emerge in all their vast glory and mystery. I would regularly sit with my mother and grandmother on the old porch swing at the front of the house, wrapped in a blanket against the chill of the night air, staring up at these sparkling beings. Even at a young age I was aware of connecting to their light, magic and beauty. I spent these evenings having conversations in the darkness with the stars, just as I did with my rock friends during the day.

One constellation in particular felt familiar to me. When the first stars started to appear at dusk, I would strain my eyes searching for one particular family group. I would feel nervous and concerned until these three old friends would appear in the sky and when they did, everything was right in the world again. Orion, the Hunter. The three stars of his belt sparked the same inner feeling of home for me that the red rock mesa canyon did. Earth and sky, night and day. My friends the stars spoke to me of being rooted in earth whilst reaching upwards towards the cosmos.

This early connection to Orion's Belt has subtly influenced my personality and character throughout my life. It connected me to the deeper mysteries of the universe and sparked regular questions of, '*Where do we come from?*' and '*Who are we, really?*'

WE ARE MADE OF STAR STUFF.

All life on earth is connected in some deep way to the stars we see in the night sky. We are family. We owe our existence to their life cycles and can dialogue with them to better understand ourselves; if you believe you can of course. If not, then feel free to head back to the 'facts' found in your biology textbooks. Both are 'true' from a certain point of view. Both help us to find meaning in the world. It is up to you which one brings you closer to your own sense of self. But more on this when we get to the Unity section of the book.

Carl Sagan,[10] the American physicist, famously said, 'The nitrogen in our DNA, the calcium in our teeth, the iron in our blood, the carbon in our apple pies were made in the interiors of collapsing stars. We are made of star stuff.' Personally, I have always felt that the stars are my family in the broadest sense of that word.

FIELD TRIP

WHERE DO YOU REALLY COME FROM?

I feel so blessed that I can still return to the red rock canyons of my youth. I often take the time to visit my friends the mountains and the stars there, who love and teach me now as much as they did when I was young.

Me – Choose a geographic place that you used to love visiting as a child. It may be a park, a zoo, a particular shop. If it's still there, go and visit it again. If it has disappeared or is difficult to travel to in person, engage the gift of your imagination and journey back there in meditation. Notice what thoughts and feelings come up for you as your journey progresses and your spark memories arise. Record your adventures in whatever way will help you to remember them.

We – Cast your mind back to key people you grew up with. These could be family members, neighbors, teachers or friends. Take the opportunity to travel back in time and, using your creative mind, imagine having a conversation with them now. Ask them how they saw you as a child. What were your gifts and how did you relate to the world? If you have the opportunity to do this in person then please take it – you may discover surprising things about yourself and re-forge old friendships and community links in the process.

The environments we grew up in as children play a vital role in shaping our story, how we see the world as an adult and the beliefs we form about our place in the world. Going back to visit them again in adulthood allows us to see their significance in new ways and discover hidden aspects of our identities and gifts that are unconscious to us.

Animal family

> Running fast, wild and free
> Untamed strength and playful beauty
> Nickered greeting, my old friends
> Gifts for you I hold, if you'll stop and stay

I was born at 1:55pm on the 2nd June 1978. It was the Chinese Year of the Horse. Horses have been one of my favorite animals for as long as I can remember. I guess you could say that they were my first 'totem' – if you take the definition of this as an animal or symbol that we feel a deep connection with and which serves to introduce us to key lessons, hinting at our strengths and shadows. Something about the horse's beauty and elegance caught my imagination from the moment I first saw one. I was attracted to their ability to gallop wild and free across the land away from potential trouble. I used to think I could outrun anything on a horse.

When I was two, my family was renting an old farmhouse on the plains of Colorado in Arvada. I remember the dry prairie grasses and playful summer winds as the backdrop to my imaginings. One afternoon, whilst my mother and I were in the garden, I decided to embark on an adventure. I could feel a strong loving presence calling me from the back of the yard and I followed it. I crawled through the dry brown summer grass, across our garden and towards the big old bay-colored farm horse that stood at the fence waiting for me. My friend. I remember the horse seeming huge to my small, two-year-old human frame, but I felt drawn to him nonetheless. I crawled right up to the fence and went through it until I was sitting underneath his huge, dark brown belly. Looking up at the cloudless blue sky either side of his big body, I felt a sense of peace and utter contentment. A feeling that everything was right in the world, because I was being protected by the horse.

It didn't take long for my attentive mother to realize that I was missing from eyeshot and to come frantically looking for me. On finding me sitting underneath the tall old farm horse, I remember seeing the understandable fear and concern on her face; that I would be severely injured should the horse move or kick out suddenly. Something told me that I was not in danger. Slowly and carefully, talking with the old horse herself, my mother reached under the fence and pulled me back into her arms. I remember starting to cry at being separated from my friend.

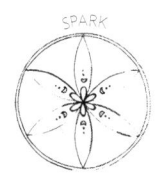

When we first encounter an animal that feels like family it is a powerful life-changing experience. Many indigenous cultures revere our animal relatives as teachers, encouraging people to listen and learn from them (something our western societies have largely forgotten and trivialized). When we stop to consider the potential gifts that our animal friends hold for us, sometimes it is easy to see where they reflect the lessons we live out in our lives: where we are being called upon to be strong like the bear, swift and cunning like the fox or elevated and far-seeing like the eagle.

When I first felt drawn to horses, I knew none of these things consciously. All I experienced was a deep sense of friendship with these majestic animals. Throughout my life, my relationship with them has changed dramatically. I rode as much as I could when I was young, until I had a couple of fairly bad falls. From that point, I developed a fear of falling and stopped riding completely. Interestingly, at the same time in my life I simultaneously developed fears of many other things and started to shut down my adventurous side in multiple ways. Perhaps at this stage of my life, I was afraid of the horse's power and my inability to control that strength. A metaphor for life, methinks. It was years later, after several wake up calls, that I finally got back in the saddle again and set a long buried inner part of myself free. Suffice it to say, my horse friends have mirrored a deep part of my psyche to me throughout the ups and downs of my life and continue to do so to this day. I am still in love with them and I am still afraid of them in many ways.

The longing for freedom that my horse friends awakened in me long ago has stayed with me and lives deeply in my heart still. Whenever I start to feel trapped by my life in some way, I escape and ride with my four-legged friends. I love to gallop on their backs across the lands of this earth with the wind in my hair. It is one of the best natural antidotes to modern social stress that I know.

The enemy of napping

> I worry if I close my eyes
> I will miss the vast beauty of this world
> I might miss something important
> That may not come again

When I was small, I used to hate naptime. My mother would try and make me and my sisters rest after lunch and I would do everything in my power to resist the call of sleep. Now please understand, the afternoons in Colorado were usually awash with bright mountain sunshine, sparkling plants, grass to be rolled in and azure blue skies to play under. I wanted to be awake, to experience these beauties and play wholeheartedly with them creating new worlds and adventures in my imagination. The thought of lying down in bed inside the house, whilst all of this was happening outside, was confounding and downright disgusting to me. So, I resisted: I cried and screamed my displeasure each and every afternoon. My poor mother!

My resistance to 'falling asleep' in life has prevailed no matter what age I find myself. As I grew up, I looked around me at the adults of the world who mostly seemed to be asleep every moment of every day as they pursued their busy goals of 'success'. Hardly anyone seemed to want to use their imaginations or go outside and play in the middle of the day. I became used to responses like, *"I'm too busy,"* or *"Not now honey,"* when I would ask grown-ups to come and play with me. It made me sad for them.

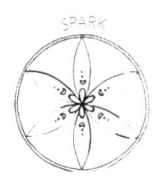

When I found myself neck-deep in my first major business job after university, one of my favorite things remained to walk outside with my lunch and gaze fondly at the trees and birds. I would find my mind wandering, during long and tedious meetings, to the window where nature would console me with its quiet, wise voice. Later on, when I grew in confidence and felt good about showing my 'weirdness' at work, I would insist (when the weather allowed) that team meetings and coaching sessions be held outside in the fresh air. Most people thought I was mad.

Nature has the ability to connect us to a place where we want to stay awake; where we want to explore both our inner and outer worlds; where we have the courage to walk down a path we haven't ever seen before or can find pure contentment in just sitting under a tree and doing nothing. After all, we are a part of nature even though contemporary culture would have us believe otherwise. Perhaps it is time we all woke up and stopped ignoring the part of ourselves that is reflected in the green earth, the blue waters and the tall trees. Perhaps it is time that we all stopped napping?

PLAYING IN NATURE

HAVE YOU STOPPED PLAYING WITH LIFE?

Me – Take a moment and remember something that you loved to do (outside if possible) when you were five or six years old. Take a couple hours off and DO IT. Enjoy the feeling of being outside playing in nature. Get curious about why you loved this activity so much and consider how it has informed your adult life. Have you forgotten a key piece of wisdom that you were born with?

We – Find some time with your family or friends and re-engage in a nature-based activity that you loved as a child. Tell them WHY you loved it whilst instructing them how to do it. Watch their reactions to your love of play in this area and see if they give you any feedback as to one of your inherent gifts.

Remembering certain things we loved or hated when we were young can help us to understand who we were/are deep down, underneath the social stories we have since constructed, and enables us to reconnect to a vital, alive aspect of our original identity.

Creating time to play out in nature is rejuvenating physically, mentally and emotionally. It is also during these times that we are able to listen to the voice of our intuition and rediscover certain things about our unique soul story that we may have forgotten in the busyness of adult life.

The darkness and light of kindergarten

> One becomes two and two becomes one
> You and me, me and you
> Are we one?
> Or are we two?

When I turned five years old, I begrudgingly started kindergarten. I remember trudging up the road with my hand tightly tucked in my mother's to ensure I didn't turn tail and run back home, locking myself in my bedroom. It felt like a prison sentence; with me the prisoner being herded behind wire fences into the school with the other cattle children. I tried to cry and scream but my parents had been resolute. I needed to go to school they said. I didn't see why.

I was often the odd one out in playground games and didn't have any close friends. Mostly I was okay with this, sometimes I was proud to be different, but more often than I cared to admit, it made me sad. The roots of the *'I'm not good enough'* belief run deep and start early for most of us. The most popular girl in our class was called Jennifer; she had blond curly hair, dark brown rabbit eyes and expensive clothes. Everyone wanted to be her friend, apart from me. She was a stark contrast to my own straight brown locks and bright blue eyes; we couldn't have been more opposite. Secretly, I now know that the same part of me that was sad at being the outcast, also longed to be like her. To be loved and accepted into the group. Outwardly however, my fledgling ego scorned her and made up stories about why I was better than the plastic princess I perceived her to be.

One day, our class had gone out for a walk and somehow Jennifer and I happened to be paired up. Walking side by side neither of us had much to say. It was as if a chasm of difference lay between us, as hard as a stone wall. As we walked back into the school playground, somehow a playful summer breeze lifted up our hair and our two pigtails became tangled with one another. After the initial surprise and painful yanking we realized that we were stuck. Brown head to blond head. Each of us continued to pull away as our embarrassment grew, shouting in pain as our strands of hair wound round one another more tightly. Whereas minutes before we had felt oceans apart, we now found ourselves thrust into the same physical space and it hurt.

It was at this point that I remember experiencing a feeling of the world slowing. It was as if time had decided to take a break and everything came to a standstill. Through the timeless fog, I looked up at my brown straight hair wound around her blond curls and was able to examine the two for what seemed like eternity. The light and the dark, the straight and the curly. Two sides of the same coin and yet distinctly different in form and appearance.

Then, as suddenly as it had come, the moment was over. Our teacher came running over to separate us and the 'normal world' came back into view. Time resumed and I was left there alone, rubbing my hurting head whilst Jennifer was surrounded by her friends. I started to cry quietly inside at the thought of being 'less than perfect'.

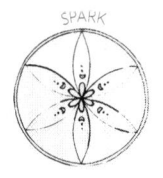

Duality is a funny thing and the concept of it comes to us at different times in our lives. Sometimes the 'other' is presented as the polar opposite to everything that we know as 'me'. I guess we go from being so unified with everything around us when we are born that it's these experiences of 'other' and 'difference' that leave a deep mark on our psyches as we grow up. As we grow and learn how to fit into the world around us, our emerging sense of individuality and separateness from others presents us with some difficult lessons. There starts to be a 'me' and a 'you'; 'mine' and 'yours'; differences in opinion; different ideas and beliefs that can lead to pain and suffering in the world. We start to see difference before we ever look for similarity.

> WE START TO SEE DIFFERENCE
> BEFORE WE EVER LOOK FOR SIMILARITY.

It took me years to learn that our 'sameness' connects us and helps us to feel part of the human and 'other than human' community on earth such as the trees, plants and animals. That it is an innate human ability to honor difference and then use love to unite and dissolve it. It's funny how, in the years to come after this kindergarten experience, I would see myself as more similar to a tree than to my fellow humans. It would be a long time before my human family would feel like home.

Earth dancing

> Deep in the earth
> She reminds us of who we really are
> Drumming eternally
> The heartbeat of life

It is the end of summer in Denver, which means hot, dry winds, brown grass and everyone talking about how we need rain. I know that it's time when I am bundled into the car with my little sister. I feel excitement that I can't name. I am going. It is time. We drive for what seems like hours across the dry prairie plains, with the mountains to my back and the wide, flat expanse of farms to my front. I know where we are headed. To an ancient memory. A vibration from my ancestors. Dances from the deep.

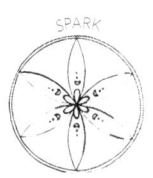

Arriving in the small railway town of La Junta my heart starts to beat faster. It knows what is coming. We drive through the streets with their small gingerbread houses to the kiva.[11] My small body and big soul knows and is pulsing with excitement.

Dusk falls as we enter into the circular ceremony. Families, couples and individuals all wait for the sacred to enter into us and dance: the Koshare Indian dances, my favorite celebration of life. The hush that descends before the dance begins is like the quiet before a thunderstorm or the silence in the deep of the night. Everyone knows that they are about to enter into a trance that will take them beyond the ordinary world; take them to places deep within their souls.

The dancers enter into the sacred circle and begin. I feel a release deep in my chest as I start to breathe in their rhythm, drink in their colors, and synchronize with their breath. The drumbeats align themselves with my cells and the pulsing of life in my veins. I grab my sister by the hand and run to the front so we can be there with them, communing with their movement, swaying with their tones. Entranced, they dance on and we move – two young girls in love with the deeper meaning of the dances that we couldn't possibly speak of at such a young age. Yet we know. We know.

The dancers are also lost, moving in and out of this world, oblivious to those in observation and yet one with them. Every so often, a dancer catches my eye; an instant of recognition of lives lived and memories lost, of lessons learned and lovers embraced. We feel our human heritage beyond the earth and into the stars, older than the sun. For these few hours, as the summer draws to a close, we stop and become true. Sacred kiva, deep in the earth, you honor me with your love. Your dancers reflect pure truth. They remind me of who I am here to be.

I remember these dances as some of my most sacred moments and it was around this time of my life that I became aware of my ancestral connection with these native peoples. Of a link that is older than culture, thicker than blood. It took years of working through my inherited western white guilt to discover the lessons and blessings that the tribes of the northern Americas could bring to me. For many years, I would burst into angry tears every time my family drove across a tribal reservation.

The dances speak to each and every one of us differently and yet they call from us the same thing: the recognition of our connection to life and to each other; of our inherent oneness with life. These sacred dances exist in every culture, for every human being. They exist deep in our psyche and collective memory. The beating of the drums evokes our earliest memories of being safe in the womb of our mother, listening to her steady heartbeat guiding us into life. We can still listen to that heartbeat. We can still dance to the beat of our Mother Earth. All we need to do is remember. Remember and dance in celebration.

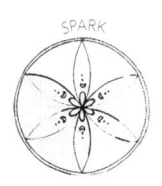

Leaving home

> Joy and pain, love and fear
> Neither can be fully appreciated
> Without the full presence of the other
> The lessons and blessings of change

I can't exactly remember the first moment that I became aware that the mountains and I were anything other than one continuous being: one soul, one heartbeat, one thought. The Rocky Mountains of Colorado were my first home. My first friends. My family. They were there when I came into this world, welcoming me with as much love as my mother in her first embrace. They are unique, wild and beautiful in ways that are incomparable (I believe) to any other range in the world. A combination of majestic, prehistoric red rock canyons in the lower foothills and carpeted pine and spruce tree peaks higher and deeper into their ranges. The highest mountains are snowcapped for most of the year and mysterious in their majesty. Breathtakingly beautiful, deeply wise and speak of hidden magic through the glistening mica crystals in the rocks that sparkle in the high-altitude sun.

In the early morning they appear in deep purples and blues, gradually turning gold as the bright golden sunshine kisses them awake. Many a morning I awoke before dawn to stare out into the darkness awaiting the daily coronation of my mountain friends. I would regularly cry spontaneous tears of joy and awe at their raw, natural beauty illuminated by the dawn light. During the light of day, they provide a constant skyline against the flatness of the Denver plains. No matter where I was in the city, I could look up and see my dear friends, solid and encouraging as they watched me grow and travel. Sunsets are awash with fiery reds, oranges and pinks, the red rocks of the foothills glowing with a light all of their own as they hold onto the last of the sun's heat, radiating and pulsing earth energy and the day's warmth with the promise of awakening again with each new dawn.

When you have loved a part of the earth with such passion and wordless joy, it is hard to imagine how you will ever love another being with the same unconditional commitment. The mountains were my earth parents, my childhood playmates and my first love. They were a constant, steady foundation in my early life and imparted to me more about the simple joys and love of life than any teacher since. They are a part of me and I of them, and I accepted them as I accepted the sun rising each day and the seasons changing each year.

It was, therefore, incomprehensible to me that I would ever leave their natural embrace. Of course, like any good quest story or myth there comes a time in a love like this where there must be a parting, where we must leave and travel separately in the wider world for a time to learn who we really are and how strong we can be away from our safety zones. And this was exactly the lesson my young self attracted shortly after my sixth birthday.

I don't remember the exact moment I was told by my parents that we were moving away. In retrospect, I am almost certainly sure that my young mind shut down in order to avoid thinking about the inevitable pain that I knew I would feel being separated from my mountain family. What I do remember clearly is the airport lounge on the day that we were boarding the plane to London. My father had decided to move our small family to Cambridge in England, so he could do his PhD in archaeology at Churchill College. My grandparents were very proud, my mother and father very excited, my little sisters confused as to what was happening. I however, was distraught. I remember tears racking my small body as I clung to my grandfather in the airport. The time of denial had finally ended and my separation was real. I was gripped by a sadness like none I had ever known before. I was being taken away. I dragged my feet, wishing they would become as heavy as lead, as I was physically pulled by my parents towards the air bridge.

On the plane, I sat next to my mother who was trying hard to soothe me and care for my younger sisters. I felt the crying subside and a moment of stillness emerged. As the plane took off, I grabbed my mother's arm and stared up at her serious face, full of conviction. I said to her, *"Mother, I WILL come back here one day, I WILL."*

Silence passed between us as she witnessed my oath and said, *"Okay Gen, okay."* Then the moment passed and I sank into a deep melancholy.

It was a subtle sadness of my soul that in truth would last in some form or another for the next thirty years of my life, until I finally understood the deep lesson of this parting.

> WE HAVE TO EXPERIENCE LOSS BEFORE WE TRULY KNOW
> THE SACREDNESS OF WHAT WE HAD.

I believe that we have to experience loss before we truly know the sacredness of what we had in the first place. We need to be pushed out into the world so we can find our own path away from our protectors. I had experienced innocence and joy as the foundation of my life for my first six years and now it was the beginning of 'the great forgetting'. The testing time in our lives when we start to forget our childlike wonder and awe at the magic of life and instead believe that we are separate from the universe and alone. All of this and more were true for me as I sat there with my tear-streaked face on the plane. I knew I had taken the first step in growing up. I had left home.

SPARK JOURNEY

REMEMBER WHO YOU CAME HERE TO BE

The journey into your spark is one of folding back the layers of memory to reconnect to the deep joys and creative fascinations that we came into this world with at birth. Why is this so important? Because it is the guiding star that will continually bring meaning and purpose to the events of your life. Once you have connected to the spark of genius that you came into this life bearing, you will outgrow any sense that your life is pointless or wasted.

Create a space and time where you can be alone and undisturbed for an hour or so. If it's helpful, you can record yourself speaking this meditation on your phone or another device to allow you to relax, listen and go deeper. You may want to get a journal, sketchbook, art materials or some other way of recording your journeying throughout the Restory Cycle. Put away your phone and any other technology that could disturb you during this process. Give yourself the gift of focus. This meditation is also available in audio download from the Beyond Human Stories website should you wish to be guided.

Begin by closing your eyes and take a few deep breaths. Imagine that you are traveling backwards down a spiral of energy that represents your life so far. Every so often you see bright lights or symbols along the line of the spiral. Notice as you breathe that you will feel inclined to stop at a certain point in time. There is no right or wrong place, just allow yourself to slow down and come to a resting point on this spiral. This is a moment in your story.

See a doorway forming beneath you and if you wish, allow yourself to be drawn down towards this door. Take a moment to orientate yourself and notice where you have landed. Re-experience this point in time whilst being aware of the sensations in your body as you re-live your experience. Do not judge or label this scene in your movie, just notice it. Remain here as long as you wish. Play with the characters and the landscapes in this narrative in whatever way you are called. Re-live the spark of your memory.

When you are satisfied, allow yourself to sense the pull of the doorway once more and ascend back up into the spiral of time, until you reach the present moment. Take a few deep, integrating breaths and when you are ready, open your eyes.

Record your experience in whatever way your inner child feels called. Draw, tell stories, write, play, roll in the grass – whatever your inner spark is calling you to express, do it with gratitude. You can repeat this exercise as often as you wish over the coming days and weeks, each time noticing which memories you have been drawn back to and what these experiences point towards in terms of the flavors and textures of your spark.

You will notice now, having read my spark stories, that universal law, magic, nature, imagination and the polarities of light and dark pervaded some of my early experiences and are core to who I am now and who I am in the process of becoming in the world.

What are yours? Are they alive and guiding the story of your life or have they been forgotten or abandoned?

Perhaps they are simply waiting for you to recognize them as a core part of you.

THE TESTS

WHAT DOES MY SUFFERING TEACH ME?

The narratives and myths within which we swim are incredibly convincing, especially when we are unaware of how pervasive they are. They drape themselves over our understanding of the world like a transparent veil. They settle subtly like gauze over our eyes and minds, so that we are barely aware of their presence. So embedded are these narratives in our socialization process that we hardly realize they are the core determining factor in how we see and what we feel about the world. They are the hidden rule book from which we make our decisions and judge our experiences. They influence us every day of our lives whether we are aware of them or not.

One of the more prevalent themes of our current human story centers around the concept of struggle – the idea that we must overcome numerous and various challenges in life so that we may earn our place in the world. Our current social ideas of success and failure usually orbit around a number of trials that we must undertake and pass in order to achieve our goals, whatever these may be. Starting from a young age, we are all faced with such 'tests' in some form or another. From the more obvious institutional ones (school and education), to the more obscure psychological ones (parental acceptance, social conformity and material status). The renowned educator and father of anthropomorphism, Rudolf Steiner,[12] spoke in depth about the major psychological transitions that we journey through in seven year cycles as we grow through childhood and adolescence, learning to develop a sense of self and independence influenced by the dominant narrative of the world. These tests of acculturation remain a core part of our growth from a child into a socially functioning adult. Initiation tests, life transition points and religious and cultural expectations influence this process and can range from the exhilarating to the traumatic, dependent on the perspective and narrative setting within which they are experienced.

Some tests we are explicitly aware of and others remain hidden in the background of our mental coping strategies. In all cases, I believe that these experiences help us to learn and grow into the person that we are destined and capable of becoming. Our sense of integrity, honor, ethics and courage are honed and pitted against the modern ideologies of separation, power, money, social belonging and individuality. Joseph Campbell[13] talks about 'the road of trials'. The part of our quest where we are given the opportunity to meet face-to-face with the forces of inner darkness and conquer our own fears. Will we bend to someone else's story and sacrifice our own inner wisdom? Yes, undoubtedly, we will – time and time again – until we learn how painful this process is. We learn to design, construct, reconstruct and wear a social mask throughout this phase of our lives whilst we play with various roles and identities that we feel will help us to survive and preserve our sense of self in the world.

Deep Ecologist, Bill Plotkin,[14] talks about this stage of human development as 'the thespian at the oasis'. Much like actors, our adolescent psyches repeatedly try out various roles in the play of life and learn to adapt and flex these masks to the wider social narratives in the theatre of the world. We play with the light and the dark sides of our own power and learn on which side of this line we wish to place ourselves. We decide whether we wish to conform or rebel against the social story of success and form our identities around this theme, choosing the characters, sets and lines of our particular play. Many people on the planet right now are struggling to move beyond this stage of human development and remain locked inside their masks, trapped in a battle for power and self-preservation. Our struggle in this stage eventually gives birth to our strength and yet far too many become lost in the midst of their pain, spending years trying to escape the seed of their inner transformation.

The Tests Stage is not age dependent, although we undoubtedly enter into it for the first time in adolescence. We can and do encounter these challenges to our character again and again as we move through life. In the face of our tests, most of us revert to the instinctive survival strategies we developed in our adolescence and close our hearts to protect our fragile sense of self from being wounded by whatever external force is in front of us. Unfortunately, rather than helping to keep us safe, this process accomplishes the exact opposite and instead locks us down, numbing our senses to the deeper story that hides inside our challenges. Our triggers hold the keys to our evolution: the question is how conscious we can become of this potential in the moment. Some stay in the testing phase all their lives and continue to carry their wounds around with them. Their perceived victimhood becomes an excuse to blame their 'failures' on the world outside of them. Of course, everything outside has its source inside, but more on this later.

> WE CLOSE OUR HEARTS TO PROTECT
> OUR FRAGILE SENSE OF SELF.

These tests can be intense. It is all too easy to project responsibility for these lessons onto the 'other' who appears in various forms as our opponent. The real purpose of these periods of our story is to discover that we are the only ones directing our experiences, no matter what the circumstances of the external event are. These 'fights' teach us our gifts. They bring to the light our deepest convictions and individual values. Our pain purifies us. There is no silver bullet in the process of claiming our authentic story. We must all keep following the trail of trials.

Arriving in a new land

> My sadness knows no bounds
> For I have lost all that I once loved
> Each moment an aching agony
> For in losing you, I have lost myself

I don't remember the plane landing. I don't even remember the journey to our new house, wrapped as I was in a 'dark cloud', a blanket of separation and grief. The dark cloud was to become an appropriate metaphor for my first memories of Cambridge, England.

> OUR PAIN PURIFIES US.

We were going to live in a beautiful, big old Georgian English house on the outskirts of the city. My father was beginning his PhD studies and both he and my mother were excited by our new life in a new land. They had rented the bottom floor and two upstairs bedrooms from our ageing English landlady, who seemed to me even more ancient than the house and gardens in which she lived. I discovered that the house, like many old English buildings, was very dark; both energetically and physically. The physical aspect of this was due to a combination of the north facing windows and perpetual grayness of the weather. To me, the house was cold and smelled of damp mold even in the summer. The furniture matched the demeanor of the house, much of it from the 1950s. The fabric was drab brown and gray, devoid of life or nature in any way. I felt alone and miserable, like a raindrop that slowly trickled down the outside of a damp wall only to be soaked up and lost in the perpetually wet ground, unnoticed and ignored by almost everyone and everything.

My sisters and I shared a bedroom upstairs which was along the long narrow hallway from my parents' room. The windows looked out onto the front of the house which was surrounded by tall Scots pine trees. Rather than bringing comfort to me, as the mountain Ponderosa pines of the Rockies would have done, they appeared dark, looming and coldly silent. In England, the trees seemed reluctant to talk to a small girl. Or perhaps it was she that didn't want to be consoled in her despair. They simply stared in silence as I lay lost and confused in my bed at night, tears rolling silently down my cheeks.

The nights were very dark due to the ever-prevalent cloud cover and my sisters and I were scared of the big old house. We had not lived in an 'old' house before and it made creaks and noises that were alien in comparison to the newly built wooden homes we had lived in, in America. We were so scared that we all refused to get up in the middle of the night to make the long voyage down the hall to use the toilet. At night, the hall seemed to go on for miles and miles and hide unseen dangers that lurked in the shadows to catch us in the cold, dark gloom. This period, needless to say, was beset by endless bed-wetting that my parents would deal with night after night with patient soothing words and hugs.

By day, we would do everything we could to escape the cold of the house by playing in the extensive, well cared for English garden. Our landlady had a gardener called, most appropriately, Mr Grub. I thought he looked and sounded like something from a storybook and often wondered if he was real or a figment of my imagination. He showed my sisters and I the secret places at the bottom of the garden where the fairies played. We would spend hours down there making up games and playing with the nature spirits. We discovered new English plant friends in the form of rhubarb, blackberries and gooseberries. We found holes, like portals, in the large hedge at the bottom of the garden that took us into new worlds and lands beyond. The garden itself was very formal and well-manicured (very different to the mountain wilderness I knew) and often I would speak with the clipped plants and trees, almost daring them to break free and grow in different directions to spite us humans. They never did. Perhaps they couldn't hear me with my American accent and foreign ways. Perhaps I didn't give them a chance to answer me. I wasn't very good at listening to anyone at this time, retreating further and further within my hardening warrior's shell to shield myself from a world I didn't understand.

On the odd occasion that I would bump into our landlady in the hall, I would feel very shy and rarely want to speak. She was kind enough in an aloof, English way. I found I could look past her wrinkles into eyes that spoke of years of enduring sadness and the suppression of her real joys in life. The story I saw in her face was one of melancholy and regret. She had found herself alone in her eighties, and all she had left were the pictures of her trip to China on her wall; a reminder of her once youthful adventure into the unknown. For my seventh birthday, she gave me an old Chinese scroll that showed an ancient painting of a vast field of horses. She knew I loved horses. Once, she told my sisters and me about the time she visited the lands of the Orient as a young woman. In those days, this was 'quite daring'. She spoke of the beautiful gardens and friendly people. It was the only time I ever saw a sparkle in her old, misty eyes and for a moment, it reminded me of the sparkling mica in the red rocks of my mountain home.

I missed the mountains every day like a deep ache in the core of my soul. It didn't go away or lessen. The ache remained, despite my mother reassuring me that, *"Time would heal."* Even when I was laughing and playing with my sisters, it was still there, reminding me of a loss that was beyond my control. When I was sleeping, my mountain home pervaded my dreams and when morning came, I woke with memories of sunshine and the laughter of my rock, pine and yucca friends. I missed them. Most of all though, I missed the sun. Colorado is known for having anywhere between 250–300 days of sunshine a year and I had grown up with its warm vital energy shining on my face almost every day. Even when it had rained or snowed, the storm would pass swiftly and the sun would reappear again, reminding me that all was well in the world. The sun was my constant reminder that there was warmth and love in the world. This wasn't the case in England. Here it seemed like we had 300 days of rain and gray cloud that would stretch on forever.

LIVING IN THIS STORY WAS ALL MY CHOICE.

In retrospect, I now realize that much of the grayness and dark clouds that I saw in England were actually only the projections of my own inner sadness and confusion. My sense of isolation, grief and separateness from the world around me was reflected back through the cold drizzle of England. My inner world had turned gray and cold and I felt as though there was nothing that I could do to make it otherwise. Of course, living in this story was all my choice.

The first testing period of my young life had begun in earnest.

CHANGE THE STORY

EVERYTHING IS TRUE, FROM A CERTAIN POINT OF VIEW

Me – Choose one of the pivotal test experiences from your life and start to tell it aloud as if you were narrating a fairy tale or a myth. Change aspects of the story as you tell it using your intuition for the areas that need healing, resolving and putting to rest. Re-tell your story as often as you need to until you feel an emotional shift in your body to a more comfortable way of experiencing this event.

We – Repeat the exercise above, this time asking a friend to be your audience and coach you through the process. Having someone to bounce your inner stories off can unlock powerful new perspective when they are seen through different eyes.

The stories we form as protection mechanisms following tough or testing times can stick with us. They can embed themselves deeply in our unconscious and provide an unseen filter for our adult experiences. We place judgments on people, places and even the weather, blaming external factors for the discontent that we feel inside. If we can become aware of them, these old stories of blame can be gateways that transform our experiences of our past and open up channels of healing in our present. Powerful reframing can happen when we take a particularly challenging memory and restory it in the moment.

Death comes early

> You have left and yet I feel you still
> I see your face smiling at me
> Reminding me that I am one with you
> And all things

We had been living in England for just over two months when the early morning call came. I remember being woken by my mother, with tears in her eyes, and brought downstairs without any explanation to the small study that my dad had been using for his work. It was early in the morning, maybe four or five o'clock, I guessed, by the pre-dawn light outside. My father stood in the middle of the room in his light brown robe and had a look of confused anguish on his face that sent a tremor through my young nervous system.

My two sisters and I sat down on the small couch at the back of the room and after a few moments, my dad turned to us and said quietly, trying to control his emotions, *"Girls, I have some bad news. Your uncle Colin has died."*

Six years old is an interesting point in life to encounter the death of a loved one for the first time. Initially, my head couldn't, or maybe wouldn't, comprehend what my father was saying. The thought that my favorite uncle, my young uncle of 19 years, the man who had introduced me to Star Wars,[15] was gone from this earth was quite inconceivable to me. I remember crying more in response to my parents' pain and grief than to my own feelings. I found myself thinking that I should be feeling something resembling loss or sadness, but I wasn't. Maybe it was the shock, maybe it was that my young self had no way of really understanding what was happening, or maybe it was because I knew, deep down, that he was not really gone forever. Either way, I realized something big had happened.

I do recall feeling guilty about the deep joy that blossomed within me when we boarded the plane back to Denver a week or so later. I was going home (even if the journey was for a sad reason). In a way, I was grateful to my uncle for providing this excuse. My soul was bouncing and leaping, flipping in ecstatic loops as we drove up the canyon road to my grandparents' house. I said a joyous hello to every tree, rock and animal that we passed. *'Home, home, home!'* my heart was beating. But my elation was cut short when we walked through the front door of the mesa house and I saw my grandmother. She looked like a wraith of her former, strong self. On seeing us enter, she dissolved into sobbing that wracked her body and had an unearthly quality to its sound. I was scared, sad and confused all at once. It was the first time I experienced grief.

Given my only reference point for death was 'The Force' in Star Wars – of which we all become a part when we die – it was not surprising that I couldn't feel the same level of pain as the adults around me. To me, my uncle was not gone, he had just journeyed to a place where we could not follow in the car. He was still there. I could feel him. I even thought for a moment that as I watched my grandmother weeping, I could see my uncle with his arms around her, trying to tell her not to be sad. My uncle had been so happy. He didn't like to see people sad.

The following week was a strange roller-coaster experience for me that moved up and down between exquisite joy as I reveled in being in my favorite place on earth, and a deep concern and confusion at the behavior of the adults around me. To me, it was obvious that my uncle was not only okay, but safe and content wherever he was. Years later, I found out that my mother had gone up to his old apartment to get some plates and turned around to see him standing there in the doorway, as real as he had been in his physical life, telling her that he was okay and happy. Had I known about this at the time it would have simply added more justification to the childhood wisdom that 'knew' there was a deeper reality than the one in which we lived in our waking lives.

As the elder sibling, I kept my sisters occupied playing, whilst I gazed fondly out of the windows in my favorite house and wandered drunk with love around the mountain gardens. I also knew that soon I would have to leave again, back to the gray, cold sadness of England and I wanted to drink in every moment I had here in my heart home.

TOUGH BLISS

MY CHILDHOOD WISDOM 'KNEW' THERE WAS A DEEPER REALITY THAN THE ONE IN WHICH WE LIVED.

On the day of my uncle's funeral, I was surprisingly sleepy. For a girl that didn't nap, I found myself an hour before the ceremony falling asleep in the library of the mesa house, on my grandmother's white embroidered pillow that had small cotton bobbles forming the shape of a heart. I dreamed strange, beautiful dreams where I was walking across the bright sunlit mesa, hand in hand with my uncle. I was blissfully happy and marvelously free. Suddenly, I was startled back into the 'real world' by my father saying it was time to go. *'Go where,'* I wondered? But I was too drowsy to cry or make much of a protest. My cheek had the pincushion pattern of the embroidered heart on it and I remember trying to say to my father that I wanted to go back to sleep and play with Colin, but he lifted me up and carried me out the front door into the sunlight, despite my sleepy protests.

The funeral was being held on the beautiful canyon-side of my grandparents' land and the whole family stood in a circle as my papa said some words that I can't recall now. Sleepily, I gazed up at the turquoise blue sky and saw my uncle's face looking down at me, smiling just as he had in my dream. He was saying goodbye to us all. I suddenly had a sense that it was time for him to go beyond this world and embark on a new adventure. As I absorbed his message, the implications finally hit me and I felt a deep sense of loss in the pit of my stomach. He was leaving us.

My grandfather started to pass the marble box that contained my uncle's ashes around the circle so we could all say our goodbyes. When the box came to me, I tried to grab it and hug it. I wanted to hold onto my uncle with all my human might but my small arms couldn't support the weight of the heavy stone. My aunt, next to me, took the box from me before I could hold on tighter and he was gone. I now felt what the adults had been feeling. I cried. I forgot my Jedi wisdom of connection. It was as if in that moment of human pain, I accepted the story that someone I had loved could be gone forever. I started to believe the myth of separation.

I cried on and off for the next day and sobbed even harder when my parents calmly but firmly guided me into the back seat of the car to drive to the airport. I was now experiencing a double loss of two things that I had loved deeply all my young life: the mountains and my beloved uncle. I felt abandoned by everything I had loved. The ache within my heart seemed to pierce all the way through to my soul in that drive to the airport and I felt a deepening of this aching pain that would persist for many years to come: the deep ache of a myth that had me believe in human disconnection with the universe.

Loss is an interesting thing. It is often deeply painful, especially when it relates to someone you have loved and accepted as a core part of your life. Even though on one level I think we all sense death as being a doorway instead of an ending, it is hard to accept some of our basic human privileges are gone forever: the ability to hug that person and tell them how much you love them; the chance to smile and laugh, to argue and fight; to share food together; to dance and play. Maybe this is what gives us our ability to experience compassion and empathy as we grow? In knowing loss, we can also know connection. In knowing grief, we can also know love.

In knowing loss, we can also know connection.

Over the years, I have learned to use my experiences of death and grief as a reminder to enter into a deeper and fuller love of the moments of connection in life, knowing that soon they will also pass. Nothing remains the same for long in this world. There is a shadow of sadness in joy, and a future of joy in pain. Both are the endless weaving of the sparks and tests of life.

School of tears

You see sadness
I feel anger
The more you push
The deeper my inner thunder

My parents found me a school a few miles from where we lived. I suspect they were initially taken by the romance of its Englishness and the cute, dark green uniforms that the children who attended it had to wear. For me though, the uniform was not cute. It represented conformity, which was the polar opposite of what I had resolved to do. I wanted to rebel as hard as I could.

The only school I had attended prior to this was an American kindergarten that had consisted of playing in the sunshine, painting, dressing-up and 'scratch 'n' sniff' stickers. This might give you an idea of how I reacted when I was told I had to sit quietly at a desk inside a classroom all day and behave just like all the other kids. To say I was unhappy is an understatement; to say that I refused flat-out to participate is more accurate – followed by floods of angry tears and a burning rage when I realized that I was being given no choice. I internally made an oath to the universe that I would make everyone's life a living hell until I found a way to break free of what I perceived to be ridiculous rules and a denial of my basic freedom. And that is exactly what I did.

On my first day, I was escorted into my classroom and confronted by a sea of staring faces. I felt like a new animal on display at the zoo; caged behind walls that no one else could see but me. I was told to sit down at a shared desk with some other children, yet I hardly saw or registered their presence. On the inside I was a churning thunderstorm of emotion: rage, sadness and a deep feeling of abandonment by my mother who had encouraged, cajoled and in fact dragged me to this strange place in a foreign country. I couldn't tune in to any part of the reality around me, and felt as though I was living in a bad movie. My teacher's voice at the front of the class sounded muted and indistinguishable.

The scene around me faded into a gray haze as again and again, waves of emotion coursed through me. I did the only thing I could think to do: I cried. I cried and I cried, for days in fact. My teacher and the other students didn't know what to do with me. I figured that if they were going to make me be here then I would do my best to make it miserable for everyone to have me around, until someone, out of exasperation, brought me home. Well, at least took me to the cold dark house that I had no choice but to call home.

In the days I was there, between the fits of tears, I found the English version of school very formal, strict and, quite frankly, boring. The energy in the school buildings was constrictive and dour. The only way that the teachers knew how to help children learn was by rote, using ragged old textbooks that looked like they had been used to teach the teachers themselves many years earlier when they were young. The corridors, for all their decoration of artwork from the students, were gray and 'fogey' (a word that I learned from a fellow student when I asked why it looked so awful). Fogey meant old-fashioned, apparently.

Occasionally, when my daily misery reached its peak, my teacher would come over and offer me a hug. I guess she could see how alone and sad I was. She totally missed the anger part. I was boiling over with hatred for the situation that I had been forced into. For the stupid weather, the stupid school, the stupid people and the stupid parents who were refusing to listen to my pain. I wanted to make others suffer in the same way that I was suffering. Not out of pure spite, you must understand, but because it was the only way I knew how to make them listen when my words were having no effect. And it worked, eventually.

My mother must have realized that I wouldn't be backing down on this, or perhaps my poor teacher said there was nothing she could do with me. Either way, my parents started to look around our neighborhood for a school that was a little more relaxed in its approach. They found one. It had friendly teachers and a large garden to the back of the classrooms where the children could run and play at break times (in sharp contrast to the concrete playground in my current prison). I actually cracked a smile when I saw it, which was obviously enough for my mother who enrolled me to start as soon as possible. And the best part was that it had no uniform!

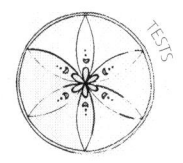

When I experienced the formal education system for the first time in England, three things struck me above all else.

1. How unhappy and joyless everyone in that system appeared to be.

2. How little school taught you about 'real life'.

3. How rarely any of my questions were actually answered, outside of the *"Because I said so"* or *"Because it's on the test"* scripted response of the teacher.

Now, things seem to be changing, I am happy to say. Our teachers, educators and innovators are starting to see the vast potential of experiencing learning in new ways. Our little people are growing into big people and creating new systems of learning both inside and outside of formal education. Perhaps there will be a time in the future where the crying of children in classrooms is no longer ignored. I am holding out for that day.

FAMILY HEALING

IS YOUR FAMILY A SOURCE OF PAIN OR A SOURCE OF POWER?

Me – Pick a 'testing story' from your family history. It should be one that still causes you emotional and mental pain, as these memories are the doorways to massive personal healing. Close your eyes and relive the story, this time stopping intuitively in moments of discomfort. Instead of staying in your story, imagine you can jump into the body of anyone else in this memory and see if you can empathize or understand what they were feeling in this moment. By walking in their shoes, you may gain a new perspective and be able to understand/forgive/release any old judgments you have regarding this story.

We – If you are brave enough and feel called, find a space and time to retell and relive the experience of a challenging time that you shared with family members. Each member involved in the experience takes time to share their story of this experience, whilst the others simply listen in silence and witness it. After everyone has shared, you can enter into a dialogue to notice how each of your experiences has changed by listening to each other's stories. What strengths and talents are now visible that were hidden before? What has transformed in your own personal story as a result?

Our families are often tricky territory, emotionally and mentally. Whether we maintain close or distant relationships as we grow into adulthood, they have the ability to offer us a mirror into our early experiences and the stories we have created around them. If one is brave and open enough, working through the memories of our younger years can offer us new insights into the lessons and blessings that our testing times provided everyone involved. Some of my most profound healings have come from sharing the stories of my tests with family members and hearing their own experience of that time reflected back to me. Rifts have been healed, pain released and new epiphanies into the gift of my challenges were revealed.

Afraid of the dark

> Afraid of the potential held in the unseen
> Unaware that it lies within my own being
> Shadow within, shadow without
> Can we face our mirror to see what the fuss is about?

I had developed a fear of the dark. It wasn't just a fear of nighttime or dark places, it was a fear of any environment where I couldn't see what was around me. My fear manifested itself in many ways. I was afraid of putting my bare feet too close to the edge of my bed at night in case there was something underneath it in the dark that would grab my ankles and pull me under. I developed a fear of deep water where I couldn't see what was around or beneath me as I swam. I had a fear of nighttime in the garden, that made otherwise familiar trees change into threatening figures and disturbing hollows. I was afraid of what my powerful imagination might manifest in the shadows. Anything I couldn't see, I couldn't control and therefore was frightening to me. Sound familiar?

We had moved away from the big, cold house in the city and out into a small cozy cottage on one of the only hills in the Cambridgeshire countryside. The house was nestled at the bottom of a wooded slope and surrounded by fields as far as the eye could see. My sisters and I had fallen in love with it immediately. Because of where we lived, the milkman came to an arrangement with my mother that he would leave our bottles up at the top of the hill at our landlady's house to save him having to make the long trip down to our cottage. This meant that if we happened to be out of milk in the morning before school, someone (me) and our dog Lucy would have to make the trek up the hill to pick up the milk. Given that it was England, high in the northern hemisphere, for at least six months of the year this trek took place in the dark. My mother would have to cajole and bribe me before I would finally accept the inevitable task ahead. My little sisters were too small to go alone and my dad was busy getting ready for work. There was only me left to take on this mission. It was my challenge.

So out of the door I would go with Lucy, my border collie companion, bounding along beside me without a care in the world. If I was slow, she would scamper back, jumping up and down in front of me with the look of, '*Come on, this is fun*,' in her soft brown eyes. But to me it was not fun. To me, it was like walking the gauntlet of my own deep fears every morning that I had to do it. I would jog past the horse stable (which was often empty of any horses) and scamper past the darkened shapes of bushes, taking a pause at the top of the hill before plunging into the scariest part of this escapade: the woods.

THE TESTS

TO WHAT DEGREE ARE WE ALL AFRAID OF THE DARKNESS WE PERCEIVE IN THE WORLD?

In the daytime, these woods were inviting and friendly, providing a safe haven for my play. However, in the pre-dawn darkness, they took on a menacing feel. My imagination created every ghost and ghoul that could exist in the human psyche and held them in the bushes and trees waiting to pounce on me. With a gulp and a prayer, I would run into the woods with Lucy hot on my heels, seeing how fast I could get through them to the relative safety of my landlady's house at the end. Having made it through unscathed (because I always made it through), I would grab the bottles of milk and race back through the woods again, my breath catching in my throat and my heart pounding in my chest. I wouldn't look back until I heard the slam of the boundary gate catching in the latch behind me. Half running, half skipping my way home, I would collapse through the front door of the cottage to find everything as I had left it 10 minutes or so before. My mother would usually greet me with a comment of, *"See! That wasn't so bad, was it?"* or something similar. Little did she know that the cause of my aversion to dark places went deeper than the morning milk run. I was starting to experience the collective human fear of the 'unknown' that drives so much of our global myths and systems today. To what degree are we all still afraid of the darkness we perceive in the world?

Around this time, I also began waking up in the middle of the night thinking about death. I would find myself bolted awake from my dreams into the deep inky blackness of the night, trembling with strong and painful emotions. First, it was the heart wrenching sadness of realizing that someday my parents would die and there was nothing I could do to stop it. Thoughts of loss, abandonment and emptiness would tear me apart inside. Following this awakening to parental mortality, I would lie in my bed wracked with tears, thinking about my sisters dying, my grandparents dying, and losing other beings that I loved, like Lucy and the trees. This deep fear and pain would eventually turn my thoughts towards contemplating what my own death would bring me when it came. Would I be lost in a void of nothingness for the rest of eternity? Would I live on in spirit form, wandering in different worlds, one with The Force, maybe? Would I be afraid at the moment of my death and regret the things I had never done? I finally vowed to myself, after months of these waking nightmares, that no matter what was to happen after my death, I would spend every moment I am here on this earth being happy and grateful for everything I am. I would live my life to the very maximum of what I was capable of (a vow that has driven me every day since and has left me feeling like I have lived one of the most blessed existences there is).

> THE ONLY THING I HAD CONTROL
> OF WAS THE CHOICES THAT I MADE.

I was encountering for the first time a deep awareness of my humanness: how fragile and delicate physical life here on earth actually is; how special and sacred living in a physical body can be. It scared me to think that things could, and inevitably would, change around me each and every day for the rest of my life and there was little I could do to control them. My nighttime mourning ceremonies continued for about six months as I subconsciously prepared myself for my initiation into the next phase of my mental, emotional and physical life. Gradually, I started to make my peace with the fact that a human life was transitory and short. I started to see that the only things I had control of were the choices that I made and the degree to which I loved my life and was grateful for my existence.

FACING OUR FEARS

ARE YOU BRAVE ENOUGH TO SEE THAT FEAR IS SELF-CREATED?

Me – Find time to go outside and take a walk in nature. Try not to think of any of your tests in any great detail. Just hold them all loosely as a concept in your awareness. As you walk, breathe deeply. Often these childhood fears lie buried in our muscles, hidden from our mind. Notice any places of tension in your body and bring awareness to them. After a few minutes, see whether any patterns in your fears become clear. Have you been dancing through specific relationship or career tests, time and again? Have you held onto old fear and anxiety from your younger years? These larger patterns are our deeper human story in action. They are our unique storylines working their way through the weave of our lives, spinning in spirals of lessons where time and again we are given the opportunity to discover and live more of our truth. Many of our test patterns begin early in life and then continue to manifest until we have the awareness to spot and shift the pattern from lesson to gift.

We – Find another trusted person who is willing to play an imaginative game with you. Face each other and take it in turns to play the role of each other's fears. The person playing fear can state out loud that which they are embodying such as, "*I am the darkness.*" The person facing their fear can take the opportunity to interview this story and find out what is hidden beneath its surface. Make sure you look for hidden gifts that this testing fear has brought to you.

Often the things we develop a fear of when we are very young persist in an unconscious and metaphorical form into our adulthood. Surfacing these early memories and the associated beliefs they create can be a fast track towards understanding patterns that continue to hold you back decades later. A sense of humility, humor and loving compassion for ourselves as adventurers is helpful here. Each soul on earth travels their story spiral and encounters its tests. It is normal to judge ourselves for our perceived failures and experience pride for our successes. This is healthy to the degree that we are able to acknowledge it and move beyond the story of success or failure. They are all just opportunities to grow and expand. Like any narrative, they are only a partial retelling of a greater pattern of truth.

The game of love

> No longer a girl
> Too young to know what being a woman is
> Lessons in power and lust
> Show us where our integrity sits

I was 13 when I had my first taste of the power of feminine sexuality. We moved away from the cottage on the hill at this time as my family was buying its first house. The area wasn't prosperous, far from it, but the small semi-detached house faced out onto a large expanse of grass, and had trees that framed the street and a park at one end. We had a small front and rear garden and enough rooms so I could have a bedroom to myself, which made me feel a little better about the transition.

Despite my initial nerves, I found myself excited to meet potential new friends my age who might live close by. After five years of being secluded in the country, my adolescence was transforming into early womanhood and I became particularly interested in dynamics with the opposite sex. Physically, mentally and emotionally (according to my father) I was already acting like a young woman in her late teens rather than her early ones. My fantasies had also taken on a decidedly adult look and feel, peppered with romance, sex and danger. I couldn't fail to notice that I was drawing the looks and attention of men of all ages around me. Whether these were the boys in my class at school or much older men who walked past me in the street, I fed off their sideways glances and admiring stares like a flower to sunshine.

In contrast, my relationship with my father during this period was dominated by numerous fights and control battles. Perceiving a lack of love from him, I sought constant validation through other men. The grown woman I was trying so hard to become was little more than a thought or an idea in my mind, but my powerful imagination convinced me otherwise and did a pretty good job of it. I already considered myself to be the wild warrioress, the passionate lover and the wise priestess. Ironically (on a soul level) perhaps I was all of these archetypes and more, but it was my human ego, not my soul, that was the driving force behind my emerging sultry teenage temptress adventures.

With increasing frequency, I found myself longing to be kissed, held and dissolved in passionate embraces within a strong masculine energy. I wanted to feel the sensation of skin on skin and delve deep into another's body, mind and soul. Essentially, I fell in love with the idea of being in love and being beloved; an easy thing to do in our society where we are bombarded with the story of romantic love and sex from all angles. This is even easier when sex is constantly portrayed as love and we assume that they are the same thing, or that one is a requirement for the other.

Beneath my longing was an urge that few have been able to define in our society to this day. I ached to express my essential feminine nature, merging back into the unity of life and dissolving the pain relating to my sense of separation. I was aspiring to 'erotic experience' in its pure tantric form, expressed through the dance between individuality and unity. I believe that the union we all long for deep inside relates to a more ancient and natural urge for an erotic engagement with the world, 'Eros' in this sense being the sensual magnetic force that draws us into a relationship with life itself – where the world and everything in it becomes our infinite, eternal lover, not just the human partners we choose to engage with. But how was I to know that at 13?

EROTIC EXPERIENCE IN ITS PURE TANTRIC FORM IS EXPRESSED
THROUGH THE DANCE BETWEEN INDIVIDUALITY AND UNITY.

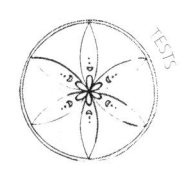

After a few months of living in our new neighborhood I had pretty much figured out the social landscape. It consisted of several different cliques of various ages, all with carefully formed group identities. There was the 'nice kids' gang which both of my sisters quickly joined, made up of sweet souls mostly with difficult parental relationships, who generally played it pretty safe when it came to social experimentation and adventure. They would hang out at the park or at each other's houses, watching movies, listening to music and laughing at each other's jokes. All in all they were good kids, with good hearts, trying to ignore the social deprivation around them and come through their adolescence relatively unharmed.

Then there were the older motorbike gangs. These kids had either dropped out of school or were in the process of doing so, and sought danger wherever they could find it through petty crime, alcohol, drugs or sex. Although I dearly loved nonconformance and was flattered when they courted me for a while, there was something inside me that steered me away from these people; an inner knowing that the games they played were a little too dangerous, even for my imagined rebel personality. The thought of spending time with them sent a shudder down my spine and fortunately I was smart enough to listen to it.

Finally, there were the 'outsiders', the stragglers, the kids who didn't fit into any neat category. It was there that I started looking for my companions. Being different myself (the natural shadow of the rebel archetype), I could spot a fellow sufferer of this affliction a mile away. One evening towards the end of the summer, I happened to be hanging out of my bedroom window watching the kids messing around in the park, when I saw a tall boy cycling around the block. He looked a lot older than most of the kids and certainly had an air of 'difference' around him. I sat up and inspected him more closely. After leisurely cycling through the park and stopping to talk briefly to the biker gang, he laughed nonchalantly at something that had been said and then took off towards a house across from ours on the other side of the green.

Over the next few weeks, I made my enquiries and found out more about the mystery boy on the bike. He lived in the house across the park with his mother, twin brother and younger sister. He didn't have a job but wasn't in school or college either (rebel box ticked for me), and he didn't seem to belong to any of the neighborhood gangs (again, tick). I was intrigued, or more to the point, my ego was engaged, so I did what any other teenage girl heading into a conquest would do: I befriended his little sister. I soon found myself invited over 'to play' and turned my developing feminine wiles on full volume. It wasn't long before he bit, hook, line and sinker, and we became an official 'item'.

I remember thinking that my parents would be more upset by the age gap between us than they actually were. My mother was worried, of course, but it is testament to her character and intuition that she knew that anything she did to try and stop me from seeing him would have the opposite effect and would push me further into his arms. So she sighed, and she worried. My father didn't seem to notice or care much, perhaps the 60s hippy side of him expected this from his difficult eldest daughter – but either way, he didn't comment on the affair. So, I was left to my own devices to work out what an intimate relationship was all about.

From the moment I started reading adult fiction, I had wanted to experience sex. In my mind, I imagined it to be one of the most exciting, fulfilling things that two people could engage in. I figured that once you had this bond and connection, breathtaking, earth-shattering love must inevitably follow. I decided that I was ready and started asking my boyfriend if he felt that way too. He almost fell off his chair when I first raised the topic, not believing his luck and pinching himself that I was the one bringing forward the request. At the time, he connected my forward sexual nature to the fact that I was American and that must be 'how they do things that side of the pond'. However, I don't believe this to be the case; I was ready for this next level of relationship early and I was bold in creating the situation in which I could get it.

We picked a quiet afternoon in the week and he came around to my house with a huge grin on his face. I bunked off school for the day pretending to be sick (an increasingly common habit of mine at this time, given my distaste for learning anything that was enforced upon me). He'd said he had 'done it' once before with a previous girlfriend, but I didn't necessarily believe him. He hadn't exactly played the field much, which in turn made me feel even more powerful. As we started to kiss and caress, I felt something ancient take over my actions. I began to move and lead our sexual dance as if remembering something I had done many, many times before. He seemed a little taken aback but went with me and displayed the utmost consideration for me at all times. I felt loved, cherished and in control. The actual act of making love happened very quickly (and somewhat awkwardly due to the need for contraception) and I have to say, wasn't anything like I had expected it to be. This had nothing to do with my poor boyfriend, who didn't have a hope of stacking up to the imaginary feelings I had built-up in my fantasies for so many years. I had presupposed that I would be swept away in waves of passionate orgasm, losing myself in the merging with another's body, when in reality, I felt slightly hurt as he entered my body.

Fairly quickly, the whole thing was over. Whereas he looked like a cat that had gotten all the cream, I felt disappointed and underwhelmed. After he left, I pondered the whole experience and wondered whether I had done anything wrong. I ran through my moves and assessed myself against the movies I had seen and the books I had read. I felt like I had done it all right; after all, my boyfriend seemed to be pretty blown away by the whole thing. In this reflective moment in my room, I am pretty sure I was thinking similar thoughts to ones echoed by millions of girls the world over when we have our first experience of consensual sex and it doesn't turn out to be what we expected it to be. We wonder why 'we' are the ones who must have been at fault.

So, with this as the unconscious psychological backdrop, I concluded that I needed more practice and that is exactly what I began doing, forever seeking the depth of presence, love and connection I expected could be found in sexual love between two people. It wasn't until my 30s that I would finally find it, having come to the brink of giving up searching completely. But for now, I would content myself knowing that the truth of what I felt was possible was out there – somewhere.

The bully

> There is voice deep inside
> That can both hurt and love
> The choice of which we feed is up to us
> It will determine who we become

I was now at the stage in my adolescence where I wanted to fit in. The trouble was that I knew deep down I had very little in common with the other kids around me. The reason for this I suspect was the fact that, like most young people, none of us really knew who we were. We had hit the point in our lives where our parents could no longer dictate our worlds (not that I had ever allowed mine to anyway) and we were striving desperately to become individuals in a society that valued 'me' above 'we'. So, we spent our days going from one social charade to another, changing our personality masks like we changed our clothes. To create added tension in this drama, my inner rebel fought against me all the way. My unconscious worship of difference and uniqueness would kick in and often sabotage any friendships that I attempted to make, keeping my belief of being alone and separate from mainstream culture vibrant and alive. Despite this, I tried to play the game of friendship anyway, and put on the various masks of acceptability to find ways of being the key in the lock of the different social groups in my school. Astonishingly, there was even a particular time where I decided to connect with the 'popular girls'. I was invited to a couple of parties and then started to hang out with them after school. This play continued for a couple of months until inevitably the script took me towards my point of exit and learning.

It was a sunny, late spring day and I had joined this group of girls for lunch. There was no space for me on the bench in the school playground with the rest of them so I had taken up a spot towards the outside of the circle and was attempting to chime into the conversation that was about boys. Not having a boyfriend at this point in my life, I didn't have any immediate point where I could enter into the dialogue, which had started to revolve around who was being taken out to what party this weekend. My ego started to dig me in the ribs and a familiar tension started in my stomach. I recognized it as the ache of being alone and insignificant. A voice softly whispered, *'You are not the same as them and they know it.'* The voice continued, gaining volume: *'You aren't as cool as they are...No one is going to take you to a party this weekend, let alone want to fall in love with you...You are different and alone.'* I felt small and insignificant in this game of one-upmanship going on between the girls. I felt like I didn't matter to any of them or anyone.

It's in moments like these that our own inner pain of separation and low self-worth creates the space for our egos to do stupid things. It opens the door to solutions that on the outside look like they will make us feel better, but in the end lead us in the opposite direction. My ego jumped in with a plan to stop me from feeling the pain of not belonging. It found me a lie. Plucking up all the bravado I could muster, I waited for a gap in the conversation and said, *"Well I am going to a party this weekend with a bunch of older kids from my neighborhood."*

Silence.

"Which kids?" one of the girls asked pointedly.

"Oh, just the boys from down the street who ride the motorbikes," I replied quickly – perhaps a little too quickly, or perhaps it was the uncertain look on my face that gave away my fabrication.

More silence and then a few giggles and knowing looks passed between the other girls. My feeling of sickness intensified as it does when we know we have been caught out.

"Oh really?" one of the ringleaders in the group said to me. *"So, what are their names?"*

I searched desperately for an answer that would seem convincing and it must have shown on my face because the giggles started again.

"*Jason and his crew,*" I replied, trying to look nonchalant. I felt waves of nausea passing through my body. I knew I had been found out and that all illusionary respect that I might have gathered before now was in tatters around my ego's feet.

"*Genne, Genne, Genne...*" the girl said, smiling sarcastically, "*...will you never learn?*"

I pretended to smile and cover over my pain and embarrassment. Thankfully, the other girls lost interest and continued their conversation where it had been left off. I sat there desperately searching for some form of redemption. Some strategy that could stop me from feeling the pain of humiliation. All I thought I wanted was to be liked and respected and I had been willing to do anything in a futile attempt to gain it. All I really wanted deep down was to feel like I belonged to something that would for a moment ease the deep pain of isolation I felt inside. I was feeling the pain that we all carry as human beings living within the myth of separation.

> IT IS IN THE MOMENT WE FAIL
> THAT WE LEARN MORE ABOUT OURSELVES.

The next day, I stopped hanging around with the popular girls. I retreated into solitude and loneliness once more, waiting for the next group of individuals to emerge with whom I would again search for love and a connection (in vain). My ego created a survival strategy during this time that would serve me well (and not so well) in the years to come, but would bring me eventually to one of the biggest lessons of my life. It created the strategy of the escape artist. Mysterious and alluring, but distant. I wouldn't stay with anyone for long, preferring to leave before I was hurt or rejected. I would retreat behind the curtains of my fickle, ever-changing personality so that no one ever had a chance of seeing the real vulnerable soul underneath the myriad of costumes.

TESTS JOURNEY

ARE YOU READY TO SEE YOUR TESTS AS GIFTS?

Tests can come in many guises and to a degree, they will be unique to your journey, meaning only you have the ability to recognize them and acknowledge the lessons and blessings that they have brought.

Me – Grab a large piece of paper, card or any other medium that you wish to work with. Now, find a quiet space where you can create some sacred time to reflect and meditate upon the different tests you have taken so far. Without overthinking it too much, write down a list of all the major lessons you have experienced in your life. These can be what you would call positive or negative tests (you may wish to split these into two lists so you can track your highs and lows).

In chronological order draw a 'story wave', with the Tough Tests you deemed yourself to have 'failed' in some way on the bottom troughs and the high Bliss Tests where you see yourself having emerged triumphant on the top. You should end up with something that resembles a waveform in some way. There is no correct way to do this; your story wave will be unique to you. Just as an oak tree wouldn't compare itself to a palm tree, each of us appears in the world as our unique story wave in vibrational form. Each vibration is connected to the wider human mythological system, and yet is also unique in its form in the time it plays out.

Each test was the resulting product of the ebb and flow of your vibrational story wave in action. You may notice that you have more highs or more lows; or that they do not balance out. This gives you an insight into your internal categorization story for the tests. Do you perceive your tests as life's struggles, or liberating comfort zone challenges? There is no judgment here, simply information. Once you have gained awareness of your vibrational mythology, you can consciously choose to change its frequency.

Once you have drawn your wave and labeled each high and low experience with a word that describes the lesson, take a moment to look for the 'gift' you received in each case as a result of this test. What did you learn about yourself? What did you discover? A strength: a belief or an ability you had and brought to bear to move through the test; or perhaps a failure to stand in your strength and be who you could be in that moment. The failures are also gifts. It is in the moment we fail that we learn more about ourselves and gain an experience that we can use when we try again next time.

We – If you wish to, find a trusted loved one and narrate your story wave, as honestly and vulnerably as you feel able to. Bring light to the highs and lows of your life lessons. See what happens when someone else listens and has an opportunity to respond. In retelling your evolving personal story, you may find that you give permission to the other person to do the same and you both grow in strength and awareness.

THE CLUES

HOW IS MY LIFE GIVING ME THE ANSWERS I SEEK?

I believe that within every being in the universe there is a compulsion to seek: a star seeks to expand its internal heat until it burns its bright life out; a plant, forging upwards, seeks the light of the sun so it can grow and expand; a bird seeks its nesting place so it can reproduce and fulfill its primal urges; and human beings seek to find our true place, story and reason for existing so we can come to peace and happiness within our hearts and souls. It's a quest that we often can't put into words yet it's ever present, lurking underneath the surface of our thoughts, feelings and actions in every moment of our lives.

This act of 'seeking' draws us continually out of our comfort zones and old narratives towards the edges of the unknown. By its very nature, if we are seeking, in some way we feel that we are lacking something – the object of our search. The alchemical process of clarifying what this object might be is core to our ability to bring our story alive in the world. We can (and often do) spend years aching on the inside with our own incompleteness, hurting with the growing pains of our constant 'becoming' as a human being in evolution. The search itself is our core story thread and we are continually exploring its elements and attributes whether we realize it or not. These can manifest in our underlying search for the 'right partner', the 'right job' or the 'right home'.

THE SEARCH ITSELF IS OUR CORE STORY THREAD.

We often believe that we may have found the object of our search, only to realize that it wasn't what we were after. The partner of our dreams starts to annoy us as our honeymoon period draws to a close; our ideal home eventually stops being so shiny; the new 'thing', whatever that may be, becomes old and boring. Thus, we spend our lives moving along the path of our own adventure, drawn ever forwards by our seeking, letting go of the objects that we come across as we find they were really just illusory pots of gold at the end of our rainbows. When we finally grasp them, their intrigue disappears like dust in our hands.

The real object of our seeking remains elusive and hidden behind its own paradoxical nature: it is the simplest thing in the whole world and simultaneously the most difficult to find. It is our search to find the truth of who we really are as a unique human being and to become this in our daily lives, bringing alive our biggest story in the world. It is our search to find completion inside that brings this about in our external lives.

The inner revelation of the essence of our authentic story leads to an outer healing of our lives that eventually ripples outwards into the communities and ecosystems of which we are a part. Yet, the process is inner to outer: in the holographic experience of life, the micro provides clues to the macro. As the ancient axiom goes, 'As within, so without', in continual cycles of awakening and evolution.

Clues that point towards this inner state of self-realization pepper our experiences, if we have the eyes to see them and the ears to hear their poetry. It can take us years to develop the reflective capabilities to 'live mythically', noticing the signs and symbols that point the way towards the source of our seeking and becoming. These clues can be obvious, for example near-death encounters, or more subtle, as in dreams, repeated emotional patterns and unexpected opportunities. The threads of our soul story wind their way through the forest of our tests, challenges and accomplishments leading us gradually towards a realization of who we are, what we are here to do and how we wish to live our lives.

> IN THE HOLOGRAPHIC EXPERIENCE OF LIFE,
> THE MICRO PROVIDES CLUES TO THE MACRO.

The real trick is to learn to spot the clues as they are happening so that we can develop a greater ability to know whether we are on or off track towards the destiny of our deeper story. The even greater gift is to know when to act on these mini-miracles to create increasing momentum and magic in our lives. I have found that in the moments when I awaken to one of my personal clues, I receive what I have now come to call 'cellular shivers'. My whole body convulses in a pleasurable wave of expanding realization that I have just 'got it' and have been given an important piece in the puzzle of my story. This is my physical way of recognizing the energy of personal truth.

The more we move towards our true identity and story in the world, the faster the universe responds with signs and synchronistic events. Our courage here determines our results. In the quantum world, our beliefs, thoughts and emotions interact constantly with the energetic matrix of the universe around us, so that we are the co-creators of our lives. Despite being told consistently otherwise, the more we believe that magic is real, the more it will become so in our worlds. I have seen it. I have danced it. There is a realm of everyday magic where our intentions and intuitions weave their way (eventually) into the physical fabric of our daily lives, catalyzed by the sustained balancing of imagination and action.

> THE MORE WE MOVE TOWARDS OUR TRUE STORY,
> THE FASTER THE UNIVERSE RESPONDS WITH SIGNS
> AND SYNCHRONISTIC EVENTS.

Synchronicities can be either ignored or worshipped. Sometimes, when something mystical occurs, our minds decide to find a rational explanation for the miracle. This usually involves us fitting the experience into the narrower frame of our prevalent cultural story. We retreat from magic. We err towards caution and conformity in our meaning-making. On the other side of this fence, we also have the ability to create and spin amazing tales around these events, so much so that those around us simply can't believe in their miraculous truth. We exaggerate and accentuate the 'facts' of an experience, so much so that we lose our ability to question and discern within them. One of the challenges of the clues phase is that we must hone our sense of discernment in order to detect self-created illusions from truth.

Integrity becomes essential in order for us to flow with the tide of our unfolding magic; for us to spot the unique nature of our own personal essence amongst the noise of the world and act from that place of our own true nature. This often happens quietly and gracefully as opposed to parades and accolades.

The world goes soft

> All my life I have been seeking a truer reality that I know there is
> Sensual softening of my soul, I melt into everywhere
> Darkness and light dance into life, the more I look and stare
> Breathe in, breathe out, release
> I find myself reflected everywhere

I started experimenting with consciousness-altering substances early on in my teenage years and was 15 when I decided to try a drug that would forever shift my perception of what reality actually was. My friends had discovered LSD (or 'acid' as it was known then) and we all wanted to try some. When I took my first 'trip' I didn't even really know what acid was or what it would do to me. Just as well really, as had I known the facts before I consumed it for the first time, I might have never experienced the phenomenon I now call 'the world going soft'.

It was a balmy summer night when we all dropped our small square paper tabs onto our tongues in the warm evening glow of my friend's bedroom. We were excited and our talk centered on the experiences that my friend's brother had gone through when he first took acid; amazing visual hallucinations and strange encounters with non-human entities featured on the list. Rather than freaking me out, this only served to make me all the more impatient for the acid in my system to work its magic or, perhaps a better way of phrasing this would be, to reveal the magic that already surrounded me.

About an hour in, I was laughing at a joke when I noticed that something strange appeared to be happening with the walls of the room in which we were sitting. Focusing my attention on what I thought I was seeing, I felt a rush of excitement as the walls in the room all started to breathe. They were moving in and out at exactly the same rate as my own breathing. If I increased my breath, they did too. With a rush of excitement, I pointed this phenomenon out to my friends who, whether by coming up on their own trips or simply by the power of my suggestion, all suddenly found they could see the same thing. This was when the fun began.

As we started to look for other things visually happening around us, I noticed a growing sense of bliss spreading from the base of my spine, upwards through the center of my body. When I moved my hands in front of my face, they appeared to leave trails of living energy in their wake, like stars shooting through the sky. The environment around us began to sparkle and shine with colors taking on a vividness that made my memory of the everyday world seem bland and pale in comparison. Textures were heightened and came alive; everything I touched seemed exquisitely sensual and delicately precise as my skin caressed it. And 'caressing' is definitely the word that best describes how I started to interact with my friends and the environment around me. Like a child who has been let out into an amazingly beautiful summer garden for the first time, everything became an exploration of sight, sound and touch. I could now see with my physical eyes things that previously had only been there in my imagination. My hearing became acutely fine. If I tuned in to things, I could hear their subtle sounds, vibrations and inner music.

The plant in my friend's bedroom appeared to be singing softly to me and the earth beneath the house hummed with a low vibration that was ever present, and yet infinitely comforting, like the soft drone of a bedroom fan turning slowly on a hot summer's night.

We spent what seemed like days (although it was only a single night) lost in this liminal world of beauty. Venturing outside of my friend's bedroom, we rediscovered a whole new landscape outside of his house, where every normal object became the focus of our newly-fascinated attention. Lampposts became trees, trees became living, breathing beings and people became angels or demons depending on the particular vibe they were emulating to our LSD-spectacled eyes. The world seemed soft and malleable, as if we were dancing in co-creation with the living fabric of the universe that manifested itself into whatever dream or imagined form we would care to play with. What would have been fairly dingy orange streetlights in our normal sight became a dancing, swaying field of energy that would shift, move and transform into amazing shapes and energy beings. We reveled in this state, like intrepid adventurers on a quest for the secrets at the center of the universe.

When the dawn finally came and my senses started to return to normal, I almost cried at the contraction back inside my body, with its mundane limitations. My acid-fueled adventure had been a glimpse of a reality beyond the everyday world. I had always known it was there and wished to exist within it. Once I had achieved it, it seemed like punishment to go back to reality.

Despite my love of the expanded view that acid had given me on my first trip, I never became addicted to this drug, nor any other for that matter. I believe that intuitively I sensed the inherent fabrication of it all. Drugs were a tiny, transient window into a vision of the world that the ancient ones, the mystics and the storytellers knew was there and had trained themselves to see with sober eyes and clear minds. I also sensed an inherent danger in the world of drugs and was acutely aware of the mental stability and control that was needed when I was under the influence of chemicals to ensure that a good time with friends didn't fast change into a waking nightmare.

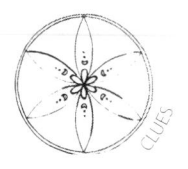

A few years later I had an experience on acid that would show me the difference between 'drug fun' and 'drug fear'. One night, towards the end of summer, a small group of us were bored and had decided to pop some trips to entertain ourselves. The acid wasn't strong (by now I had taken enough of it to know the difference) but I started to notice the usual telltale signs of it taking effect, like the walls breathing and colors coming vividly alive. We were also all smoking joints (marijuana) and I happened to be sitting next to a boy that I didn't like very much. He had a snake-like energy that made me feel jumpy and anxious whenever I was around him. A recipe for trouble was brewing and yet I chose to ignore my intuitive hunches to get out of there. As I took a long deep toke on a spliff, I noticed that he had started to lean in towards me and was looking at me in a way that made my skin crawl. He was speaking, but I couldn't focus on what he was saying. From reading his change in energy however, I surmised that he was trying to flirt and this sent a shiver of disgust down my spine. It was the first time I allowed negative emotions to come into my body whilst I was tripping and boy did I FEEL it. I started to experience the cold, dark fingers of fear creeping in around the edges of my awareness. The thing with LSD is that your emotions fast become visions and sensations, which can seem ultra-real no matter how much your rational brain tries to take control again and tell you otherwise.

The closer he leaned in to me, the more uncomfortable I became and in an attempt to label this feeling, my creative imagination came up with a dangerous metaphor: the fear I was feeling suddenly became a solid line of pain in my left shoulder that I fatefully imagined to be a tiny drill. The closer he came to me, the deeper the drill started going into my shoulder and the more I felt the associated pain. I started to get really scared. Even though I 'knew' that the drill wasn't real, it FELT real and knowing the power that imagination has to create reality, there was a growing feeling of doubt in my ability to keep control over my brain and body. As soon as the doubt appeared, the fear doubled. I started to breathe deeply and slowly thinking that if I focused on the air entering and leaving my lungs that it would save me. It didn't. The pain kept getting worse and worse. I knew I had to do something before my sense of reality cracked in two and the normal world was gone for good.

Without thinking, I stood up and started to walk out of the room. Moving quickly through my friend's dark house, I instinctively followed the scent of salvation. I didn't recognize my surroundings and yet knew that somewhere in the darkness there was an environment that would save me. Unknown shapes rose up as I moved from room to room and I knew that if I stopped to examine them for a moment I would be lost in the dark forever. Moving, seeking, longing, I found myself grasping a door handle. Turning it and opening the door, a rush of cool, life-giving air told me that I had found the object of my quest: the night garden. I fell outside, gasping in breath after breath of the refreshing air, the scent of the grass, and the flowers as they lay sleeping. I stopped, crying with relief as my heart rate started to slow and I felt myself surrounded by nature's friends and allies. The drill in my shoulder ceased and as I stood, my fingers reaching for a nearby tree. I started to regain my sense of control on the illusory world. The touch of bark on my skin grounded me back into my body and I knew I had been saved.

I never took acid again after that night and it would be years before I discovered my natural inherent human ability of lifting the veils of illusion to the 'world gone soft' once again. At least I now knew what the door to the real world looked like and it had a name: nature. All I had to do now was remember how to connect and commune with her. Terror had led me back to an important clue in my soul story.

Lessons in loving

> I look into your eyes and you carve me open
> There is nowhere I want to hide
> I pull you in deeper and deeper
> Together on the tides of love we ride

My middle name is Ninon: after Ninon de Lenclos,[16] the famous 17th century Parisian courtesan and teacher of sacred relationship. Perhaps this is where I inherited my interest and ideas on love and relating; perhaps it came with me from previous lifetimes. Either way, early in my teens I learned to swing my hips, pout my lips and swish my hair in ways that would send most boys crazy (and I unashamedly loved the power and control I felt when doing it). Walking down the street, I would count up the admiring stares that I received and it would make me feel special. Somewhere inside, the wounded little girl was saying to herself, *'See, I do matter, I am special. See how pretty and special I am to attract all this attention?'* The irony of all this attention seeking behavior is that at the same time that my ego fed off it, there was an even deeper part of me that hated the superficiality of the whole situation. I felt disgusted at being looked at 'like a piece of meat' by men who saw me only for sex, and I hated feeling cheap and preyed upon.

It was around the age of 15 when, in response to this deep-seated hate, I developed another behavior to contrast and complement the flirtation: dubbed the 'fuck off eyes', if, on any particular day, I didn't want male attention but received it, I would raise my eyebrows, stiffen my shoulders and jut out my chin, sending out waves of 'you are looking but you can't have me' energy. This was of course just another way my ego had found to make me feel attractive and superior all at once. Oh, the games we play to protect the wounded one inside us! I now know after years of working with women who have shared similar experiences to my own that this tends to be a learned female behavior which allows us to exert power over the masculine. After centuries of male domination, we have developed ways that allow us to control the men around us, yet very rarely are these practices healthy or honoring to the true essence of men or women. It takes maturity, openness and a desire to heal our inner stories about power and sexuality for us to seek and find balance in our relationships.

OH, THE GAMES WE PLAY TO PROTECT
THE WOUNDED ONE INSIDE US!

Despite all of these contrasting and uncomfortable experiences of growing into womanhood, I continued to dive back into the fray, learning and practicing on the playing field of one relationship after another. I was perpetually longing for and seeking a feeling of connection, love and completion in every fiber of my being. In my early teens, I had a string of unfulfilling and short-lived love affairs with different guys, each time bringing it to an end because I realized that this mask of masculinity in front of me was nothing like the image of the 'god' that I carried within my heart and psyche: for I wanted a man who could balance my feminine energy; who could be strong and yet sensitive; bold and secure in who he was, but courageous, adventurous and vulnerable at the same time. When I was 16, the universe decided to bring into my world a young man who would teach me some of my earliest and yet most powerful and profound lessons in love. It was with him that I received a glimpse of what it is to feel like a goddess in human form.

He was devastatingly unique, boldly carrying views that were counter-cultural and expressed himself in ways that made him stand out from the crowd. He listened to music that called to your soul in the dark of the night and carried himself in a way that was both mysterious and alluring. He was the most authentic person I had met in my short life and I fell head over heels in love with him.

I remember distinctly the first time he made love to me. Lying on the bed, he asked me if I had ever been kissed before. I laughed playfully and said, *"Of course!"* with a coy smile. He paused, the silence heavy with sexual tension and then repeated his question.

"No, I mean have you ever been really KISSED?" and with that he proceeded to ravish me open into a place that I had only ever experienced in my dreams. The subtlety of his movement across my skin took my breath away, connecting me to a place deep inside that was beyond any human experience. I felt loved, honored and utterly feminine for the first time in my life. It was as if I had been shown the secret door to the mystery of sex that I had been searching for and it wasn't long before I became addicted to this love. Together we danced for months in the dark, warm recesses of our sexual fantasies. We broke every sexual taboo that we wanted to and in doing so, shattered the illusion we had been sold by the mainstream culture as to what was an acceptable, normal sexual relationship. I felt the wild temptress being set free in my consciousness and I reveled in her sacred dance.

This relationship was the first I experienced in the category of what I would now call a 'soul contract'. I believe that we meet and connect with people in our lives for a reason, in order to learn, grow and let go of old, outmoded ways of thinking and acting. This lover helped me to open and allow myself to be utterly vanquished by a masculine love. I taught him the value of entering into the sacred sexual dance with a partner who was both playful and adventurous. I was loved by someone and was willing to be melted by him, growing stronger from the experience.

Yet once we had drunk deeply of each other and our lessons had been received fully, it ended as quickly and as intensely as it had begun. One night after making love, we both lay exhausted under the light of the moon streaming through a skylight in a friend's attic room. I was filled with a sense that we were complete. We were done. I was also surprised that I didn't feel more sadness at this realization and that I could now say goodbye with gratitude and love. As he kissed me one last time the next morning before heading out the door to the next part of his journey, I shed just one tear in farewell to a soul that I would remember for the rest of my life. With the unspoken parting complete, we never saw each other again. There was no need. I had been taught what it was to be truly loved by a man. I had also started to find the clues to my own feminine sexual power and for this gift I will be forever grateful.

> OUR RELATIONSHIPS CAN BECOME SO MUCH MORE
> EXQUISITE WHEN WE LIVE IN THE PRESENT.

What would human relating be like if we could engage, love and trust this fully and with as little attachment? Perhaps it would lead us to our liberation from many of the social narratives that currently keep us trapped, suppressing our inherent sexual creativity. Stories of fidelity, morality and social convention often restrict our natural impulse to love and express our affection freely without boundaries. Our relationships can become so much more exquisite, adventurous and ecstatic when we are willing to be vulnerable and play, when we live in the present just to see where it may lead, without allowing expectations of what 'should' happen in the future to intervene.

GRATITUDE

WILL YOU CREATE YOUR FUTURE
THROUGH GRATITUDE FOR THE PAST?

Me – Create a daily gratitude list in your journal or on your phone. Write down anything from the small to the big things that make you feel special, thankful, joyful and abundant in your life. What we focus on increases, and making a daily space to bring awareness to the blessings in our life will exponentially increase them!

We – A gratitude exercise that we have practiced for years in our family is that of Sunday night 'claps'. After dinner, each person gives the others an individual 'clap' for doing something during the week that they are proud of, grateful for or feel is worthy of recognition. The rest of the people around the table clap too in communal appreciation. Over the years, as my step-kids have grown, the practice has become deeper and bonded us in love and gratitude for each other. It also ensures that we never take each other for granted!

Most of us know from experience that gratitude is an energy that fuels our sense of health, well-being and freedom but how often do we use it to communicate directly with the universe? If our thoughts and feelings eventually become the experiences and physical reality of our lives (which I believe is true), then the emotions we feel act as powerful channels of communication to the energy and essence of the world around us. The more often we become conscious and deliberate in our use of emotional energy, the faster we become co-creators of our authentic story.

Shocked awake

> Shocked awake by my own dark dreaming
> Fear that clenches me in its icy grip
> Time to wake up and take a new path
> One that leads me back to me

Most of us spend our lives actively trying to prevent what we perceive as 'bad things' happening to us. I believe, however, that when we stray too far from the path of our purpose, our true story has a way of kicking us back on track. Sometimes this happens gradually, but often it comes in dramatic or painful ways and frequently through events that we never even considered could happen. When I was 17, I chose to bring on one of these cataclysmic events that would change the course of my life forever. I brought it on in the form of a full-blown tragedy, from circumstances that made me feel fear like I had never known existed. I needed it. It was my first real spiritual breakthrough, the first of many 'dark nights of the soul'.

It was the summer after I had finished college (which again I had managed to pass through the merits of my photographic memory, as opposed to time spent in the classroom) and I had decided to take a year out to work before applying to go to university. In truth, I had no clue what I wanted to study and given my track record of disengagement with education, university didn't seem like an exciting prospect. I found myself working in a lingerie shop to make some money and was hanging with my latest group of 'friends' who were all four to five years older than I was. By day, I would work in the store and by night I would go out and party. On the surface, life didn't really have any more purpose to me other than the next club, the next party or the next encounter with a man who captured my attention for a while.

Bubbling in the underworld of my thoughts and feelings I felt lonely and empty. Despite the fleeting experiences of connection I had been given through recreational drugs, I was lost and sinking in the waves of social expectations about what could and should make me happy, none of which were proving to be true. Instead of facing the fear that would come from admitting that I needed to create a different story, I buried my anxiety and intuitive warning signals deep inside. If I couldn't hear, see or feel the fear then I could pretend for a while I didn't have any. I could fabricate the mask of a smiling, gregarious socialite and fool everyone around me. But there was one part of me that wouldn't be fooled. It was my heart that would cry in the dark of night when there was nowhere else to hide. It was the part of me that was screaming for relief from the façade of social games that pervaded my waking existence. It was the voice of my real story trying to be heard.

One afternoon, I was hanging out down by the river with the boys. They were all joking about my job in the lingerie shop, saying how sexy it was. I had a badge as part of my uniform that said 'Qualified Bra Fitter', and one of them asked if I could steal some for them to all wear. I laughed and thought, *'Yeah, why not?'* After all, they were only little items, not worth much and they weren't closely watched-over by our manager. The next day at work, I took a couple of extra badges and hid them in my bag to take home. No one noticed and it felt good to make the boys happy. This seemingly small act, however, started my ego along a dangerous track. The story in my mind went something like this: *'If I steal a couple of small things from the store, the only one it really hurts is a big multinational company that doesn't pay its employees enough as it is. In truth, I am really only supplementing my small income in a way that I deserve for all the long hours that I put in there.*' Tenuous logic indeed. The next day, I took a couple of pairs of pants and snuck them out in my bag at the end of the day. The week after that I took a couple more. Not lots, just a few things to give as presents to friends so we all felt good. However, the ego's style of feeling good on the surface can mask our intuitive sense of danger and blind us to the signs that we need to hear. I had become incredibly adept at ignoring my warning signs.

A few months later, I was finishing up work for the day. We had tidied the store and were grabbing our bags and coats to go home. I had snuck a few pairs of pants and a bra into my bag and as my manager was pulling down the shutters, she turned around and announced that she wanted to do a random bag check. I choked inside. She hadn't done this before. A cold, icy wave of panic washed down my entire spine from the top of my head to the ends of my toes. I couldn't breathe. The sounds of the other shop girls opening up their bags were muffled as my body went fully into a dark, deep ocean of fear. Time slowed down and I couldn't move. Lastly, she turned to me. I knew I was caught and there was nowhere to run. Accepting the inevitable, I slowly opened my bag to reveal my stolen loot. Both shame and fear hit me in waves and I couldn't even raise my eyes to meet those of my kind manager. I knew without looking that she was shocked and saddened. Without any anger, she took the items from me and quietly said that she would see me at work the next morning.

I don't remember the other girls leaving. I don't really remember much about my walk home from work that day. I must have been in complete shock. I was empty, as if the world around me had ceased to exist and I could remember nothing about who I was or what I was doing walking down this street. I arrived home and slowly made my way upstairs to my bedroom. I fell down on the bed and powerful emotions poured in: fear, guilt and shame washed through me. I wanted to scream and cry and beat myself into oblivion all at once. '*How could you be so stupid?*' my ego shouted wordlessly through the language of my turbulent emotions. I was lost in the dark swirling of a whirlpool of self-hatred stronger than I had ever felt before. I was drowning and choking on the churning waters of my mistakes. At one point I even grabbed a large book that was lying on the bed and hit myself over and over again on the head with it. Fortunately, this act – combined with the physical symptoms of the adrenaline flooding my system – had the effect of spinning me out of the current of my inner war. I dropped the makeshift club and collapsed, exhausted and pitiful, a victim of my own ego's story. The storm of emotions had done its worst and passed, leaving only gray ominous clouds in its wake. The rest of that evening I was subdued and internally desolate. I had, however, accepted my fate. I didn't mention what had happened to anyone in my family and went to bed early.

The next morning I walked to work knowing that I had to face the consequences of my actions. On arrival, the girls were doing their best to pretend that nothing had happened and that everything was going to be okay. For a short couple of hours, I was able to pretend with them. About mid-morning, just as I was wondering when I would have to have 'the conversation' with my manager, into the store walked a tall, imposing policeman. I looked up from the underwear table where I was folding pairs of pants and gulped hard as another wave of fear and shame hit me. I realized that my manager wasn't going to have any conversation with me and that I was about to be arrested. Somehow, I had not predicted this particular outcome the night before and now I was glad that it hadn't occurred to me, as I doubted I would have had the courage to come into work if I had known this would happen. I took a deep breath and followed the policeman's instructions to get my things. I was escorted out to a waiting police car and got into the back, noticing that there was a policewoman in the front. She smiled at me and I was surprised. I weakly smiled back.

It was from here on in that this experience became somewhat odd. I was super scared – panic-stricken probably summed it up pretty nicely – but at the same time, I started to have a strange dual experience that almost felt like I was outside of my body and normal consciousness. Driving to the police station around the corner, I noticed what a bright sunny day it was outside. I noticed the beauty of the golden rays streaming through the leaves of the late summer trees and the warmth as the sun hit my skin through the window of the car. As we pulled into the station, I found myself noticing intricate details of daily life occurring all around me such as women taking their babies for a walk in the sunlit park and police officers greeting each other as they went about their day. I almost felt calm as we entered the police station.

Everyone I encountered in the police station was very kind to me. They all seemed to see me through the eyes of pity and compassion, not contempt and judgment as I had expected. The police lady from the car took me to a side room and said that she had to search my things. I allowed her to do whatever she needed to do and even helped her to empty my bag. I was then escorted into another room where the policeman who had arrested me asked me a number of questions about why I had taken things from the store. I saw no reason to lie and for the first time in many years, told the complete truth as far as I could see it. He listened without comment and recorded my answers. I still felt very afraid and yet it was as if my soul was there, holding my hand through the whole thing. It felt like I was experiencing all of this for a reason beyond my conscious control.

After the official paperwork had been done, I was informed that I would be charged and would have to go to court – something that threw me momentarily back into the whirlpool of fear I had experienced the night before. I was then escorted to a small but clean cell towards the back of the building. I walked in and sat down on the hard, cold metal bench. The door scraped shut behind me and I heard a heavy lock drawn across to bar me from getting free. My heart sank. I felt both imprisoned physically, as a result of my actions, and mentally as the consequence of the psychological stories that had driven my choices. I was lost and alone – the two feelings that I had been desperately trying to ignore. Now they had me trapped and I had nowhere to run. I started to cry. Tears rolled down my face and I held my head in my hands. *'How has it come to this?'* I asked myself, over and over again.

My young life started to roll 'movie-like' in front of my inner eyes as I saw event after event in my life leading me right up to this point in time. I saw how I had felt isolated and abandoned ever since I had been moved away from the mountains. In fact, for the first time, as I sat there I realized that I had been in a prison cell of my own making ever since I had decided to hate England and my life there so very much. My inner story had become the physical reality in which I was now sitting. I gulped and sobbed. I had created the whole thing and I only had myself to blame.

Slowly, from the fog of my pain, I heard footsteps coming down the hallway and stopping at my cell door. *'What now?'* I wondered. I heard the heavy metal bolt on the door being slid back and looked up as a tall policeman came in and shut the door behind him. I hadn't seen this man before and my heart started to pound as he approached. As he sat down next to me, I realized that he hadn't yet said anything and panic started to flood through my body all over again. Thoughts of rape and molestation came into my head and I started to wonder what I could do to defend myself, when I noticed that he was smiling at me. His smile was kind and soft. I breathed deeply trying to calm my racing pulse and wondered again why he was there. We sat in silence, side by side, for what seemed like an eternity (although in reality I'm sure it was less than a minute). Finally, when he did speak, his voice was gentle and yet so resonant it seemed to echo right through the cell and out into the hallway and car park. The words he said to me in that moment would stay with me for the rest of my life. They were the exact words that I needed to hear for everything in my life to make sense: *"Gen, you are worth so much more than this."*

Silence – apart from the deafening beating of my heart. These words echoed through my bones and drummed in my ears. *'You are worth so much more than this...'* became a vibration that rippled through me and out into the world beyond.

Then the policeman stood up and silently left my cell, shutting the door behind him and locking it once more. *'Did that really just happen?'* I asked myself. I wanted to pinch my arm to check I was awake and not dreaming. It really had happened, I realized, as I heard footsteps retreating down the corridor outside. Shock hit me once more, but this time it was the sort of shock that I imagine a person experiences when they have just witnessed a real-life miracle. I felt peace enter into every cell in my body and at the same time, a quiet sense of elation. He was right, I thought. He was right! I breathed a breath of fresh, sweet air as I realized that I had just been given the keys to my freedom.

YOU ARE WORTH SO MUCH MORE THAN THIS.

The next person to enter my cell was the policewoman who had carried out the search of my bag. She came in carrying my things and a hot cup of tea, announcing that after a few final bits of paperwork I would be free to go. I cried a few more tears of gratitude at her human kindness and she smiled once again. It would frequently make me laugh in the months to come as I went through the trials and tribulations of the English court and probation system that by bravely 'paying my dues' and being willing to stand up in front of a judge and tell the truth, I was completing the final bits of my own 'inner paperwork' before starting a new life. A new life and a new story; one that would leave behind the belief that, by conforming to rebellious teenage peer pressure and social expectations to be something I was not, I would be happy. No, I was signing the final goodbyes to all the false friendships, superficial lovers and lies to myself and others. I was saying 'Hello' to a future in which I valued my personal integrity and freedom above all else.

    That night at our kitchen table, I told my mother what had happened. She held my hand, cried when I cried, and breathed a deep heartfelt sigh of relief when I told her of my awakenings to my own personal power and responsibility. We hugged for the longest time and I knew that something significant had shifted within us both. I had taken my first step off the well-trodden path of habitual human life and onto a hidden trail into the mountains of my real adventure. I had no idea where it would lead but I knew that as long as I had the courage to keep putting one foot in front of the other, I would come to no real and lasting harm.

Digging the girl

> Knowing without knowing
> The veils between worlds thin
> Connection across the ages
> Intuition opens the door to our ancestors

When I was growing up, my parents were archaeologists. In the subsequent years, they have both moved on in their careers and expanded into new fields, but back then they dug for clues: clues that would point us towards an idea of what our society and culture might have been like in the past; how our ancestors would have acted, interacted and related to each other; clues that point towards the roots of our current narratives and ways of seeing the world.

I thought that this was super-cool. My parents didn't spend their days tied to an office desk but rather out in the field running excavations, curating exhibitions in the museum or in a 'Finds Lab', cleaning and studying artifacts. The best bit about all of this was that when my friends were busy doing paper rounds or waitressing for spare money, my sisters and I would tag summer jobs with the archaeology unit and make our cash by washing ancient pottery and bones.

After my brush with the law, I retreated once more to the comfort and safety of people who had known me since I was a child; good people who empathized with my teenage angst and were compassionate in my hour of need. I landed a job working for the archaeology unit. The days started early: I would get up and put on my oldest, dirtiest and warmest clothes, grabbing my lunch on the way out the door. Arriving at the unit, I would join a cheerful band loading survey gear, mattocks, shovels and the tea-making kit into the back of the old battered and muddy site van. Stories of the previous night's drinking, joking and loving would all be shared around cups of tea and hand-rolled cigarettes, before climbing aboard and heading out for a day's digging in the field. Any grumpiness I might have felt at getting up so early dissolved as soon as I was lovingly embraced into the unit family. In comparison to other groups of people that I had worked and played with, this one was always laughing and cheerful. After all, we were headed out to work at something we loved and were genuinely interested in, as opposed to the majority of the long, gray-faced disenchanted workers and students we passed as we drove out of town.

Arriving on site, tasks would be allocated to everyone according to skill-set and desire for that day. Digging on these sites was rarely the kind of thing that you would imagine from watching archaeology programs on TV. Rather than delicately brushing away sand and soil using paintbrushes and precision dental equipment, the sites that I dug on were mostly ancient residential complexes that had ditches, middens (large refuse heaps or pits) and post-holes to be explored. The thing with ditches is that they are big, so to dig them in sections takes a lot of hard work with a mattock and shovel. On one site, I was allocated a ditch section that went down a meter and a half before I hit the natural soil layer into which it had originally been cut. By the time I had finished, I had blisters on my hands and was shoveling soil out of my section above my own head. It was tiring work.

Although I loved the hard honesty of digging, I also loved to plan. Planning involved taking a large A2 drawing board mounted with graph paper and creating a scale image of the area of the site that had been excavated. Armed with my measuring tape, pencils and bulldog clips, I would trek out to the trenches that had been dug the day before and sit down quietly for a couple of hours of meditation. I wouldn't have called it meditation if you had asked me at the time, but since developing a practice in the years that have followed, I now know that this was exactly why I loved this activity (or inactivity) so much. To draw an ancient landscape with integrity and artistry requires that the drawer lose their rational mind. Yes, I was checking the tape for accuracy of placement and scale but after

20 minutes or so, my mind would go quiet and my hand would just draw. With my imagination set loose, I would feel into the land and people as they might have been, recreating the houses, ditches and trees of times gone by. When entering into a semi-trance-like state, images, feelings and thoughts would pass through my awareness like clouds moving across a clear blue sky. Sometimes, when I was left alone for a whole morning undisturbed, I would even find myself imagining the lives of the people that must have passed through the very spot where I stood and drew: their challenges and fears, their love affairs and dreams. The very idea that someone (me) was thinking of them after they were so long gone, seemed to honor their spirits and existence on the earth.

During this time, I started to change psychologically in many subtle ways. Surrounded as I was by loving, caring and playful adults, I found I could breathe again. I stopped trying to be someone that everyone would like and started just being me. The members of the unit treated me as an equal among friends, not as just the kid and as a result, I started to act as an adult. I stepped into a larger world and began to take responsibility for who I was and the impact I was having on others. I became proud of doing a good job and as a result, wanted to work hard to prove my worth as a part of the team. This was my new way of bringing to life the oath I had taken in the police cell: to be worth more than the mask that the old Gen had been wearing.

By working hard and showing a willingness to learn, I was offered increasingly harder tasks at work. First, I was allowed to help run the 'Finds Lab' where all the artifacts that were dug up on site were cleaned and catalogued before going into storage at the university. It was here that I came under the instruction of one of my first female mentors and role models, a feisty lady in her 60s who smoked mini-cigars and took no prisoners, while making sure that her lab was shipshape. It was this guardian angel in disguise who taught me how strong a mature woman, secure in her wisdom, could be. Over the months I worked with her, I would watch even the most senior members of the unit show her deep respect and come to her for advice and healing. She helped me connect to my own inner strength and intuition.

Then it came. A moment in time that would provide me with a big clue to one of my strongest human gifts: that of my intuition. We were out on a Bronze Age site early on a misty, gray October morning. There had been excitement the day before when we had found cremated bone inside some large pottery urns. I was hoping I might be asked to assist on this area of the site. As the jobs were being allocated, my heart sank in disappointment. My name wasn't mentioned in the group digging the urns. Instead, the site manager gave me a wink and asked if I would like to take on one of the oval looking features that had been found to the north of the site. Hiding my disappointment, I agreed, and grabbed my digging kit to make my way over to the feature.

Before something is dug, you can usually identify it by the different color soil that was once used to backfill whatever that original space had been. On this particular morning, as the wind swirled fog and mist all around me, I looked down at a dark, oval shape in the lighter natural base soil and tried to imagine what this might once have been. Before I even placed my trowel to the earth I had a strange feeling that this one was something different.

Bending down, I found a comfortable position to the left side of the feature and I started to remove the top layers using my trowel and a small shovel to clear away the soil. I slipped into my familiar trance and became 'mindless', enjoying the simple movement of following the edge of the oval pit and removing layers of earth as I imagined a sculptor might move away clay or stone as they uncovered the work of art waiting inside.

As I worked, I allowed my imagination to expand and sense into what I might be digging. I found myself thinking of a girl about my age. I imagined what she looked like and what tasks she might have been set by her elders around the encampment. About half way down, as I was digging gently around the top of the oval closest to my right knee, I felt the tip of my trowel hit a material that was distinctly harder than that of the soil. I stopped and savored the moment of discovery. Breathing in the curiosity of what might be uncovered with the next stroke of my hand, I waited a brief moment and then moved. I gasped as the soil fell away revealing bone. Smooth bone. Convex, delicate pale bone: a skull.

My heartbeat quickened as I realized what I had discovered: a burial site! I hadn't dug a burial site before. They were usually reserved for the most experienced and skilled diggers due to the fragility of human bone. I ran over and grabbed the site manager, dragging him back to my oval prize. Grinning and as excited as I was, he gave me another wink and with a backwards admonishment to be careful, left me to continue my adventure. *'He must trust me,'* I thought and with a small puff of pride I sat down again earnestly continuing my delicate work.

Carefully, I started to remove the soil from around the skull. I was enchanted by the tilt of the head to the left. It was almost as if this human was curling into my right knee for comfort. I worked with great reverence, knowing I was to reveal them to a future time and vastly changed world than the one they had left when they were buried here. Over the course of the morning, as I moved gradually down the body and uncovered more and more delicate bone, I found that she had been buried in a curled, fetal position known as a 'crouched burial'. I was struck by the beauty of the human skeletal form as I worked. I felt a growing connection with this human being that intensified with each exquisitely curved rib that I brushed open to the sky. I experienced a depth of emotional current that moved me in waves, like the ocean. One moment I would be riding high on the elation of digging this delicate, amazing, once living, breathing individual and the next, I was bent over in quiet mourning for a life lost to a place and time that I wasn't a part of.

Up and down I swayed between light and dark, joy and sadness, excitement and reverence until I was done and she lay there, open and radiant for everyone to see. I am not sure at what stage in this process she naturally became a 'she' to me. It just was. At lunch, the rest of the team came over to admire her beauty and complimented me on my work. I found myself lacking in words to describe the experience I was having and instead, like an ancient priestess overseeing a ceremony of great magnitude, I just smiled and acknowledged them.

That afternoon I was allowed the privilege of drawing her and in a space of silent awe I created by far the best plan that I had ever done. Precise and intricate, each crack and indentation was drawn and preserved. It was almost too beautiful to disturb her resting place and as if she could sense my reservation, my friend (the unit bone specialist) came over to help me complete this final stage of the task. As we worked, carefully lifting bone after bone, I found my voice once again and started asking her all kinds of questions. How do we know the sex of the skeleton? How old was she? Was she sick when she died? Had she had a baby? Laughing, my friend assured me that once she was back in the lab and had been cleaned, she would be able to answer some of these questions, if not all of them.

A few weeks later, the daily life of the unit had taken over and I had become busy with new projects and tasks, losing a large percentage of the memory of my burial experience. I was sitting outside at lunch, enjoying the late autumn sun sinking into my bones, when my friend walked past me on her way into the Finds Lab. Stopping at the door, she addressed me in a casual way and said, "*Oh Gen, I forgot to tell you. I finally got to look at that skeleton you dug a few weeks ago. You know, I am pretty sure that she was a girl about your age.*" With a knowing smile she turned around and continued inside. I stopped chewing my sandwich and ceased breathing for a moment as the words sank into my awareness. I remembered my feeling of the girl as I had dug her. My knowing that she had been my age. The connection I had felt to her. '*Holy shit!*' I thought, '*Was that more than my imagination?*'

I smiled in awe and gratitude as I took another bite of my lunch. I had stumbled across a completely different way of knowing that transcended time and language. I couldn't wait to try it again.

Following the magic we find in life
is what gives us energy and purpose.

DAILY MAGIC

WILL YOU BECOME A RESPONSIBLE MAGICIAN?

Me – Daily magic is the process of creating new stories through awareness and adaptation of our beliefs, thoughts, feelings and actions. We are magicians in every sense of the word when we are able to transform negative experiences in our lives through changing our expectations and beliefs about them. Next time you spot a story you dislike, take a moment to reflect on how your inner beliefs about that situation end up creating the thoughts, feelings and subsequent actions that fuel it. By taking personal responsibility for our inner narratives, we also take back control of changing them.

We – Next time you experience something magical in your life, find someone with whom you would rarely discuss such occurrences and share your story of synchronicity. Be courageous in your articulation of the event and how it made you feel, think and act differently from what was expected of you by the prevalent social narrative of how adults should think. Notice what happens for the other person. Are they surprised, supportive or scornful? In telling your story of magic, did they in turn share one of their own? Often when we have the courage to speak authentically and honestly, we automatically give the person or people we are speaking to permission to enter into the same space.

As adults, we have often had decades of being taught that magic 'isn't real' or is something that moviemakers utilize to sell us merchandise. Overcoming the feelings of childish stupidity or naivety that hold us back from speaking about natural moments of synchronicity or miracles takes a brave soul and a tough spirit. When we realize that it's actually this universal flow of interconnection that makes us feel alive, we will see the socialized joke that we have all been fed in the western world. We won't be as fast to eat the junk food of society and the media. Instead we will start to see that following the magic we find in life is what gives us energy and purpose.

Changing the story of school

> Do what you love, not what makes sense
> For it is here that our power is found
> Passion and purpose combine
> As our heart leads us to our gifts

I moved away from home when I was 17. I don't really remember it being an overly emotional moment for me or my parents. It was simply time. In finding my new family at the archaeology unit and the closest thing to a safe environment within which to explore being me, I had also opened up the doorway to a new lover in my life. Following the general trend in my romantic affairs, this man was four years older than me and reflected a safety that I craved after years of dangerous liaisons in love. It wasn't a particularly passionate affair but it was fun and comforting to have someone adoring me again. After a few months of practically living together, we decided to make the move more permanent and with a tinge of sadness (and more than a big sigh of relief), I finally left my parents' home.

I found the simple things to be the most exciting. The feeling of maturity and responsibility that came with having to contribute towards rent and bills, the freedom of shopping for my own food and choosing what I wanted to eat at night (after years of negotiating with my siblings) brought a smile to my face every time I went to the store. The ability to do my own laundry, clean the house and have a bath at midnight if I wanted to brought with it the sweet, sweet taste of liberation. Who'd have thought that the basic act of living would bring me more joy than parties? It's not something I have ever lost in all the years that have come since. The ability to revel in the smallness as well as the bigness; the beauty in both simplicity and luxury.

After six months of good living with my boyfriend, another big transition loomed on my horizon. Through blind intuition more than anything else, I had decided to apply to go to university. Historically, I hadn't been a good academic student nor had I particularly enjoyed learning in the English school system and yet something had driven me to move towards this particular path. I remember sitting with my parents late at night around our kitchen table with a number of university brochures spread out in front of us. Not knowing where to start, my father asked me, *"So Gen, what do you want to study?"* No one had ever asked me that before. My education since leaving kindergarten had seemed like a form of enforced punishment rather than choice and now that I had the freedom to pick I didn't know which way to move.

"Well," I said, *"I would love to go and study archaeology but perhaps I should do something like business studies instead."*

A moment's silence. *"Why would you want to study business?"* my father asked.

Another short pause whilst I thought of a good response. *"Ummm, well, it will make me money and will probably open up a good job."*

A fatherly smile. *"And why archaeology,* kiddo?"

"I'm not sure...I guess because I love it."

Smiles all around.

"Well, I'm sure you will know which one is more important to you honey," my father said and with that he stood up and went to bed.

I was so grateful to my father in that moment. This choice had to be mine and mine alone and he knew that. I wasn't just choosing my university degree, I was choosing the foundation for how I would approach my work in the world for the rest of my life. Not really knowing why, I made my choice on the basis of an intuition and intelligence greater than my brain or a socially programed story. A year later, I found myself packed and in the car with my mother, traveling to Sheffield where I would begin a three-year bachelors' degree. And the subject? Archaeology and Prehistory of course!

As soon as my course lectures started, I discovered the magnitude of the change that this one choice had wrought within me. For the first time in my life, I LOVED what I was learning. I found myself waking up in the morning, jumping out of bed and looking forward to the day's lectures. I made a beeline for the library in between classes and actually enjoyed doing the reading for my essays. I attended every lecture (whereas before I would have been lucky to motivate myself to make it to 60% of them). I completed every essay on time and took pride in my work. By the end of the first term, contrary to popular belief (including my own), it had become obvious that I was, in fact, a very good student. I was learning about a subject that I was passionately interested in and I had teachers that were equally as passionate about passing on their knowledge. Life was good and I was free in a way that I had craved since I was very small.

I was learning an important life lesson, one that I would go on to teach other students a decade or so later, as well as being given an important clue to my own path into the future. In dedicating my time, energy and imagination to something I loved, my whole life was expanding as a result. My health, happiness and levels of fulfillment were at an all-time high and the enthusiasm and creativity that flowed out of me was both surprising and addictive. And the spiral went ever upwards. The more fun I was having, the better my work became. The better my work became, the more I tended to attract the 'right' people to spend time with. People who stretched me and brought with them new experiences and cultural histories. People who wanted to be with me, because of who I was becoming, not because of who I had been. It was intoxicating, a high wave that would inevitably crash. But for a time, I was surfing its crest and loving every moment.

Danger signs

> Psssst – wake up, don't forget who you are
> The universe calls us continually back home
> The question is, will we listen
> Or learn the hard way

Some behavior patterns die hard, particularly those that make us feel good. A few months into my newfound university freedom I made friends with a lively group of locals. Being from 'up North', they were kind, genuine and thrived on mischief. Of course, I liked them immediately. They knew all the cool hangouts, how to get into the best clubs (always on the guest list) and where to go to meet the most interesting people in town. I was adopted into the clan and found myself in the privileged and unfamiliar position of being one of the 'cool kids'. Needless to say, my ego loved it. I fell easily back into the recreational drug culture that I had thought I had left behind, this time telling myself that I was older, wiser and more able to spot the safe zones and genuine people from the chaff of petty criminals and space cadets. It was a naïve story, but one that served its purpose in keeping me safe – at least for a while.

Weekdays consisted of me thriving in my studies and academic exploration. Then Friday night would roll around and I would switch into full party mode. The club would have been picked, our cocktail of amphetamines selected and outfits planned well in advance. Walking through the front door to my shared house, I would dump my uni gear and head across the street to my friend's apartment to prepare: spliff rolled, snack eaten and phone on full battery receiving calls from our tribe about the night ahead. The flutters of excitement would start to churn in my belly and rise gradually up my spine as the evening turned into the night.

One by one they would start to arrive. Smiles spread wide across faces full of anticipation. Friendly hugs and jokes filled the air along with the inevitable undercurrent of sexual tension playing out between boy and girl. Whether attached or free, clubbing creates bonds between people that transcend the usual relationship rules. When the music and ecstasy take hold, the world outside dissolves and you enter into communion with those around you. You connect to each other in the simple joy of shared expression, dancing and appreciation. Once this has happened for the first time, each repetition with your new tribe only serves to strengthen the bond between a group of party buddies. Between letting yourself go on the dance floor in reckless abandon to a beat, or sitting curled up together in a dark corner sharing your deepest fears and longings, this environment strips you bare of all your normal protection patterns. It hurls the carefully constructed mask of your personality hard out of the window for the night and allows you to run free like the innocent child you once were. Occasionally, amongst this free, orgasmic, fickle love, deeper connections are also formed.

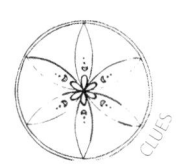

I had been playing with my new friends for about a month when I found myself being consistently drawn into close connection with the ringleader of the group. A cocky, roguish guy, he was unusual in both character, look and appeal. Older than the rest of us, he was looked-up to and wore the role of leader easily. My rebel persona was hooked once again and quickly I started to forget about the nice, safe guy that I had left behind at home. My new love went out of his way to find me on the dark dance floors and I was the first person he would come and pass his joints to, the one he would seek out to share stories with in dark corners and the hidden niches of clubs. I felt like a queen who had been chosen by an outlaw. I was in a love story again and the transition was fast. After a few weeks, I found myself saying a difficult goodbye to my old boyfriend from home. He took the transition with as much grace and acceptance as he could muster.

As soon as I became 'his girl', I gained in status and notoriety simply by association with my outlaw. I stopped hanging around with any of the uni students I knew and entered fully into the underworld of local clubbers and party addicts. I found myself once more spending time with people older than me and with significantly more experience of the drug culture than I had. Life was lived for the weekend. Conversations centered on the next party, score or DJ set that was being put together. Rather than being a purpose or aspiration, work was simply a mechanism to fund our weekend frolics and I rarely met anyone during this period of my life that had anything close to what I would call a 'vision'. But then, I was having so much fun that this wasn't a major problem for me right away. I was on guest lists and given regular after-party invitations. I was befriended by DJs and drug dealers alike. I was high as a kite on my perceived social status and hedonistic lifestyle and donned big fat blinkers to block out anything that was signaling danger as I flew down the tracks.

I found that the people of my new tribe had an unparalleled ability to focus on the fun and joy in life. Like every generation who discovers drugs, we entered into 'the garden' free, in love with each other and with all of life. For a time, whilst the illusion seemed real, we felt like the richest people on earth and superior to all those wage slaves and conformists who worked their tails off only to be miserable at the end of every day. We also knew how to play like the innocent children we had all once been and that many of us had been forced to cut short due to early trauma and abuse of one kind or another. Unfortunately, the 'play' was more often infantile than healing.

After a year or so spent in a drug-infused honeymoon period, life started to kick me awake again. At first I noticed changes in my relationship. As with most relationships, initially the two of us had felt like a modern-day Bonnie and Clyde, madly in love and completely in sync with each other. However, this had inevitably started to fragment and crack – a prelude to the day that the mirror of illusion would fully shatter. He started to regularly throw out hurtful, derogatory comments about how I looked, how I spoke or the choices I made that conflicted with how he thought things should be. And these weren't just petty, normal bickering comments, these were verbal ninja bombs designed to hurt; to gradually dig their fangs into my consciousness. These barbs would be hurled my way usually during a come down in the early hours of the morning. In my fragile, post-drugged emotional state, these comments would push me into a turmoil of confusion, making me want to hit him full in the face at the same time as running away never to be seen again.

Very quickly this confusion dissolved into frustration and then full-blown anger on my part. My warrior spirit was ignited and I found myself biting and fighting back. Sometimes I would bite so hard that it would draw mental blood from us both. The fights became louder and more violent, often dissolving into a screaming match and me kicking him out of whatever house we were in at the time. Once, I even left my own house with him in it for two days and made no attempt to come back or speak to him. On another occasion, I was so angry that I called a friend and made him come over so I could pack up and move out, only to find myself back there a few days later, the incident seemingly forgotten. Our egos had declared war on each other and we took it in turns to prove who could be smarter and more stubborn in our skirmishes. Loving the drama (and fearing what would happen to our constructed social status as a couple should we break up), we mostly found a way to make up after each battle, although peace was a façade and only ever a temporary and fragile state.

The undercurrent of tension and fear in life that had created the fractures in our relationship started to ripple out and spread wider than the two of us before long. First, a couple of close friends were arrested for dealing Ecstasy. One of them went to prison. It sent a shock wave through our group and we were all forced to open our eyes to the fact that it was no longer a safe game that we had been playing. I lay awake at night with waves of remembered panic coursing through my body: police cells, court cases and the words 'guilty by association' rang in my head.

Shortly after this, a boy in my year at university died of a heroin overdose. Once more, panic and confusion resonated out across our community and I found myself facing the fact that perhaps we were not invincible after all. I felt a strong sensation of awakening from a dream that had pervaded every area of my life. It felt very similar to the moment that you walk out of a darkened club at 6.30am and realize that there is a regular world existing outside of the strange dream-like reality in which you have been dancing for the last seven or eight hours. The sunlight starts to shine and you raise your hand to shield your eyes from the daylight, yet gradually you start to accept that you need to remember how to function in the normal world again if you are to survive. I realized that something had to change if I was to get myself back on track.

When we are on a path that is leading us inexorably to disaster, life has a way of kicking us (repeatedly) until we finally listen. The kicks are gentle at first, like a growing sense of worry or nervousness; an unexplained inability to relax or smile as often as you once did. Then, if you choose to ignore them, the nudges start to ramp up in both force and speed. Anxieties in life infiltrate your dreams and you find yourself unable to sleep or retreat from the messages attempting to find you. Friends are arrested or die, fights happen more regularly and people around you start acting crazily, as if they are losing their minds. You wonder which way to turn, and start to see that you must *do something* rather than be paralyzed.

Then come the larger metaphorical kicks from left of field and when you are least expecting them, in the form of sudden ill health or accidents, the breakup of relationships and friendships or the loss of jobs. If you can stop and hear what the universe is saying to you at any one of these points, then you will maintain the ability to save yourself and correct your course before it's too late. These kicks are clues, asking us to listen. I got to stage three before I finally heard what the universe was saying to me.

> WHEN WE ARE ON A PATH THAT IS LEADING US
> INEXORABLY TO DISASTER, LIFE HAS A WAY
> OF KICKING US UNTIL WE FINALLY LISTEN.

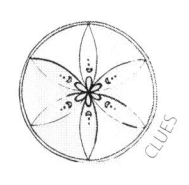

It was late and the night was dark like ink. If the moon or stars were still shining they were obscured by thick, heavy clouds. My boyfriend and I had gone over to his dealer's house to score. I had felt on edge all night and jumpy, as if there was some imagined danger around every corner ready to spring out and engulf me. On arriving at the house, the air was thick with smoke and I did everything I could to hold my breath, politely refusing joints. On this night, the last thing I needed was to be hazy from bush weed. After courtesies had been exchanged, his dealer casually mentioned that he had hidden his stash and we needed to go out somewhere with him to retrieve it. I gulped. This didn't feel good and yet I found myself nodding numbly as my boy agreed to the plan. It was one of those moments when I hated myself inside for not finding the inner strength to refuse and go home and yet later, I would thank my intuition for taking me on this particular jaunt.

As we left the house and started walking down the street, the black air seemed to take on an unearthly, toxic glow from the orange streetlights that illuminated our path. The night felt sick and fevered – or perhaps that was just me. We turned a few corners and started walking up back streets that I no longer recognized towards an expanse of black vegetation held back behind an old wall. I wondered where the hell we were going and perhaps 'hell' was the best word that I could use to describe the area towards which we were walking. As we drew close enough for me to finally see what it was, I almost laughed at the surreal nature of the story that was unfolding. He opened an old gate and held it open for us to follow him inside: A graveyard. *'You have got to be kidding,'* I thought to myself. *'You just can't make this stuff up.'*

I hesitated for a moment before following the boys inside. *'Fuck it,'* I thought. *'Get in, get out and then return to normal as fast as you can.'* We walked into the darkness and with each step the orange glow from the streetlights faded behind us. Having lived for a while in a house that had backed onto a graveyard, the location itself wasn't particularly scary for me. I had several pleasant memories of that graveyard, including staying out past curfews, sharing first kisses and making up stories about the lives of the people whose names we saw engraved on the headstones. But we weren't in that place now. The one that I found myself stumbling through the dark in with two men, neither of whom I trusted, felt totally different. We walked along nonexistent paths, round and round in what seemed like repetitive circles whilst searching for the elusive stash. My mind tried to engage its usual defense mechanisms to fight back my sense of fear and vulnerability: *'No one will see you'*, *'He'll find it in a moment'*, *'You can say you had no idea what they were looking for if you are all caught'*. All forms of, *'Don't worry, it will be alright.'*

Suddenly, as I was walking, I felt the world drop away from my feet and my chin hit the ground with a jolt. Shock kicked in and for a moment I was completely still with confusion, my mind slowly grasping for an explanation of what was happening. As if in a dream, I started to do a head to toe diagnosis of my body and realized that the whole of my right leg up to my hip socket had dropped into a hole in the earth. Instead of being disgusted or scared, I found myself initially curious and intrigued by what I had literally stepped into. *'I have fallen into a grave,'* I calmly thought as my boyfriend ran back to grab my hand and pull me up.

"*You alright?*" he asked, genuinely concerned.

I mumbled a "*Yes*" and nodded forwards to indicate that we should carry on. As he moved off in front of me into the dark again I realized that neither of my companions had comprehended what had just happened to me. The message was for me alone. As I brushed the fresh, dark soil off my leg, I knew what the universe had just gifted me. Words flowed into my head: *'You are at the brink of falling into an early grave and yet you still have the ability to pull yourself out and change course.'*

I got it. I listened. I knew that it was time for things to transform once again.

Time to walk out of the darkness of death towards the light of the life that I had promised myself I would live.

'Okay... Let's do this,' I thought.

I smiled and in that smile was strength. In that smile was courage and the spirit of saying "Yes" to my adventure once again.

STORYBOARD

WILL YOU PUT TOGETHER THE PUZZLE PIECES
OF YOUR TRUE STORY?

Me – Create a journal, vision board or wall dedicated to celebrating your moments of magic. Document in words, images or sounds (perhaps with a music playlist) the moments where the universe was giving you a big clue to your deeper story.

We – Put your personal storyboard up somewhere in your home where others can see it (or if it's in musical form, you may wish to share your playlist with others). Watch the reactions of other people to your collage of clues and notice whether this catalyzes aspects of their story through the mirror of yours. After all, we share a common human narrative and our experiences can help others understand their own.

Spotting the clues to our deeper story can be tricky, especially with the human tendency to immerse ourselves in the drama of life with every opportunity we get. However, the practice of bringing clarity and conscious awareness to the patterns that play out over and over again in our lives helps us to tune into the moments of epiphany that we may have failed to spot at the time they happened. Moments of extreme fear can be the universe speaking to us just as clearly as the moments of joy, realization and bliss.

Integrity

Tell the truth and be kicked out
Or lie and stay in the club
Our whole lives rest on these decisions
That might change the course of our lives

I finished my bachelor's degree in Archaeology and Prehistory and passed with flying colors despite the turmoil of my social life. After looking unsuccessfully for a job in archaeology (there were limited options!) I fell into an administration role in a beaten-up warehouse in northern England. It more than paid the bills. I had also managed to untangle myself from the messy relationship with my previous boyfriend with relative ease (which surprised us both) and had struck up a new relationship with a beautiful, poetic soul who worked nights on the same contract as I did. He was kind, deep and provided me with safety after the rollercoaster relationship I had just exited. It was a blessing that left me free to concentrate on a new passion: my career.

With little to no practical experience of corporations or leadership, my youthful tenacity and enthusiasm created a new 'mask' as a successful young businesswoman within a very masculine leadership culture. Inside 12 months I had been promoted twice and was now leading a team of 17 people of assorted ages and backgrounds. I was scared and exhilarated on a daily basis and starting to discover that I had an innate gift to connect deeply with people and make them feel special and loved. Whether these were members of my own team or my expanding network within our customer's business, I quickly became loved and trusted by almost everyone who did business with me. But why? Looking back, I believe it was very simple. I kept my promises (even when it meant putting in late hours) and I respected everyone, at least initially. I also really enjoyed what I was doing and my fun was infectious to those around me. Despite the fact we were working in a gray old warehouse on the edge of Sheffield, a beaten-up, poor industrial city, I chose not to see it negatively.

When I looked around me I saw kind, loving colleagues; I saw opportunity and the potential to progress, if I was willing to work hard. There was fun to be had in solving problems. I put my active imagination to work, setting my team a vision and making sure that they all had a voice in how we were going to get there. Now please understand, this is definitely not to say that I got it right all the time. I most certainly didn't. There were days when I made every leadership mistake in the book and spent nights awake, riddled with stressful stories, worrying about how I might have pissed off this person or damaged my reputation or given my team too much power...or blah, blah, blah. But, for the most part, life at work was good and I was growing.

My team was responsible for the tracking of expensive electronic equipment for a large multinational media customer. Like many other 'young leaders', I took myself and my job very seriously (often too seriously) and worked ridiculously hard to protect my reputation. My ego was tempted into patterns of protection on a daily basis: I played the internal political game that many senior managers do, always endeavoring to look good and say the right thing, so that people felt I was a dedicated member of the company – even when secretly, deep down, I disagreed with them. *"Compromises are a part of a successful leader's makeup,"* the office manager had once said to me. Being young and inexperienced, I had halfway believed her, but my rebel saw to it that it was only ever halfway.

One afternoon, I pulled on my warm coat and started off down into the warehouse to investigate some discrepancies that had shown up on the computer system. The warehouse had a deep chill about it. It was dark and cavernous. I walked from rack to rack with my clipboard and a red pen, scribbling big crosses where pallets of stock were supposed to be. After a long, cold afternoon and sheets full of red marks, I started to realize that I was looking at a potentially serious problem. If my investigations were valid then the company I was working for had either lost, misplaced or misappropriated a large amount of our media customer's stock that they believed was currently on the racks in our warehouse. Worried, I did the sums and saw that I was looking at a loss of almost a million pounds sterling. After the initial wave of disbelief had subsided I did a very English thing and went and made a cup of tea. Life's challenges, I have found, are often made better by a good cup of tea. After warming my bones a little, I wandered around the warehouse and triple checked everything. I was scared silly to make an accusation if there was any chance I could be wrong. Naïvely, I started asking around amongst the warehouse staff to see what was going on. I was told, in no uncertain terms, to mind my own business, but this only served to deepen my interest. Concerned and like a detective on the scent of a mystery, I went and spoke with my line manager. To my surprise, he could not have been more dismissive, shrugging it off as warehouse system issues.

'*Does no one care?*' I thought to myself, surprised at the lack of interest in something that I felt deep down was going to be a big problem. '*What if our customer found out?*' I left that thought trailing off into the distance as a sinking feeling started deep in the pit of my stomach. It had an increasingly familiar note, the one that I recognized as the emotional 'stop sign' of my conscience. My inner signal that I was about to do something scary. That night as I sat at home, staring blankly at a wall, I knew that the right thing to do was to report the facts to our customer, but, like most people I knew at work, I had developed a very deep, trusting and honest relationship with my main contact there – I would have even described it as a friendship – so, it felt like I would be betraying his trust. I also knew deep inside that in doing the right thing, I would probably lose my job. I gulped and went to bed, trying desperately to ignore the churning feeling in my stomach as I contemplated my options.

The answer didn't come fast – or perhaps it did and it simply took me a while to gain enough courage to act on what I knew I had to do. I spent three days in pure fear. I was scared of losing everything: my job, my source of income, my reputation, my credibility, and my career prospects. My mind had a field day creating every dark story of career-related doom it could imagine. I was beset at night by vivid dreams that helped me to eventually come to a decision: the only decision that I was ever going to make. I emerged from those dark days knowing I really only had one choice. If I was ever going to be able to live with myself again, I had to tell the truth. So I did.

On the morning of the third day (forgive the biblical tone), I walked into work very early and locked myself in the computer control room. With the hum of the servers all around me I breathed deeply and summoned up the courage to pick up the phone and call my contact at our customer's company. Hesitantly at first, but then growing in speed, I told him the truth of what I had discovered. There was a moment of silence when I had finished before I heard him say, "*Wow Gen, thank you!*" I was surprised. There was no anger in his voice. He was super-grateful that I had told him and promised to protect me if he could, although I remember feeling as he spoke that the fingers of destiny were wrapping themselves around the situation. Everyone would know that there was only one person who could have found out the truth and reported it – and that was me. I had been the one who had tenaciously been asking lots of questions. It wouldn't take long before the gossip machine's arrows found their marks on me.

As I suspected, the news broke quickly and my working life became hell. The worst part was the fact that everyone at my company suspected that it was me who had reported the situation to our customer, but they had no proof. So, they acted the part of treating me as a manager, but systematically started to cut me out of everything. I would walk around corners and see people having hushed conversations that would hurriedly cease as I approached. I would catch the accusing stares of people in the office whenever a stock-related issue was brought up and I tried hard every second of the day not to slip down a rabbit hole into the dark depths of feeling like a powerless victim. I had chosen this and I knew that I had done the right thing as far as my conscience was concerned.

After a few weeks of living hell, I decided to do the only thing I could, which was to leave. '*I have done the right thing*,' I kept telling myself over and over again. I knew it was time to move on, no matter what that move into the unknown would bring me. After I had set up a couple of interviews for other jobs and was preparing to go, I called my friend at our customer's company and told him I was leaving. After a shocked silence on the end of the phone, he said, "*Don't move, someone will call you back in half an hour.*" Surprised and more than a bit intrigued, I waited. Half an hour later, the phone rang and it was a voice I didn't immediately recognize. The voice said something that I didn't expect in the slightest. As I listened, every word that reached my ears warmed and excited me. The voice was expressive and clear. He wanted to create a job for me within our customer's business because he was so impressed by the way I had handled the relationship and my recent decision. He had even made up a title for me: 'Stock Integrity Manager!' I had to laugh. Isn't it funny how sometimes, even when things look like they are falling down around you, the courage to keep going will bring you to a new and truer path? In the years that followed as I launched into my new career in the media industry, I couldn't have imagined the path of learning and exploration that unfolded before me. The choice to be 'in my truth and integrity' changed my life forever. But I am getting ahead of myself.

> EVEN WHEN THINGS LOOK LIKE THEY ARE FALLING DOWN AROUND YOU, THE COURAGE TO KEEP GOING WILL BRING YOU TO A NEW AND TRUER PATH.

My definition of integrity changed forever following this event. Beyond honesty, it means the integration of the values and gifts that we each hold in our core. It is a weaving together of our essential human strengths, bringing these into reality with the actions we take. In addition to 'walking our talk', we begin to 'talk our walk' as our way of living becomes integrated and aligned with our spirit. We start to step into our bigger story in the world and create ripples that will come back to us again and again.

DREAM WORK

ARE YOU IGNORING A VAST RESERVOIR OF CLUES?

Me – Our dreamtime can be a rich unmined well of insight when it comes to working with our stories, particularly core themes, our deepest visions, longings and essence. There is a wealth of material available that can help you to engage in conscious dreaming. It's something I now use regularly in my retreats and journeys with people. If you wish to play with your unconscious in this way, start by setting the intention just before you sleep that you will remember the important elements of your dreams. Then, ask yourself a question that you wish to work with whilst you rest. State the question and hold it in your mind and heart as you drift off to sleep, like a mantra. When you wake, before doing anything else, take some time to relive your dream experience in your mind. Then record it in whatever form works best for you (this could be a voice recording on your phone, a notebook or drawing). Keep returning to your dream throughout the following days to see what messages appear in relation to your question and your bigger story.

We – Sharing our powerful dreams with others can help us to explore them in a deeper way. If you feel called, share your dreams with trusted friends or family members and get them to explore the dream landscape with you. Enter into your dream in as much detail as you both can and see if you can spot clues/messages/ideas that were previously unseen. Try and avoid 'interpretation' as this can limit the extent to which the messages of the dream can be assimilated.

Sometimes, when we are in the middle of a particularly challenging test, it becomes hard for us to stop long enough to hear the voice of the universe speaking to us, showing us the clues that will lead us forwards, out of the mess in which we find ourselves. When our conscious brain is in overwhelm, we often find that we can gain more clarity through the realm of our dreams, working directly with the unconscious realm of experience that holds all the inner answers that we seek.

The marriage game

> The story of success is subtle
> Offering us many different masks to wear
> It is only when we try them on for a time
> That we find out what we cannot bear

After whistleblowing, I had been working in my new job in media for just over a year and had fully donned the mask of a successful corporate businesswoman. I had a great salary, my first company car and had assumed the dominant position of the main earner in my relationship. My boyfriend had tried to find work when we relocated for my new job but he discovered that this was harder than expected so he ended up taking a role in a different department, but working at the same media company. Not only did he earn less than I did but he was also in a more junior position within the organization. At the time, I didn't really notice the shift in dynamic that this created between us, focusing instead on us being a 'modern couple' who could handle this move away from traditional gender roles quite easily. However, there was a perceptible change in energy nonetheless. In becoming more confident and assertive in my work interactions, I started to play this out at home too. He was a soft, sensitive soul, which was one of the things that had most attracted me to him at first, but the more 'masculine' I became, the more 'feminine' he had to become to balance us out.

We couldn't have articulated this at the time, but looking back, a number of things stand out clearly to me now. I was working in a very male-dominated environment and in order to survive and thrive there, I also emphasized the masculine part of my nature. Like a chameleon, I changed shape to fit in with my colleagues and peers and became decisive, opinionated and developed a talent for moving fast through any conversation or conflict. The problem was that I was so invested in my career, and so enjoying the sense of power and freedom that it gave me, that I lost sight of the other side of my inherently feminine nature (the softer, gentler, more accepting person that my partner had initially been attracted to). This narrative all played out under our radar whilst we continued with the busyness of our lives...at first.

This dominant tendency of my persona even carried over into one of the most important decisions of our life: marriage. I was the one to ask him. On a stormy windswept night in the Lake District (where we had gone for a camping trip), I wrote a card and popped the question that most girls dream of their whole lives: of being asked for their hand in marriage by the man of their dreams. And yet, here I was asking him. In true feminine fashion, at first he looked stunned, and then with a look of intense joy on his face said, "*Yes!*" Strangely, as I fell asleep afterwards listening to the rain and wind lashing our small tent relentlessly, I remember thinking that this was supposed to be one of the most joyful moments in my life. And yet I felt no different than I had before. It was another anticlimax, just like the first time I experienced sex. Perhaps, if I had been more aware at the time, I would have spent longer thinking about that particular inner clue, but I didn't. After all, during this time in my life, my thoughts were as fast as my actions. I didn't dwell for long on anything.

At about the same time, I received a promotion at work. I felt proud and excited about my new role, as well as more than a little scared that I was not experienced or old enough to do it. My boss reassured me that he had been promoted at a similarly young age and that he trusted that I would jump in the deep end and swim. I took his faith in me very seriously and focused all of my attention on 'doing my best'. Unfortunately, this was yet again at the expense of my personal life. I quickly forgot that I had a wedding to plan. One morning at work I found myself in a conversation at the coffee bar with a friend who almost fell off her chair when I said I was going to email out our wedding invitations.

"*You are going to do what?*" she asked me incredulously.

"*What's wrong with that?*" I said.

"*This is a wedding not a weekly meeting,*" she responded, a shocked look writ large on her face.

Again, I probably should have seen the danger signs, but I had a reporting deadline to hit that morning. I didn't have the time to think about such niceties.

> I PROBABLY SHOULD HAVE SEEN THE DANGER SIGNS,
> BUT I DIDN'T HAVE THE TIME TO THINK ABOUT SUCH NICETIES.

The situation at home started to become increasingly strained. Understandably, my fiancé was feeling neglected, like he had taken a back seat in my life. When he confronted me with these things, my ego would leap to my defense and I would become indignant and protective of the businesswoman lifestyle and persona that I was acting out. Thoughts like, *'You're the man in this relationship, why are you acting so needy and weak?'* would run through my head, but I wouldn't say them to his face for fear of hurting him. The more he tried to pull me back into his life, the more I perceived him as smothering me and trying to restrict my freedom. I started to feel increasingly trapped, and like I was the 'bad guy' (you notice all the masculine metaphors entering into this narrative, right?). I started to think that if this was what marriage was going to be like, then I wanted no part of it – but fearing where that train of thought would lead, I quickly shoved it to the back of my mind, ignoring the discordant feelings it brought up. There was no value in having such thoughts; we had already booked the ceremony and invited our families. What would they think if we backed out now? In truth, I let the fear of what others would think of me completely override my own intuition, which was screaming at me in the silence of the night. Unsurprisingly, I was sleeping very little at this time.

I LET THE FEAR OF WHAT OTHERS WOULD THINK OF ME COMPLETELY OVERRIDE MY OWN INTUITION.

It was in this co-dependent pattern of deep discomfort and willful blindness that I shuffled through the next few months, until our wedding day finally arrived. It was the morning of the registry office ceremony and my sisters had come to stay with us to be our witnesses. As I put on my wedding dress and did my hair I was excited in the way that any girl coming to the conclusion of a fairy tale story in her life is. The problem was, I was excited by the thought of *playing the role* of the fairy tale princess bride; I was excited by looking beautiful in a wedding dress – more so than I was by the thought of spending the rest of my life with the man I was about to marry.

As I did my wedding makeup, I remember looking down at a snow globe that I had been given as a child. A white fairy castle sat inside its glittery waters. I failed miserably to spot the clue my childhood toy was giving me. If I had allowed my overactive mind to slow down for a single moment that day and found the silence within me, I would have heard my own inner voice telling me the truth. But I didn't want the truth that day, I wanted the fairy tale. I ignored the clues that my inner wisdom was shoving in front of my nose and dived headlong into another big life lesson. Perhaps this was the way it had to be.

> I IGNORED THE CLUES THAT MY INNER WISDOM
> WAS SHOVING IN FRONT OF MY NOSE.

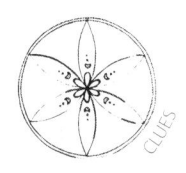

It was raining and we all had to run to the car to avoid getting our wedding finery wet. I hated the rain but consciously chose to ignore the omen. In the registry office I felt surprisingly calm and resolute. I was going to go through with this no matter what. After all, what was the worst that could happen? My husband to be was beaming and I tried to absorb his obvious happiness into my heart. It worked to a degree and I was smiling as we walked hand in hand into the room where we would be married. We sat down and I smoothed the folds of my simple cream wedding dress out around me and set my self-made bouquet of roses down on the mahogany table. As the registrar started the legal bit of the ceremony, I found myself looking mindlessly out of the window at the pouring rain that was hitting the windows, detaching from the scene around me. I don't know how long that moment lasted but I was brought back into the room just as it was time for us to read our vows. I went first and as I started to read, I noticed that my husband was shaking. Curious, I looked up from my paper and saw that he was crying. I was confused and unsure as to what this meant. There was a small part of me that thought, *'Man up, would you!'* but that voice was quickly smothered and subsumed by another within me that asked a pointed question. Why was I not nearly as emotional as he was? In fact, why was I not emotional at all? I became interested in my apparent lack of engagement. What did that mean? The registrar gave my husband a tissue and I continued reading my vows, forcing out a smile that I hoped covered my sense of discomfiting detachment. I felt aloof, like an actress playing a role with professional precision.

I know this may sound cold and harsh to some of you reading this and yet it is the ultimate truth of how I felt that day. All the time leading up to my wedding, I had distracted myself by being too busy at work, or convincing myself that once we were married all the little niggles of our incompatibility would somehow be magically solved. None of these stories were true and it took me many subsequent years of self-reflection to see the clues I was ignoring as clearly as I present them to you now. What person can say that, never at any point in their lives, have they chosen the superficial 'right thing to do' over the messages from their heart? Nor do I mean for you to walk away from this chapter thinking that I never loved my husband. I did love him. But the reality was I didn't see him as my equal and despite the love I felt, I lacked respect for who he was choosing to show up as in the world. It was these two primary things that would end up slowly poisoning our relationship in the years to come. But for now, I had a family party to attend and a honeymoon to go on. I could pretend for a while that things were how they were supposed to be: the fairy tale. For now.

> I LACKED RESPECT FOR WHO HE WAS CHOOSING
> TO SHOW UP AS IN THE WORLD.

CLUES JOURNEY

CAN YOU LEARN TO SEE THE MOST IMPORTANT ASPECTS OF LIFE?

The Clues Stage can be subtle and hard to spot. In many ways, the period is a continuation of the theme and vibe of The Tests, but this time with interjecting moments of magic and synchronicity that call your attention to the traits of your deeper narrative. It takes awareness and reflection to tune into the harmony of your story.

Take a walk through your home, looking for any objects or pictures that remind you of a particular moment of synchronicity in your life; a moment when your soul gave you a clue to your real story. If possible, look for a physical object that you can touch and take in your hands (if you don't have this ability at the time you are reading this, you can do this exercise in your imagination also). Pick two or three things that represent miracle moments for you.

Next, find a quiet space and take a moment to really look and feel each object. Remember what was happening in the moment that this magical experience happened for you. The magic can be either light or dark, tough or blissful; the clues we receive cover both of these polarities. Take your time and enjoy this remembrance. Magic makes us feel alive when we experience it. It is healthy for us to reflect and savor its power in our lives.

After you have relived these moments fully, write down or draw the properties that these magical moments or clues hold for you. How do you feel when something synchronistic occurs? Where do you feel the sense of awe and wonder in your body? Does magic have a color for you? A taste? A sound? Go into as much sensuous detail as you possibly can.

Now, in the spirit of fun, give your experience of magic a name. A word or phrase that has meaning for you. Write this on a piece of paper and you may also wish to decorate this to bring to life the experience it represents. Next time you notice your soul speaking to you in the form of a synchronistic sign, miracle or clue, speak your word aloud. Sing it, dance it, laugh it alive! What's mine, you may ask? *'Tough Bliss'*.

Each time you celebrate natural magic unfolding in your life, you will remember how this feels and in your remembering you will be magnetically attracting more of your soul story into form. You will learn to recognize the clues that the universe gives you more and more.

METAMORPHOSIS

ARE WE PREPARED TO LET OLD PARTS OF US DIE SO THAT WE CAN BE REBORN?

In learning to recognize the clues to our story that are being given to us by the universe, we are presented with a pivotal choice. The mask of our identity has by this stage often started to fray around the edges. In quiet moments, we find ourselves asking new questions about the emerging shape of our future. This can be a time of new vision, a new purpose and new vocational callings – if we are brave enough to create the space for them.

A useful metaphor for this section of the restory journey is the process by which a caterpillar transforms into a butterfly. Most of us are familiar with this tale, however, for those that are not I wish to focus on one particular element that I continually find powerful. Once the caterpillar is interred in its self-made cocoon (it is important to note 'self-made'), it responds to the pulse of evolution and willingly surrenders its former identity. It starts to melt. Literally melt! The caterpillar's body starts to decompose – whilst it's still alive – into a 'soup' of the various components of its new life. It must let go fully of its previous form and identity as a caterpillar in order for its 'imaginal cells' (I love this term) to fire and form the new DNA and physical structure of the butterfly. Thus, the caterpillar must willingly die in order for rebirth to happen.

I believe that we also reach this stage as humans, during major transitions and transformations prompted by events that deeply challenge us in our life. Once we have started to sense within us the new person wanting to be born, we have to go through a process of letting go of our old selves, allowing our previous habits, ways of being and masks of personality to melt away so that a new skin of our story can be revealed underneath.

> IN QUIET MOMENTS, WE FIND OURSELVES ASKING NEW
> QUESTIONS ABOUT THE EMERGING SHAPE OF OUR FUTURE.

To do this, we need to prepare ourselves for death. The cycle of death and rebirth is a core element of the mythologies of almost every culture across the world. Needless to say, this initiation into our true story and self is far from easy, especially when we have very few elders, teachers and wise people available to us as guides. What are we being initiated into? I believe that during this stage, we are given the opportunity to remember and embody who we really are. To reconnect ourselves back into the vast web of life in the universe, restoring our original spark and unique gifts that we came into this life bearing. It is perhaps the most challenging stage of the entire narrative life cycle. I certainly have found it so, and continue to, every time I am invited to step willingly into its arms. Yet the creative process of the metamorphosis stage is also one of the most exciting – if we want to evolve beyond our adolescent skin, then we can't escape its breakdown which ultimately results in a breakthrough.

What happens when we sense that we are close to physical death? I guess the answer depends on the circumstances in which we have come to that place. Have we arrived at the major transition point consciously, knowing that we are about to die? Are we at peace with the transition, trusting that there is a new life that lies beyond the old one? If the answer is yes, then the death is often relatively peaceful and full of grace. If no, then we tend to panic, fight and try to run away for as long as we can. When we reach this stage of our soul's journey, those of us who have felt deep inside the longing to grow, evolve and show up into the world in an authentic way, will have been attempting to prepare ourselves in a variety of ways. We may have stumbled across or sought out teachers, information or assistance and will have begun to prepare our cocoon. If, however, we have been ignoring the pulse of transformation calling in our lives, then by this point we often reach 'crisis' or what is also known as a 'dark night of the soul'. Perhaps our relationships are breaking down, or our work may be in the process of massive change, or our health may have come into question in some way – or perhaps we find ourselves thrust into an experience that combines all of these things.

I have found that my own journey has been a seesaw between crisis and creation. One moment I was scared of my imploding personality, or the death of a phase of my life, and the next I was excited like a little child for the coming of the new. Some days I was conscious of the changes being called forth within me as my imaginal cells began to awaken, and on other days I ran and buried my head in the proverbial sand, telling myself that my job/my marriage/my health would be okay if I could just make it past the next milestone. Of course, more stones would pile themselves heavily one on top of another, until the way ahead looked more like a looming mountain of challenges than a clear road into the future. I oscillated between elation and trepidation on a daily basis.

One of the most difficult parts of melting within our cocoon is the process of letting go of old guilt, shame and self-judgment. These self-flagellating emotions stem from moments when we felt we had failed or were not good enough in some way. In order for us to activate the imaginal cells of our greatest human story we cannot cling to self-judgment. Instead, we must let go and come to our Metamorphosis Stage with humility and a large degree of surrender. We must move deeply into the practice of forgiveness, of ourselves and others, which involves us willingly transcending the role of the 'victim' within our old story. We must release old hurts, wounds and the sense of injustice that often accompanies our narratives of righteousness. To forgive requires compassion and an ability to move beyond our stories of right/wrong and me/them. We are asked to find compassion in our hearts for the process of being both human and divine – of being both 'me' and 'we' – in order to relax the narrative defenses that are holding us in our self-made cocoon of the past.

> WE MUST COME TO OUR METAMORPHOSIS STAGE
> WITH HUMILITY AND A LARGE DEGREE OF SURRENDER.

This is a scary time, a time when those around us sense our impending death and rebirth to a new phase of life and can become conscious or unconscious saboteurs attempting to keep us tightly enclosed within our old shells. Sometimes we listen to their fears and attempt to halt the process of evolution: to keep ourselves in the uncomfortable but well-known place of safety within our old story. Some people do this so successfully that they remain a hungry (and often angry) caterpillar their whole lives. Eventually, however, every real adventurer comes to the tipping point where they must choose; where they must rebel against the past. If we persevere and conquer our fears of the unknown story attempting to be born through us then we can't go back. Once heard, we can't un-hear the deep pulse of our purpose. If we choose to listen to it, its voice will be there guiding us through both the darkness and the light. My guess is if you are reading this book, you have already started to form your cocoon in some way. You may even be melting. All you have to do is choose to say 'yes' to the call of your real story. Choose and then let go.

> ONCE HEARD,
> WE CAN'T UN-HEAR THE DEEP PULSE OF OUR PURPOSE.

The moment I awoke to and accepted the metamorphosis that was attempting to break me, my evolution was inevitable. I knew in my bones that I wouldn't choose to remain small and in pain when a greater expression of my story was being offered. The journey was painful in places and ecstatic in others. It continues to be so. Truly our process of metamorphosis is one of tough bliss where we must for a time walk between the worlds of the old and the new. Our task here is to bring spirit into matter. To combine our authentic passion and purpose with our grounded ability to survive and thrive in the world in which we find ourselves living. Gone are the days when we could 'awaken' and then run up a mountain to meditate and retreat from the world. Butterflies are desperately needed: those who are willing to land in the dirt, take action in the world and inspire others to enter into the process of transformation for themselves.

The mask falls off

> Sinking, I find myself choking on my old face
> "Let go" my voice in the dark shouts
> I make the choiceless choice
> And rise to the surface of a new story

There comes a time when the call to transform becomes so loud that we can't ignore it any more. Starting as a whisper at the edge of our consciousness, it grows in intensity and volume akin to bird song in the pre-dawn light, gradually awakening us to our inner disturbance. If ignored for long enough, it becomes a crashing, shouting cacophony of pain experienced through the challenges of our life. I was 27 when my soul decided to serve me with a notice that I couldn't help but accept.

Since the wedding, I had become increasingly aware that certain parts of my life were seriously out of alignment. I was frustrated by my so-called successful business career, wondering how I had ended up spending up to 70 hours a week of my life trying to make a warehouse operation run more smoothly, a pursuit that had started to feel more and more trivial as each day passed. My days were spent running from meeting to meeting accumulating lists of actions, most of which wouldn't get done due to the fast-paced nature of change. Amongst all of this, if I had a spare moment, I would be glued to my phone attempting to reply to the thousands of emails that had accumulated, rehashing the same conversations that had taken place in the meetings. Often, I would find myself mid-yawn questioning the validity of attempting to bring any semblance of structure, process and order to chaotic humans. Yet I was so exhausted by this very process that I rarely had time to give it more than a passing thought. It would be some years before I would start to discover the secrets to creating change, but for now I was overcome and overwhelmed by the mass of responsibility and information that flowed to me on a daily basis.

Because of the demands from work, my relationship with my new husband was suffering. The slightest comment from him, seeking love and attention, would spawn instant hostility from me accompanied by a feeling of suffocation. I would react with outward anger and scorn towards his advances, whilst inwardly knowing that the object of my difficult emotional reactions lay within myself. It was confusing for us both. I knew that I was holding the main part of our problem and yet it was too scary to look for the source of my discomfort within my own psyche. It was far easier to blame my husband for being 'too needy' or 'too demanding' than to turn around and look at my own shadow. So, I ignored it, or at least, I tried to.

Because of the stress I found myself in, I retreated into old comforting habits. This repertoire included eating unhealthy but convenient food, shopping for things that made me feel good temporarily and watching TV to numb my mind and drown out the difficult questions that sprang up from silence and dreams. The toll this took on my physical and mental health was severe. I found myself getting sick a lot and struggled onwards despite my body's attempts to get me to be still and listen. I was in a constant state of exhaustion, with feelings of unexplained despair and sadness bubbling up at regular intervals. When quizzed by my family, I would attempt to articulate the grief that I felt and yet failed miserably to give it a name. I didn't have the words. All I knew was that I wasn't happy and something big was calling me in the middle of the night. The ever present voice was also growing louder by the day, reminding me that my purpose here on earth was something far greater than that which I was currently living. I was successful but miserable; I was making a living but not 'living' in any sense of the word. I was struggling to survive in the midst of a dying narrative of success. I'm pretty sure my family and friends thought I had the beginnings of depression or I was embarking on an early mid-life crisis. No one ever mentioned it directly.

> I WOULD ATTEMPT TO ARTICULATE THE GRIEF THAT I FELT
> AND YET FAILED MISERABLY TO GIVE IT A NAME.

My discomfort was preparing me to find the courage I needed in order to leave the comfortable home and social structures of my life behind. It was time for a new story.

Opening my eyes after a night of broken sleep, I switched into behavioral autopilot and turned over to grab my mobile phone from the bedside table. As my eyes slowly focused on the screen in front of me I saw with a sinking feeling that eight missed calls had racked up overnight. Flicking to my emails, I discovered that another work crisis had unfolded during the night and that I was being asked to fix it – yesterday. A sigh of stressed despair worked its way from head to toe and escaped through my mouth as it dawned on me that my weekend was blown again.

My husband stirred in our bed next to me and I felt a wave of annoyance wash through my nervous system as his arm reached out to encircle me. Such was our relating these days. I neither wanted nor needed his touch and had reached the point where the less I was around him, the easier it was for me. I was far too stressed and distracted to see that the escape artist, the child and the bully were all at work in my inner shadow and I didn't want to see or own any of them. Projection after projection had played out between us for so long that we had lost our ability to see the real humans underneath them. In that moment, as I moved away from his embrace, a sad realization hit me full in the face. I didn't want to be with him anymore. Our relationship was about to enter its death.

I slowly freed myself from our bed and got up, grabbing my robe. As I moved silently out of our bedroom I happened to glance at myself in the mirror as I walked naked into the bathroom, and shuddered with self-revulsion at the image I saw. I hated myself for being overweight, shrouded in a protective layer of fat. I also felt anger that time after time, year in, year out, I had chosen to eat foods that I knew were slowly killing me. I grimaced as I thought of the number of times over the years that I had sworn to myself to change my unhealthy eating habits and then relapsed into the comfortable routine of processed and poisonous foods. Deep in my reverie of self-loathing and despair I failed to notice that the last piece of the puzzle was marching swiftly towards me.

Opening the bathroom window, I looked out onto the view of the street and was taken aback as I found myself hit by a wave of hatred that broke over the top of my already high wall of darkness. At this time, we were living in a rented house on an old estate in the city of Coventry. Dubbed the 'shitty city', it was bombed flat in WWII and had been rebuilt almost completely from concrete and pebbledash. I found the town depressing but, given it was convenient for getting to work, my husband and I had settled for it. I suddenly felt as though my soul was crying out in agony: *'I SHOULDN'T BE HERE ANY MORE!'* it screamed in my ears. I fell down on the floor of my bathroom wracked with sobs, unable to move. *'Why am I here? Why am I so miserable? Why can I see only darkness all around me?'* I wanted to grab my bag and run away from this life as fast as my legs would carry me, but I simply didn't know where I would go.

After allowing myself to cry long and hard, I finally pulled myself up from the floor and stumbled down the stairs to our living room. Sitting on the edge of our sofa I once again went into autopilot and grabbed the remote control for the TV set. However, this time, I was about to receive an answer to my desperate call for help. Somehow the TV flickered into life on a channel that I hadn't seen before. As I slowly looked up and started to pay attention to what was before me I saw images of a sunny beach in some far-off tropical island. Athletic, muscular surfers were braving monster waves and surfing across the face of ocean swells with such skill and grace it looked like they might have been born into water and had never left its fluid embrace. I became entranced. I hadn't watched surfing before nor even considered it as a viable pastime and yet here it was in front of me, speaking to my inner longing and desire.

Such is the language of our souls: it speaks in metaphors and moments of synchronicity, leading us to apparently random coincidences that set us up to hear the voice of our bigger story, just when we need to hear it. On this dark morning, as I sat in a trance watching the sunshine and aquamarine waves roll across my TV screen, I was caught by the meaning it held for me. My longing suddenly became crystal clear within the frame of the surfing competition playing out in front of me. Like a scroll uncurling with an ancient message, I finally understood the meaning behind the darkness I had locked inside me for so long.

> **SUCH IS THE LANGUAGE OF OUR SOULS:**
> **IT SPEAKS IN METAPHORS AND MOMENTS OF SYNCHRONICITY.**

It reminded me of the story from my childhood when I would spend hours imagining that 'when I grew up' I would travel this beautiful earth and see new and wild places. I ached for sunshine and inspiration in my life. I longed to be pushed out of my comfort zone on a daily basis and do work that was meaningful and fun. I was hungry to discover my own genius and then throw myself headlong into its study and practice – in service to the world.

I finally realized that I yearned for freedom from the self-imposed prison of my current identity that had been wrapping itself tightly around me for years like a cocoon. It was time to shed my skin and be reborn anew. The scary part was that I had no idea what creature would emerge from the darkness into the world, but I knew I had to find out. As this realization coursed through my veins, I sat on the sofa and watched episode after episode of the surf competition putting my 'work' on the back burner for the first time in years. I felt a mixture of excitement and fear, of trepidation and courage. I knew I would do what had to be done to move into the next phase of my life, come what may.

Later that day as the mood took me, I went online and spent my bonus money, as the first tangible step in a period of my life where I would be apprenticing myself to the journey of my story. I bought myself surfing lessons.

CREATING A COCOON

ARE YOU READY TO LET GO OF THAT WHICH YOU HAVE OUTGROWN?

Me – Carve out 24 hours where you can be alone and undisturbed. Consciously create a cocoon environment. This can be inside your home or outside in nature if you have a certain place that you love to spend time in and feel safe.

Prepare for your own metaphorical metamorphosis by gathering together objects that represent the part of you that is preparing to die (these could be old photos, clothes or objects that represent an old and dying story for you). Spend 24 hours (one full day and night) in your own self-designed ceremony to let go of your old self and create space for the new butterfly version of you to be reborn. You might wish to burn or bury your old things, symbolically letting go of the old narrative. Alternatively, you can also celebrate your life so far and spend some time reflecting on the new aspects of your story that you wish to manifest.

It's important to have appropriate materials with you to ensure your comfort and safety for the full 24-hour period. Let someone know where you are and that you will be offline and not wishing to be disturbed for this period of time. You will definitely want to bring a journal and pens to record the messages you receive throughout this period. You may choose to bring special foods or to fast – you must decide whatever is best for you. Ensure that you have plenty of water to keep hydrated and appropriate clothing for your environment.

When we encounter a crisis of the soul, we can choose the extent to which we enter into the process of transformation consciously. The more we can see these challenges as opportunities and nurture them (by creating a space in our life for the initiation to occur), the more graceful and painless the process will be. If you are hungering for a deeper cocoon experience, you can check out facilitated vision quests or nature-based retreats. I have put a number of recommendations on *www.beyondhumanstories.com*

Walking with angels

> Remember beyond time
> The things that have been lost and forgotten
> Awaken your childhood abilities
> Reignite your wider vision

I was driving across town in my company car, wearing my company suit and ignoring my company phone that was racking up missed calls and messages. Left, right, left again; heading towards an unknown house and an unknown woman.

Since awakening to my 'dark night of the soul' process, I felt like a ghost walking through my own life, detached from the narrative and identity that was in the process of falling away. I had finally decided that 'enough was enough' and that I needed to create massive change in almost every area of my life. The only thing was, I had no idea where to start, so I had stalled. Like a rabbit caught in the headlights of the oncoming car of destiny, I didn't know which way to move first.

SINCE AWAKENING TO MY 'DARK NIGHT OF THE SOUL' PROCESS, I FELT LIKE A GHOST WALKING THROUGH MY OWN LIFE.

So, there I was, driving into the unknown. Number 12, 14, 16 – there. This was the house. This was the street. I parked my car and got out, standing alone on a chilly, gray afternoon looking at the door that I hoped would change my life for the better, just as my intuition had whispered it might. Walking up the garden path I noticed the hotch-potch planting and overgrown grass, reflecting on how beautiful the chaos seemed amongst the uniformity of the other houses. Working up the courage, I raised my hand and knocked firmly. My friend had suggested that I come here. She said she thought I would really love this healer. As the door opened and I saw a middle-aged, kind face looking back at me, I felt immediately that my friend had been right. I was meant to be here.

Inviting me in, her eyes scanned me and I wondered what she could see. I was here for a Reiki healing. It was my first and I was excited. I was also desperately hoping that it would begin to heal me of some of the inner turmoil I was feeling. The lady started by asking me a series of questions regarding my medical history and my knowledge of the techniques she was about to use, and then she smiled as I described my work and home life challenges. After listening with her silent smile for a few moments, she requested that I lie down on a massage table set up in the middle of her living room. Taking a moment to center herself, she began to place crystals on my body and as a big piece of clear quartz was placed gently on my heart, I felt a buzzing sensation activate. I was surprised at the physicality of the experience.

"Relax and close your eyes," she said in a soft voice.

I happily complied. The humming took over my senses and I felt energy flowing up and down my spine. Letting go of my conscious mind, I gave myself over to the waves of vibration that coursed through me. Vague memories of similar sensations I felt as a young child touched at the edge of my awareness like a comforting promise of familiarity. I slowly lost track of time and reality, drifting on an ocean of softly swaying, liquid frequencies.

Minutes, hours or days later (I didn't know which), I heard a soft voice calling me back into the strange living room. I slowly opened my eyes to see the kind face looking down at me as she removed the crystals from my body.

"*You left for a while there, didn't you?*" she said to me with a smile. Not feeling able to speak yet, I smiled in acquiescence. Gradually I stretched, feeling life returning to my limbs as if I had been asleep for many years. Sitting up, I looked at my healer, my eyes silently asking for information regarding my diagnosis.

After a pause to consider her words she said, "*Well, you are one of the healthiest people I have ever seen.*"

"*Good news then?*" I asked in return, bemused as I noticed that the room behind her appeared to be softly pulsing with energy.

Again, another pause before she continued. "*Your energy centers were completely blocked, however – it took me quite some time to clear them.*"

'*Clear them of what?*' I thought to myself as I looked down at the aged and worn 1970s carpet where the patterns were writhing and moving before my eyes.

"*You should take it easy for a few days, drink plenty of water and get lots of sleep,*" she said as she started to move across the room.

"*Thanks,*" I said as I stood rather shakily to my feet, feeling the floor bend and give beneath me as if it was made of marshmallow. I breathed deeply, trying to center myself. The world felt different yet not unfamiliar. I remembered being used to a world of vibration and light somewhere in the depths of my consciousness and was not afraid, more curious. Somewhere in the back of my mind I remembered having perceptions like this years earlier when I had last taken acid.

> I REMEMBERED BEING USED TO A WORLD OF VIBRATION AND LIGHT SOMEWHERE IN THE DEPTHS OF MY CONSCIOUSNESS.

Turning around to say thank you to my healer, I found myself involuntarily reaching out to give her a hug. Surprised, she returned my gesture with real warmth and strong arms. Stepping out of the front door, the fresh air hit my face and danced across my cheeks, caressing me as if I was a long-lost friend. Smiling, I turned to say goodbye.

I was met with a hesitant, "*Wait...I have to tell you something.*"

Intrigued, I paused, aware that a burst of excited energy exploded in my solar plexus like sunbeams breaking through clouds.

"*I have to tell you...*" another pause as she looked as though she was listening to a voice behind her right shoulder. "*You are completely surrounded by angels. I wasn't going to tell you, but they insisted.*"

Angels? This was a relatively alien concept to me. Despite my mother's Catholic upbringing, religion hadn't really featured in my life and we certainly had never talked about angels.

"*Ummm, thanks,*" I replied, not really knowing what else to say.

She could tell I was confused and to remedy this, she continued, "*You see, I can tune into the earthly realm and speak with ghosts, entities that were once human, and nature spirits and so on, but you – now your energy centers are clear – you are vibrating at a very high level. The level of the angelic kingdom. They are all around you, trying to get your attention. Perhaps you should spend some time meditating – you will be able to open a channel very easily to them now.*"

I didn't know what to say and felt a combination of excitement and skepticism at hearing her revelations.

Knowing I was going to have to take the next steps of the journey on my own now, she simply gave me another hug. "*It is a great gift that you carry and you know where I am if you need help in learning how to use it.*"

"*Thank you,*" I said, and meant it. I turned out to the street to walk back towards my car. As I heard her front door close behind me, I was struck by the thought that perhaps I had also just closed the door on a chapter in my life: one where I had tried to pretend that I was a normal, fully-functioning member of an insane society. I started the engine of my car and noticed that I was still humming all over.

'Angels,' I mused, as I pulled out into the rush hour traffic. *'I wonder what she meant?'* Something other than me drove my car that night because I ended up getting lost and going a different way home. This route went directly past a big bookstore on a retail park. Instinctively pulling in, I got out of the car and wandered into the store wondering whether I would be brave enough to ask the attendant for help finding books on angels. In the end, I didn't need to. The sort of synchronistic magic to which I would become very accustomed in the following years was working in full force that evening and the first book stand that I came across on entering the store was labeled 'Mind, Body, Spirit'. I glanced across the piles of best sellers on the table and breathed in sharply as I noticed there were several books relating to angels, including by authors such as Rudolf Steiner [17] and Rupert Sheldrake [18] who I filed under the mental category of 'new science and education'. *'Perhaps this topic isn't as odd as I thought,'* I said to myself. I started picking up books to see which ones resonated. After half an hour or so of looking, I ended up with a handful of titles that I couldn't seem to put down, despite the skepticism of my intellect.

The books picked up where my kind Reiki healer had left off and I was more than aware that this information had come into my life at just the moment when I needed it. With every paragraph I read, I was reminded of things that I had *known* intuitively as a child, yet had buried during the period of my tests and in my struggle to fit in. These memories saved my life. In the next few weeks, the doors inside me were unlocked and thrown wide open. To the astonishment of my mind, I found myself connecting to and speaking with angelic beings of all kinds in various different forms. It was as my healer had said – I was surrounded with loving energies all waiting to help.

For anyone who has looked into these things, it is easy to find out (like I did that night on walking into the bookstore) that the theory and practice of communicating with angels isn't as strange as we might be led to think. In fact, mystics, priests/priestesses, wise men/women and many 'normal' people have been practicing and documenting it for centuries. The existence of 'other than human' beings in the universe that we can connect to, communicate with and learn from, is something that has been written into the ancient narratives of humanity. It's a fairly recent phenomenon of post-modern reductionist mythology that teaches us to mistrust anything that we cannot measure, prove and repeatedly demonstrate in the three-dimensional (physical) world. Things get even weirder when we start to delve into the world of quantum physics. Here, atoms, particles and energy behave in non-repeatable, random and 'weird' ways that are constantly baffling us. This 'not knowing' is the new science.

As this kind of angelic interaction gradually became normal to me, I realized that the angels were like the 'imaginary' friends I had played with as a child (in fact, they told me on many occasions that they were one and the same). My communication with them ranged from spontaneous auditory dialogues in my head (that I could never make up myself) to moments of grace and 'gnosis' where I would suddenly be made aware of answers/wisdom and universal laws from a source outside of my human knowledge. One of my now favorite authors, Richard Rudd [19] describes angels as, 'layers of consciousness, far more organized and complex than our own that can only be communed with when we develop the higher faculties latent inside us.'

My Reiki healing had thrown open the floodgates to my natural latent human abilities and I was now aware of some of the gifts that I had buried in the pain of my forgetting. With angelic guidance, the weight of hopelessness that I had been carrying slowly started to lift as I moved forwards into my new adventure. I had opened a fresh chapter in my life, and was starting to see a path appearing in front of my eyes that had previously been hidden by my slumber in the human social drama of 'attempting to make it' in the world. Where the path was leading I didn't know, but at least I felt safe again walking into the darkness surrounded by new, ancient friends.

Remembering beauty

> Wiping the sleep from my eyes
> I awaken to see a world from my past and future
> When did I decide to forget this beauty?
> When did I start to doubt life?

I believe that most of us long for experiences that break us out of normality, revealing the truth and depth of life. These pivotal moments forever change us, catalyzing new identities and ways of being and acting in the world. These experiences are to be savored and are never forgotten.

The foundations of the third dimensional, rational world were starting to crack beneath my feet. I was on the edge of going into free fall; of jumping off a cliff into the unknown. A new me. I was both excited and scared shitless. *'What if I am making all of this stuff up?'* was the thought that came to me several times a day as my experiences of the 'more-than-human world' (to use a phrase coined by David Abram[20]) pervaded my experiences with increasing frequency.

I had been deeply unhappy in the ordinary world of marriage, business and material life for some time, so was acutely aware that anything representing a more meaningful and magical existence would be highly attractive to me. When I bounced this story off my angelic friends using the lens of my imagination to communicate my questions and intentions, I was immediately assured that everyone who remembers their connection to a bigger world experiences this fear initially. *"You are not insane, you are awakening,"* they repeatedly told me. I wanted desperately to believe them.

I became very careful to whom I spoke of these things. In an attempt to be honest and authentic I tried to share my experiences with my husband. Unfortunately, the more I told him, the more I caught him giving me searching looks. Stories of *'Who is this woman who was once my wife?'* were written across his face. Although he tried to listen, he didn't understand and probably thought that I was losing my mind. In fact, the only two people who did immediately 'get it' were my grandparents in Colorado. Having been out of touch for many years, bar birthdays and Christmas, I felt a sudden urge to reconnect with them as if I instinctively knew they would be among the few people who would understand what was happening to me. I called them a few times, getting braver with each conversation I had, revealing more of the magical encounters I found myself having. They listened, reassured me and encouraged me to explore this newfound connection. They even started sending me books and articles from other 'angel friends', assuring me that I was both sane and part of a growing group of people across the world who also had this connection. Without their loving support from afar, I don't think I would have been courageous enough to continue. But continue I did. It was far too late to turn back and after all, what was there to go back to?

I did my best to navigate between these worlds. The more I opened up my spiritual senses, the more magical and vibrant my life became. 'Daily magic' infiltrated my world through synchronistic events and 'coincidental' meetings. Spontaneous wisdom emerged through dreams, visions and messages. I would find myself opening books to exactly the right page to read the answers to my questions. People would say things to me at just the right time to help me make decisions. White feathers (commonly attributed to angels) would appear in the most unlikely of places. The more I fell in love with the world around me again, the harder I found it to be 'normal' or put on the mask of the person I once had been at work or at home. I was creating a chasm between my old world and a new one and I had no idea whether I would ever be able to bridge the two.

A few months later my husband and I traveled to the Lake District in England to visit his parents for a long weekend. They lived in a rambling old cottage by the mouth of Lake Coniston in an area of stunning natural beauty. I looked forward to going there as an escape from the city and an opportunity to breath clean, fresh air. On this particular trip we arrived after dark and, parking in the usual place by the old barn, grabbed our suitcases and started to make our way up the path to the house. I had been practicing connecting with beings of nature that week and as a result sent a silent, energetic 'hello' to all the spirits that I imagined lived in this location. To my surprise, I immediately felt a very tangible response that could be described as a warm wave of love and welcome that washed over me stemming from trees, river, lake and plants.

AT WHAT POINT DID I DECIDE TO FORGET?

Struggling to see the pathway in the dark, my husband disappeared in front of me and I found myself pulling the heavy case alone. As if they sensed my disorientation, the spirits responded immediately. Looking down, I saw small green footprints appearing on the path to the right of my feet. Working through my amazement I realized that they were guiding me to the door of the house that I was about to miss in the darkness. I sent a wave of 'thanks' to these now very real spirits of the lake and tried to put aside my astonishment as I was met at the door by my mother-in-law. Later that night as I lay in bed pondering my experience, I realized just how much of the world I had been willfully blind to for so many years. I was overcome by the emotion of gratitude and joy, like a grown woman who has forgotten her favorite childhood toy and discovers it hidden in a box years later. '*At what point did I decide to forget*?' I wondered as I drifted off to sleep.

    The next time my eyes opened, bright sunlight was streaming into our bedroom through a gap in the curtains. My husband was soundly asleep next to me as was the rest of the house judging from the sounds of snoring coming from the direction of his parents' room. I could feel the vibrations of the birds and the trees awaking to a gorgeous sunny morning outside and I was drawn like a magnet to it. Slipping quietly out of bed, I threw on some clothes and tip-toed downstairs. Failing to find my boots anywhere, I abandoned my search and let myself out of the back door barefoot. The bright, cool air swirled around me and I felt like Dorothy in *The Wizard of Oz*[21] when she first emerges from her old house into the technicolor magic of Munchkin Land. Every leaf I beheld was sparkling in the morning sun with vivid colors and flowing energy; the grass twinkled with dewdrops that reflected a multitude of rainbow colors; the sounds of the stream that ran down the hill and through the garden were heightened and glided musically to my ears. Combined with the sweet songs of the birds, the humming of early bees and the gentle breeze, I was entranced by the natural symphony that was being played out all around me. There were no signs of human beings anywhere, no cars on the road and no planes in the sky. All was nature celebrating the simple and exquisite joy of life and I was being allowed to witness it. Reaching out energetically to the more-than-human beings, I felt their joy echoing my own. I danced with them, delighted in every living thing that existed right now, had ever existed in the past and would yet exist in the future. Everything was beautiful and pulsing with the ancient impulse of joyful creation.

Feeling somewhat overwhelmed by my experience, I sat down on a rock ledge that overhung the small stream winding its way down the garden to the river. Leisurely I reached down and dipped my fingers in the cold flowing waters. The subsequent shivers of delight as the water caressed my skin sent me further into my reverie. This was the level of experience I had sought through drugs. *'If only I had known that I was capable of achieving this unassisted all along,'* I mused. What a clever trap of the ego to tell a story that our natural human birthright is only accessible through the modern chemicals of a disenchanted society. I drifted in and out of thought and space for some time, my mind sending impressions across the pool of my awareness like the reflections of clouds on still water. A waking dream. A blissful open-eyed meditation.

After what could have been moments or hours sitting on my rock, something caught my attention enough to make me raise my gaze from the flowing water and look up across the garden. Amongst the dance of life in the garden something or someone was moving. At first I couldn't quite focus on what it was, but as I looked in its general direction, the image solidified and I observed the unmistakable figure of a man moving slowly through the sunrays. He was tall, very tall; taller than any human man and he was glowing with a soft golden-white light. I recognized this being from the depths of my heart and a place beyond any mental stories I held. I would have recognized his spirit anywhere in any time or any place.

He was walking surrounded by angels, nature spirits and moving lights of all colors and vibrations. I was dazzled, yet despite the complex dance of energies, I noticed that I was able to perceive him precisely and he, me. As his gaze caught and connected to mine, I felt as though I was being lifted gently into the air and held in strong arms of pure love and compassion. The rest of the world melted away and, probably for the first time in my life, I was completely and utterly in the present moment. I was held by him, this being of pure light and love. Almost immediately I heard a resonating voice echoing through every part of my body as if a light was being shone into every cell, activating and opening it. The musical, golden voice said many things to me, some of which have passed beyond the realms of my conscious memory directly into my soul to be resurrected at the appropriate moment in time. However, there was one part of his message that I remember well to this day.

He said, *"Sister, you have a remarkable gift of seeing the inherent beauty in all things. Of seeing the truth at the core of life. You must teach this to your brothers and sisters, so they too can walk in beauty."*

I smiled with deep love and gratitude, silently singing my joyful acceptance of the mission he had presented to me. His eyes heard and witnessed, smiling in return. A smile that was as deep as the oceans and as wide as the universe. Eternity was held in that smile.

THERE IS NO TURNING BACK ONCE YOU HAVE SWORN
TO FOLLOW YOUR REAL STORY.

It was one of the first times in my adult life when I felt a complete and utter sense of unity and oneness with the world around me. I was held, loved, seen and understood beyond all time, stories and space. Words alone are but pale attempts to connect you to the depth of this experience, but use them I must. The essence of his message to me on that blessed morning was a call to my deeper purpose and unique soul identity. His invitation called me out of all stories and into truth.

That's the thing with accepting the call to your adventure. You rarely know where the path onwards will take you, but once accepted, walk the path you must. There is no turning back once you have sworn to follow your real story. It is the choiceless choice.

Meeting my match

> Know with me, be with me, love with me
> Be brave enough to walk with me
> I have found my truth within
> And now I see it reflected in you

My marriage was dying. Despite trying to find common ground from which to move forward, my husband and I had walked towards the edge of a metaphorical cliff that was crumbling beneath our feet. The deeper we looked into our psyches, the more it became obvious that we both wanted very different things in life. I craved adventure, freedom and a purpose greater than myself. He was longing for a simple, quiet life of comfort and what I call 'living for the weekend'. My growing passion for making a difference in the world and being of service was taking the majority of my focus and energy and I saw no reason to change this. He craved my undivided attention; something I couldn't give. We both knew it was the end of our dance and we were in mourning for the loss of a relationship that we had invested seven years of mental, emotional and physical energy into. I still loved him but it was no longer enough for me. I loved freedom and authenticity more.

I was determined to be honest in dissolving my contract with my husband. This was scary for someone who had long carried a pattern of lying in order to protect the feelings of others. I had once been told that 'lies are bandages for the soul' and accepted that story completely, believing that by withholding my truth from someone that I was protecting them from getting hurt. I now know that this is rarely true. It was time to dissolve this story for good and regain my integrity. It took a lot of courage to admit that I had been too young, too naïve and too scared to see what was happening years ago. It took tenacity to break free from my discomfort zone where familiar unhappiness was less scary than the call of the unknown. Tenacity transformed into dedication has saved me more than once. I had gone too far in my metamorphosis now to turn back now. The insistent call of my deeper story was growing in every moment, drawing me forwards like a siren. I knew what I had to do: I had to leave.

> THE INSISTENT CALL OF MY DEEPER STORY WAS GROWING IN EVERY MOMENT, DRAWING ME FORWARDS LIKE A SIREN.

Amongst all the emotional turmoil, life went on. Work was still tough although I had started to cherish the weekly opportunities of travel – it provided a welcome break from the difficult conversations with my soon-to-be ex-husband. One Friday afternoon as I was boarding a plane home and reviewing my game plan for the next divorce tournament, I was snapped out of my self-reflective (and somewhat self-pitying) reverie by a familiar voice behind me saying, *"Looks like I'm sat behind Gen. Magic, I am going to pull her hair and crack bad jokes all the way home."* Turning around with a smile, I looked into a familiar and friendly face.

I had known Euan for five years. He had been the voice on the phone, the one who had hired me after I blew the whistle over lost stock. We'd had a warm, easy friendship and I had come to deeply admire and respect him as one of the most human leaders I had ever known. I smiled and said, *"The jokes had better be funny this time."*

Laughing like mischievous kids and causing a scene, we took our seats and started swapping stories. The conversation flowed easily and we quickly ended up talking about our personal lives. Seeing no reason to hold back from him, I shared in a more subdued tone my decision to leave my husband and get a divorce. Looking surprised for a moment, he glanced from side to side and then in a hushed voice told me that his relationship with his wife was in a similar state. He stopped speaking and we simply gazed at each other in understanding of our mutual pain.

"*You know, I am midway through my psychology course and need to do some coaching. Maybe some of the techniques I have been using would also help you?*" I suggested.

"*That would be great,*" he replied with a cheeky wink. "*But what can I do to help you in return?*"

"Well, I also need to do a role-modeling project for my course," I continued. "*I want to understand authentic leaders and you are one of the best I know.*" Fortune favors the brave I thought.

"*You've got yourself a deal,*" he said. "*Now back to those jokes.*" I groaned out loud.

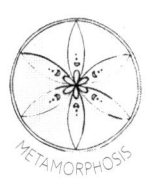

"*So, what is it that you long for in your career?*" he smiled at me, as I turned my head to look at him perched next to me on the bench, a beer in his hand. We were watching the pink and orange sun set in shining streaks over the Forth Road Bridge in Scotland, a rare sight in this rainy country.

"*Why, to live for a cause greater than myself,*" I replied smiling right back.

"*But what does that mean in the greedy, ruthless world of business?*" he asked.

"*To live according to my values. To help rather than hinder. To be a person of integrity. To shine the light of compassion into the darkness of the old capitalist stories – all of these things and much more. To be honest, I am still working that one out for myself,"* I said with a giggle.

"Admirable and challenging isn't it?" he mused. *"I sometimes feel like I am an island of sanity in a crazy, ego-driven world: the only one who is trying to do the right thing."*

"Not the only one," I said softly.

"No, not the only one," he replied.

We talked late into the evening or, more accurately, early into the morning. Drunk on more than just alcohol, we spoke about many things – things neither of us felt we had permission to speak about in our previous relationships or friendships. We conversed on what it means to be a spirit in human form; how we each learn to hear the voice of our story drawing us forwards towards adventure. We moved through our human egos, fears and desires, the grand nature of the universe and our place in it. It was like the pouring of clear, clean water onto parched ground and we were left gasping for more. It was a real connection with someone who shared the same values, desires and passions as my own and I was intoxicated.

When we are brave enough to open up to another person without expectation or agenda, we find ourselves rising above the level of mind chatter and projected judgments that form 98% of most human inner dialogue. We become vulnerable and untouchable in the same breath. It is the most risky route to ultimate safety that you can ever take. It is risky in that your ego fears the breaking of boundaries and lack of social conformance. It dreads the deep listening that comes when we are open because in the silence, all our protection mechanisms drop away in the light of real human intimacy. Deep down we all crave this openness of expression and shared appreciation. When we have the courage to leave our egos chattering behind and risk showing up naked, it is better than any drug, better than any movie or love story. It's so simple and yet so hard for most of us to achieve. Why? Simply because we are afraid. We are taught to be afraid of this level of connection from a very young age. All it takes is one or two experiences of being teased or bullied for speaking your truth before you learn to shut up and keep it all locked down. I, like many of you, shut up and shut down early in my life.

> ALL IT TAKES IS BEING TEASED OR BULLIED
> FOR SPEAKING YOUR TRUTH BEFORE YOU LEARN
> TO SHUT UP AND KEEP IT ALL LOCKED DOWN.

When we finally accepted the inevitable closure of the night's engagement, we looked at each other in silent appreciation.

"*That was the best conversation I have had in years...Seriously!*" he said to me.

"*I know, me too. Thank you.*" I was struggling to put my experience into words. I stepped forwards to give him a hug goodnight and to this day cannot explain what happened. There was no obstacle in my way, no reason for me to fall and yet I felt a strong push in my lower back that caused me to tumble into his arms. Confused, I suddenly found myself in a closer embrace than I had intended, tried to recover my 'cool shield' and failed miserably. He, on the other hand, embraced me as if it was the most natural thing in the whole world.

"*Thank YOU,*" he said as he bent his head down and kissed my cheek. I leaned into that kiss and savored the moment. In the background I could feel the angels smiling.

Back in my room I texted him a "*Thank you for tonight*" message. He replied, "*Thank yourself – you manifested me.*"

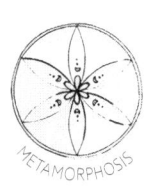

I looked out of the window of my hotel room at the bright, late summer evening sun, drinking in the rare beauty of the Scottish Highlands drenched in seldom-seen golden light. '*Funny, it's been sunny up here a lot lately,*' I thought curiously to myself. My eyes turned down the driveway and I saw the first glimpse of what I had been expecting for the last half an hour. I smiled, my heart beating faster and the butterflies in my stomach dancing. The car pulled up to the front of the hotel and after a moment the door opened. Euan got out, mobile phone glued to his ear and laptop bag hanging from his other hand. It was all I could do to stop myself running headlong down the stairs and flinging myself into his arms. I drank in the sight of him and the anticipation of an evening of diving into sensations of being physically close and moving together in a rhythm of male/female, giving/receiving, in breath/out breath. I knew I was caught headlong in the grasp of Eros and yet something was different. I had never been stripped bare like this. I had never put so much on the line. All my protection mechanisms were down and for the first time in my life I had no inclination to raise them again.

I waited for his text to say he was in the bar and then tried to slow my descent down the stairs, in an effort to appear like I was holding it together far more than I actually was. And then there he was, smiling broadly at me as I slid into his arms for a hug.

"*I would like to say I have missed you but we have hardly gone more than a couple of hours without a text this week, huh*?" he said. "*People are going to talk.*"

"*People are already talking,*" I replied with rebellious defiance.

"*Yes, they are, but tonight let's just you and I talk, huh?*"

Bottle of wine in hand, we strolled outside under the stars. Walking towards a gate leading across a field, I grabbed his hand, "*Come on, I am going to teach you how to talk with the trees.*"

Laughing, we jumped the gate and made our way across the field, selecting a large oak tree, its verdant leaves a vivid green. Sitting down next to each other on the roots of our new friend, I settled in and started to breathe deeply, connecting to the energy of the tree, feeling its protective vibration surrounding us. I also felt Euan's strong male energy humming next to mine and knew that he was far more tuned into me than anything else.

In an effort to refocus him, I said, "*Okay, now tune in and breathe – what can you feel?*"

There was a moment's pause and then the hair on my skin electrified as I felt his arm winding its way around my waist.

"Your lips on mine." He paused. *"We both know that's where we are going."*

I opened my eyes and looked deeply into his even though it was dark and the only light around us was that of the stars peeking through the canopy of leaves. Not knowing what to say, I just looked at him. I mean *really looked at him*; this man sat next to me, offering his love. Swirling around us, I could feel the energy of our past and our future hanging as history and potentiality to be solidified. A story in motion all waiting for my next move. Reaching out, I wound a hand around his neck and in a single motion, rolled us off the roots of the tree and onto the grass. All I could see was his face and the stars above his head framing the perfect moment. He moved towards me and the space between us became electric, tingling with the energy of anticipation and communion. Then after a sweet, bliss filled moment, I surrendered, pulling him to me, feeling his lips touch mine with a kiss that was sweet and surprising all at once. Familiar, comfortable: *'I know you'* was the knowing that suffused me as we melted into one another in the grass.

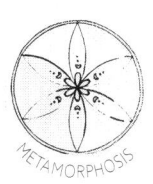

Giddy. Glowing. Humming. I sat at my desk filled with a feeling of completion and excitement. In one way, I hadn't known a love like this before: a love where everything else melts away and I was in complete unity with another human soul. It is the sort of love that we are brought up to expect as kids, bred on the Disney version of romance, and yet hardly ever find in the 'real world' when we enter into the teenage dramas of human relating. On the other hand, I felt as though I had always known love like this. My early love of the mountains, sunshine, nature and play. My soul's infinite love for the mysteries of the universe and the journey to living this in human form.

To contrast this romantic reverie, my ego was busy telling me stories of career suicide. *'You are sleeping with the boss'*; *'You will be hated by people who think you are playing a power game'*; *'Your family and friends won't understand: they love your husband too much and will make you into the bad guy'* etc. I really wasn't listening much to this nagging voice though. Instead, I was focused on the light I felt inside me. What I was doing felt right. No matter what human drama was trying to unfold through the two of us, I knew on a deep inner level that this was supposed to be happening. The irony that this had been the very same man who had 'rescued' me years before when I had told the truth, wasn't lost on me. No one else that I could ever recall had rewarded me for my courage and truth-speaking. I felt as though finally, after all this time, someone valued the real me and simply wanted me to be even more of that (as opposed to a mask of the perfect lover, the sexy rebel or the successful business woman). We had entered into this dynamic a long time before it had blossomed into sensual love and it felt to me as though destiny or karma was in full flow.

My wishful thinking that no one would notice the shifts in me was shattered a few hours later when my mobile phone started to ring. It was my mother's number. Amused (nothing of importance in her daughter's life ever seemed to escape her intuition), I was smiling as I picked up the call. The smile soon faded when I heard the tone in her voice.

"Gen, what is going on with you? I've had you on my mind all week. I have a terrible feeling that something is happening."

"Ma, everything is okay. In fact, it's wonderful. Remember I told you that Euan and I had been coaching each other? Well..." I proceeded to tell her everything. There is no point in holding back from my mother as she has the ability to see right through to my soul.

There was silence for a moment. We both held our breath. And then the torrent came and swept over me. *"Oh Gen, how could you do it? Your husband is a good man. He deserves better. It's the same old cycle of you being bored again and this time you are putting your whole career in jeopardy. How can you be so hopelessly romantic? It will all come to tears in the end. Has he even left his wife? Well, at least that's something, but how do you know he won't go back to her again? He has kids and you know how you get with kids..."*

I stopped listening six minutes in. She was right from a certain point of view and I would be lying if I said I hadn't had each and every one of those thoughts in some form. Through my mother, the voice of my fears was speaking loud and clear, in a way that I couldn't avoid listening to.

"*Ma – I've got to go. I have a meeting,*" I said, to interrupt her monologue. I knew she was worried and wanted me to be safe. I also knew that if I listened to her version of this story then I would be turning my back on my own inner voice of truth; betraying the woman inside who was unfurling her butterfly wings.

"*Okay honey, promise me you will call me later?*"

I didn't promise. I knew the more I listened, the weaker my resolve to stick by what I knew was right would be. I hung up and grabbed my things. I had a meeting with the trees and the wind to attend to outside, to clear my head. They didn't judge me or try to make me see the world through their eyes. I needed their quiet unconditional acceptance to gather myself.

Later that evening, Euan and I were sitting underneath the same oak tree where we had kissed for the first time. I got there first with a picnic and wine and sat watching the sunset, mulling over my tangle of mixed emotions and waiting for him to join me. As before, I felt him energetically and found myself looking at the exact spot where his physical form emerged from behind the trees. From the look of his body, he had also been through the emotional ringer that day. Doing his best to hide it, he gave me a long, lingering kiss and hunkered down next to me on the tree stump, grabbing a handful of cherries. I knew instantly something was up, as Euan dislikes cherries. Waiting no longer, I instantly told him what had happened with my mother and my encounter with her stories. After a brief look of surprise he focused all his attention on me and admitted he had been having a similar experience of guilt, worry and fear during the day. Stories of other people's assumptions and the potential of hurting those we love had run through the movie of his psyche too.

Gulping, I was silent. I needed to know whether he, like me, was going to have the courage to walk this path despite our inner fears trying to divert us.

After a moment he turned to me, taking my hand and said, *"Real or infatuation?"*

His question hung in the night air, suspended in time as he waited for my answer to come. When it did, it surprised me. I looked at him with love, studying every aspect of his face as I said, *"Both."*

He smiled, *"Good. Me too."*

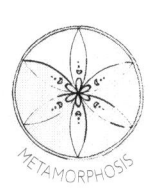

During the weeks and months to come, I learned much about the dual nature of bliss and pain. I was more in love than I could ever remember and I was also experiencing excruciating emotional pain, doubt and confusion. I was receiving daily phone calls from my mother and sister telling me how much they were worried about me; that they were convinced I was doing the wrong thing and could see it all crashing and burning around my ears.

I had also found the courage and the voice to tell my husband the truth about what was happening and why I was leaving him. That conversation was one of the hardest I have ever had to instigate. I think deep down he was desperately hoping that my mother and sister were right and that I would come to my senses and go back to him. I knew that, true to my previous patterns, once I walked out of a door, I wasn't coming back.

I found a flat in Glastonbury – one of the only places in England that had ever felt like a sanctuary to me – and moved out of our marital home, taking only the barest minimum of my things and leaving him with the lion's share of our possessions. My logic was that I earned a higher salary and could better afford to replace them. To be honest, I oscillated between feeling like a divine guided saint and a selfish sinner. This was one of the few ways I could think of to show my compassion.

When I moved out, it was the final straw for my mother and sister. Their anger, denial and confusion at what I was doing caused me to make one of the most difficult decisions of my life. I stopped talking to them for almost a year – an agony given they are the people closest to me in the whole world. I knew that every negative interaction we were having was creating energetic and emotional pain that was fueling their fear stories. I also knew that if I could create silence between us for a time, then perhaps my deep intuition that I was doing the right thing would eventually start to be seen and that actions would do a much better job than my words at showing them the truth.

The depth of my family's pain took me aback, but equally I was aware that my mother and sister were doing Euan and me a great service by voicing their fears. They never said anything that one of us had not thought at some point during our coming together. By them holding up the mirror of our inner fears, we were able to come back again and again with stronger inner resolve. Over the long term, we knew we were on the right path and we chose to walk it together. In the short term, all anyone apart from us could see was the immediate pain that our decisions were causing.

I was squarely in the middle of a real-life initiation and was being tested to see whether I would walk my talk and live my real story. Sometimes in pursuit of integrity, you have to risk losing the people and parts of your life that you love the most, but in letting them go, those that are worthwhile will return to you in a truer form. You have to trust that a higher, wider, deeper narrative is playing out through all of you.

> You have to trust that a higher,
> wider, deeper narrative is playing out.

It would be another year before my family came to see the myriad positive ripples that my courage to be with Euan would create. My health, my career, my relationship with him and myself would all improve exponentially, allowing me to step boldly onto the next stage of my journey. Yet I had to trust that, with time, my actions and their associated consequences would speak louder than any words I could have said. Eventually, they did. My family and I came back together closer than ever and we were able to dialogue with honesty, respect and compassion leaving behind the childhood ways of operating that we had outgrown. Trust would become an important partner for me in the years to come.

CIRCLE WORK

Can you listen beyond judgment to the lessons of conflict?

Me – Working with the people in our lives who we find challenging is often where the greatest potential for transformation of our stories and prejudices lie. If you feel unable or uncomfortable dialoging with people face-to-face, this can also be done metaphorically as a meditation. So, imagine that you have a circle of people around you and enter into a 'council' regarding a challenge you are all experiencing. Take the time to imagine each person's perspective and really try and 'stand in their story' without judgment, as far as you are able to. You will be surprised by the power of this exercise and the effect it has on your relationships with these people.

We – If there has been, or is currently, an issue within your dearest circle of family or friends, consider how you might change the narrative. If appropriate, gather a group of friends, family or companions and enter into a dialogue circle. Please ensure that a clear framing for the circle discussion is set before entering into ceremony and that the traits of listening, suspending judgment and compassion for all stories are emphasized. Hold a circle council where each member of the community speaks from their heart on a topic related to transformation, death, rebirth or metamorphosis. You may wish to explore as a family or community how you are blending your own personal experiences with that of the wider group and how this can be utilized to help transform the social, educational and communal structures around you all.

When we are in the middle of a metamorphosis, our friends and family can be either our supporters or saboteurs. If it's the latter, it's often a result of them projecting their own unconscious fears and stories onto our life. These triggers can act as powerful transformative catalysts for them as well as a whole community of people, if explored in the light of compassionate dialogue. A collective healing can take place if everyone involved is open to exploring different sides to the shared story.

A new vocational story

> Don't give up, don't stray from your path
> Tenacity and faith are powerful friends
> The universe will move mountains when required
> For us to grow and expand

I remember when I was in school, my teachers would talk about a 'career' as if it was a once in a lifetime decision that I absolutely had to get right otherwise I would end up miserable, living out my days in a job that I hated. I couldn't buy into this idea. It just didn't feel relevant for the world that I saw around me and certainly not to a girl who had a bucket list four pages long.

After falling into media operations (working in Supply Chain and Logistics), I didn't really give my career path much thought. Because I had become 'successful' against the benchmark of western society, I hadn't dropped far enough out of that narrative to consider whether that success was what I wanted. I drifted from one opportunity or promotion to another at work, making my decisions on the basis of the best option that was in front of me at the time. After all, how could I choose something that wasn't there yet as an option?

This mindset prevailed long before I understood that our vision and imagination create our future.

Having started to awaken to universal law versus human law, I soon learned that I didn't have the option to look at/re-engineer some parts of my life and not others. I was being asked to integrate my learning across all areas of my life simultaneously. The concept of 'integrity' had become a mantra to me and increasingly represented 'wholeness'. If I was out of alignment to my inner truth anywhere in my life it resulted in energetic jabs, like stepping on a stone in my shoe. Increasingly, I found that I was rarely allowed the luxury of burying anything for long and that my discomfort would increase until I stopped and confronted whatever it was.

My recent ride towards integrity had been in the relationships sector of my life. To use a surfing metaphor, now that I had ridden the rough waves and was coasting in smooth harmonic waters once more, it was time to sit up on my board and take another look around. My surfing lessons had taught me to become finely attuned to my inner and outer environment. The danger that I saw in the distance this time was of my career looming towards the rocks and I knew that, fairly soon, I would have to paddle my board into fresh waters or risk a painful psychological collision.

By now, I had outgrown the skin of the old media job but was still loathe to release it. I had worked damned hard over the years, winning the respect and admiration of my colleagues. Let's face it, success and admiration feel good to us, right? Yet, underneath my ego's need for recognition, I had started to feel a different desire pushing its way to the surface. I knew in my heart that worldly success was no longer enough. My daydreaming increased and I found myself longing to use my growing transformative skills with new people and in new places. I started to dream about writing books, working with people across the world and becoming a teacher and coach. My imaginal cells had fired and the best thing I could do was to follow the trail to my next assignment.

One evening after yoga, I was lying on the floor of the living room and felt a strong compulsion to look on the company website for new jobs. Intrigued, I connected to our company's careers page and said, *"Okay intuition, show me where I am supposed to go next."* Scanning down the list of possible jobs, I tried to clear my mind of any preconceptions or judgments, knowing that if I had seen any of my previous three roles advertised then I probably wouldn't have looked twice given their impressively boring job titles. I had scrolled to the bottom of page three when something caught my attention.

The role's title itself didn't appear to be interesting at first glance (it was listed simply as a 'project manager') but the department caught my eye. It was a job in the Corporate Social Responsibility team. Clicking through for more information, I started to get excited – this could be it! I uploaded my CV and was hitting the submit button just as Euan walked through the door. *"Babe, look what I found,"* I said.

"The job looks interesting," he responded, *"and it's based in London which is a serious plus."*

I felt a building excitement in my stomach.

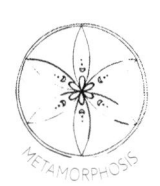

A week had passed and I hadn't heard anything back from the HR department. Had my application gone through okay? Had they managed to review it yet? Not being known for patience, I picked up the phone and called the recruitment team when I got to work the next morning.

"Wait a moment please," a girl's voice said to me after I had explained the reason for my call. *"Oh yes, I see it here. We did get your application but it was rejected from our filtering system on the basis of a lack of relevant experience in the area."*

My heart sank for a brief moment but almost immediately my tenacity kicked in. *"But what about all my transferable skills?"* I asked. *"I mean, I have proven experience in every one of the areas that the role will be responsible for."*

She replied saying, *"Well, that's true but I'm afraid the parameters of our system are set that way for a reason, to avoid irrelevant applications."*

'A stupid reason that also filters out unusual people with talent,' I thought silently to myself but then she continued, *"You could give the recruiting manager a call directly and have a chat with her. Perhaps she would be willing to see you for an interview?"*

"Thanks," I said putting down the phone. I walked towards the kitchen to make myself tea and mused on the situation.

'What do I know to be true?' I asked myself:

1. I know I can do that job really well.

2. I felt that synchronicity had led me to it and therefore there was a bigger story at work.

3. All my life I have been tenacious and taken risks rather than accepting fate. So far, this had paid off every single time.

'Okay, let's give it another try then,' I said to the universe. But before I picked up the phone to the recruiting manager, I stopped to do some homework and gather my thoughts. There is much to be said for winging it, yet at the same time I know I flow better when the 'seat of my pants' has been prepared as much as possible before they fly. I also penned a couple of questions of my own relating to the role's breadth and responsibilities. I knew from the listing that the salary was less than what I was currently being paid, but I was following my spirit this time and not my wallet.

I got up and took a walk outside. After breathing deeply for a few moments I imagined the soul of the woman I was about to call and asked the angels to send her love. I set the intention that I was about to enter into a connection with her that was above and beyond the normal human interaction. No matter what happened, the outcome would serve the highest potential for both of us. After spending a few moments standing in the morning sun in this meditation I felt peaceful, having consciously made the switch in my mind and emotions from what I could 'get' from this conversation into what I could 'give'. I was ready.

Sitting down on the garden wall, I put my notebook on my lap and dialed her number. '*Here goes,*' I thought.

"*Hello,*" a warm and pleasant voice answered.

I let my mind go and my heart speak, trusting to a flow of conversation coming from somewhere or something beyond 'me'.

After about five minutes of explaining who I was and why I was calling her she butted into my monologue and said, "*Okay hang on, this is great actually. Are you available for coffee this afternoon?*"

Two weeks later I sat at a desk in a London hotel room looking out at the bright sunshine of a clear morning. Euan had left for work moments before with a squeeze and parting comment of, "*Show 'em how special you are, babe.*"

I was composing myself for my interview with my new boss in a few hours. I had prepared my vision for the role and practiced presenting it to Euan the night before, just to make sure I had everything covered. He was a tough audience and even with the love filter on, had given me some useful feedback and adaptations that I was in the process of making.

As I looked out of the window at the sunlight sparkling off the water in the canal, I felt the normal butterflies kick into life in my stomach. And yet I welcomed them. I had recently learnt that rather than letting fear hold me back, it could actually be the fuel that propelled me into a high state of performance. Beaming golden energy into the areas of tightness in my body, I sent a firm instruction to my ego to let my soul lead on this one.

A couple of hours later, I walked into the interview room to be greeted by a smiling lady a few years older than myself. Looking into her wide brown eyes, I immediately relaxed. I decided quickly that I liked her. She had a real warmth and genuine sense of humor as well as a huge amount of experience that I decided I could learn from. After chatting for half an hour in total honesty, I stood up and gave my presentation. I could tell from the look on her face about five minutes in that I had prepared way more than any other candidate that she had seen so far. She stopped me a couple of times to digress into avenues of inquiry that moved us from monologue into a real human dialogue. I thought, *'If this is what it's going to be like working for her then I'm in!'* By the end of our allocated time we both knew that we had matched each other's energy well. Smiling, I almost hugged her and yet normal business etiquette kicked back in. We warmly shook hands instead.

"Well, I will be in touch really soon," she said. *"Thanks Gen, that was wonderful."*

It's funny how small comments from a place of authenticity can make us feel like we are floating in the clouds. I walked out of the room feeling super-proud of myself and grateful to the universe.

My phone rang the next day and I already knew what would be waiting on the other end of the line. It was my new boss (I had already decided that she *was* my new boss) offering me the job.

"Seriously Gen, that was the best interview I have ever witnessed. You beat ten other candidates to the role, all of whom had more experience in the field than you do, but I was so excited by your passion and vision that I know you will do a great job."

I felt my chest swell with love and pride. *"Great, I can't wait to get started,"* I replied, full of excitement.

In the years to come, this woman would go on to become one of my lifelong friends and mentors.

OUR TRUE WORK ACTS LIKE A MAGNET, CONSTANTLY PULLING US FORWARDS ALONG THE JOURNEY OF OUR STORY.

Amazing things happen when you start to believe that anything is possible, no matter what barriers get in your way. I refused to give up or be swayed by rejection and created magic as a result. If we continually create a life that gives us and others joy, then I have found that the universe will move mountains (or simply change minds) to support us. Our true work acts like a magnet, constantly pulling us forwards along the journey of our story. We just have to be brave enough to overcome the obstacles sent to test our resolve.

Partners in crime

> Time to stop running away
> Step into the story that I have tried to escape
> Embrace the transformation it brings
> Welcome the love that unfolds

There are moments in life when we are asked to let go of our resistance. To stop trying to escape the parts of us that we have spent years running away from. The very things that we have sworn over and over that we are 'not', are often the parts that we have hidden deep inside as the result of a wounding in our past. For me, one of these was the role of mother. From an early age, I had sworn that I would not have kids of my own, nor want the responsibility of caring for others. I had grown up in the western model of the nuclear family where mothers absorbed enormous amounts of pressure due to the lack of a community support system and I wanted none of this. I had adamantly stuck to the path of this opinion – at least until now. As can often be the case, it seemed that the universe had other plans.

I was super-aware of my old story around motherhood as I drove my car over to Euan's house that evening after work. We had been together for a while now and both of us knew we had discovered something special. Not a fairy tale (even though it was that too, at times) but for the first time ever in the deep caverns of my inner heart where there can be no lies, I could admit to myself that I wanted to spend the rest of my lifetime with this man. My ego had been a little shocked by this at first as if I had never really thought it would happen in 'real life'. Surprisingly, rather than being scared, I was excited. I was elated. More importantly, I was at peace: the quieter and more intense form of love that sits behind infatuation and lust. It was an odd dichotomy. I felt more free, alive and authentic within my relationship than without it. And so it was time to meet Euan's kids.

After my recent experiences that had necessitated the casting off of the old masks of adolescence, I was learning how to show up as who I really was for anyone and everyone. I was determined to do the same tonight. *'Kids know,'* I thought to myself, smiling. Their intuitive dials can sense adult fakery a mile away and even though the thought of openly talking about the 'weirder' things in my life – such as angels, true dreams and seeing energy – scared the crap out of me, I resolved to still go there if the topics came up. *"After all, if we deny our gifts then ultimately we are giving them away,"* I said out loud to myself and the universe (but there was still definitely a side of me that feared what others would think if I spoke openly about it).

I pulled up into the gravel driveway and parked my car next to Euan's. A little thrill of nerves ran down from my throat to my solar plexus. *'Calm down,'* I said to myself and breathed deeply as I swung my legs out of the car door. Working up my courage, I walked up to the large old door and knocked firmly three times before my ego gave me any chance to stall further. Inside the house, I immediately heard the excited voices of a girl and boy, followed by Euan's deeper tones. I heard footsteps and muffled laughter and then the door opened wide. I was greeted by the warm glow of the old English kitchen and three grinning faces. Something in me relaxed.

"*Come on in,*" Euan said grinning. "*Guys, this is my friend Gen.*"

"*Hi,*" said the nine-year-old boy confidently. "*Would you like to join us for a game of Tummy Ache?*"

"*Tummy Ache?*" I said grinning back. "*You don't mean your dad's cooking do you?*"

"*Noooooooooo,*" said the little five-year-old girl shyly from behind Euan's legs.

Laughing, we all relaxed some more.

"*Wine?*" Euan asked as we walked into the warmly-lit sitting room that I had become familiar with over the last few months.

"*Yes please,*" I replied, "*although this time I will try not to spill it all over the white rug, huh,*" referring to the accident of the previous week.

"*Oh no, go right ahead...Dad does that,*" said the boy mischievously.

"*Oh really? He didn't let on to me,*" I said smiling conspiratorially.

I sat down on the aforementioned white rug and was instructed by the kids on how to play Tummy Ache, the popular family 'game du jour'. Euan left and went into the kitchen to get the wine. A moment later I heard from across the room, "*Gen, look what I can do.*"

Looking up from the board where the little girl and I had been carefully arranging our playing pieces, I saw Euan's son, sitting in the lotus position on the couch with his forefinger and thumb touching. Slightly taken aback, I grinned. At which point he started to chant and raise his hands up into the air.

"*Om, jom, bajuba, jai...om, jom, bajuba jai... om jom, bajuba jai.*"

My jaw dropped.

"*What have you done to my son?*" came Euan's voice from the doorway, looking equally as surprised as I was.

"*Seriously, nothing to do with me,*" I said, wondering if that was actually true. The little girl had dissolved into giggles at my side seeing her brother's strange behavior. Her pleasure was infectious and all four of us started to laugh, yet there was a strange feeling deep in my chest that started to suspect I might have encountered these souls before.

After several rounds of Tummy Ache and much humor at who could create the worst board game dinner, Euan announced that it was way past his little daughter's bedtime.

"*Awwwwwwwwww, Daaaaaad, can't I stay up and play with Gen some more?*" she whined.

"Come on, you have school tomorrow – you don't want to be too tired, do you?"

"Well, can Gen do my story then?" came the reply.

I was taken aback by the level of trust and connection she must have been feeling. Smiling, I confessed, *"It would be my honor...storytelling is something I do very well."*

"Okay...but no messing around you two," Euan grinned, obviously pleased that his two kids had taken a shine to me so fast. *"I'll come up and give you a kiss when you are done,"* he said to her.

"Come on Gen," she said, her small perfect hand grabbing mine and pulling me towards the stairs. *"I wanna show you my bedroom."*

My heart melted even more.

Arriving on the landing at the top of the stairs, we proceeded into the room she was sharing with her brother. She pulled her pajamas out from under her pillow.

"Okay, I'm going to go to the bathroom whilst you get changed," I said thinking she might want some privacy.

"I'll go with you," she said sunnily – and this was the first instance of an endearing habit she continues to this day; that of accompanying me to the bathroom, without a shred of shyness or embarrassment. Chatting at a million miles an hour, she haphazardly got changed for bed and even managed to brush her teeth through a muffled explanation of why she hated macaroni cheese.

Giggling like a kid, I automatically slipped into the role of friend and playmate, bantering back and asking *"Why?"* a million times. We moved gradually back into the bedroom still talking as we went. As she was plumping her pillow, she turned to me with a look of great seriousness and slowly presented me with a ragged pale cream-colored cloth. It was obviously something of great value to her and I guessed that it had been totally loved over the short years of her life, given the various holes and threads that hung off it. I adapted my mood to hers with equal respect, and gently took the proffered item.

"What's this?" I whispered in reverence.

"This is Byshee," she said. *"She was my baby blanket when I was little and now she sleeps with me every night."*

"*Hello Byshee, it's an honor to meet you,*" I said prompting giggles from my companion on the bed. It was obviously a response that met with her favor.

"*You're not like any grown-ups I know,*" she said as we lay back together to read her book.

"*I made a promise to myself when I was your age, that I might get older in years but I will never, ever grow up,*" I said. "*Growing up strikes me as very boring most of the time.*"

"*That's really cool,*" she said and snuggled down into her duvet.

After another 20 minutes or so of giggles and regular interruptions in the story reading, Euan finally came up the stairs and peeked his head around the doorframe.

"*Right you two! Time for Daddy to intervene otherwise you will both sit up here talking all night.*"

"*Grown-ups always spoil our playtime,*" she whispered to me and we both burst out laughing.

"*What was that?*" Euan said with mock severity.

"*Nothing,*" we both said in unison as I winked slyly at her.

"*Goodnight lovely,*" I said. "*Can we play again soon?*"

"*Yes pleaseeeeeeeee,*" she smiled.

I felt all warm inside and this time winked at Euan.

"*See you downstairs in a sec,*" he said as I walked past him in the doorway.

I descended down the stairs and slumped down on the couch next to the boy who was playing on his dad's phone.

"*Hey,*" I said.

"*Hey,*" he said back.

"*I don't suppose you like Star Wars do you?*" I asked.

"*Yeaaaahhhhhh, it's really cool! Have you seen Episode Three? It's my favorite.*"

"*Yep,*" I replied thinking a silent '*YES!*' in my head. "*I saw it three times at the cinema.*"

"*Wow, REALLY Gen?*" His eyes widened. "*I don't know any girls who like Star Wars THAT much.*"

I laughed. "*Do you know when I was smaller than your sister, I watched Episode Four every weekend for a year."*

"REALLY?"

Deep admiration and respect was flowing my way, so I decided to hit this one out of the park. *"You know, when I was four, I loved Star Wars so much that for a period of six months, I refused to answer to my own name and would only come if someone called me Luke Skywalker."*

"Woawwwwwwww," he said, looking at me with his mouth wide open. *"High five?"* he offered, grinning.

I high fived him just as Euan came down the stairs with a strange look on his face.

"Dad, Dad! Guess what Gen's favorite movies are?" the young boy said excitedly wiggling on the sofa.

"Yeah, I know...Star Wars," Euan said, smiling.

"Totally cool," he whispered as he went back to playing on the phone.

In the years that have passed since our first meeting, my 'partners in crime' (the kids' proud title for our relationship) both continue to astonish me at the lessons and blessings that they bring into my life. They have helped me to let go completely of my adolescent story that attempted to reject the mother archetype from my life and turned it into a beautiful narrative that has transformed the idea of a stepmother into a friend/teacher/guide. Hidden in the roles that we reject are often enormous gifts, if we are brave enough to find them. Whenever I need advice, I go to them and respect their humorous wisdom as some of my greatest teachings. I am blessed to have these two special souls in my life to walk beside me as I grow into my butterfly.

> HIDDEN IN THE ROLES THAT WE REJECT ARE OFTEN ENORMOUS GIFTS, IF WE ARE BRAVE ENOUGH TO FIND THEM.

Reunion

> To come full circle and see a place with new eyes
> Is one of the greatest gifts of the journey
> To see that joy and agony are one and the same
> That lead us back to our spark of home

I allowed tears of joy to come freely as I drove carefully up the winding canyon road. They were a reflection of my inner celebration. It was 2011 and I had been on quite a rollercoaster ride to arrive at this place in time. The late afternoon sun shone down in golden rays through the spruce and Ponderosa trees, caressing the majestic red rocks that sparkled their mica and quartz skin at anyone who happened to be looking. Like sentinels, they lined the valley that led towards my destination, each one of them familiar and smiling at me like an old friend whom I was finally seeing again after years of separation. Cottonwoods and aspens along the creek edge swayed in the gentle breeze, reaching their branch arms out to embrace me in welcome. My soul was rejoicing in this return. I was back in Deer Creek Canyon once again, almost 20 years after being torn apart.

After winding carefully up into the foothills, I turned onto the bumpy mud road and could hardly contain the grin spreading across my face. My hire car jiggled across the dirt surface and I marveled at how little had changed from the images of my childhood memory. Taking the right-hand bend, I passed the old, tumbledown white outhouse and the pullover that was a godsend in the winter when the road was slippery with ice. I knew what awaited my eager eyes around the next corner – Sprucetree Restorium, the cabin adjoining All Faiths' Chapel, the magical place where I had been christened, was waiting for me.

Pulling up into the small lay-by beside the red wood cabin, I paused and took a deep breath as I switched off the engine. Opening the door, I listened. Crows, blue cardinals and mountain jays greeted me alongside the occasional chirps of the chipmunks and the scuffling of busy squirrels. The scent of pine needles and hot red mountain soil filled my nostrils and I shivered in delight. Grabbing my bags, I made my way across the small footbridge that spanned the creek; now dry and dusty from the arid mountain summer. Unable to contain myself any longer I dropped my bags and like a six-year-old, ran to each of the huge grandmother spruce trees in the front yard, flinging my arms around them in turn with a joyful *'Hello!'* My heart beat strongly with reconnection and memory and I felt their ancient loving welcome flooding through my body and soul. If you have ever stopped to 'be' with a tree you will know the feeling I am talking about. It's the sensation of being enfolded into the embrace of nature and loved unconditionally as a daughter, friend and companion. Trees radiate silent wisdom and knowledge of the cycles of earth for anyone who stops long enough to listen.

When I had finished my hugs, which took a while as there were many trees to be greeted, I made my way towards the cabin itself. Opening the creaky screen door, I smiled at the familiar sights and smells that greeted me inside. The old, worn and much-loved red-striped velvet armchair and footstool that had once been in my Papa's library at the mesa house; the wide stone fireplace, blackened with decades of use; the wall-to-wall books that had once belonged to various people within our family, speaking to me of human adventure in all its multidimensional beauty. The cabin had a smell that reminded me of my happy childhood days spent in these mountains. A mixture of aging wood, books, leather and pine. I did a little dance of gleeful gratitude and delight.

I WAS BEING WELCOMED HOME INTO THE SILENCE.

The Sprucetree cabin (as it has become known in our family) was built in stages between 1954 and the early 1980s by Laurel Elizabeth Keyes,[22] her husband Caryl Chivington and later, her son, Paul. It sits along the side of a small, sacred spring, nestled amongst huge ancient blue spruce trees that have been guardians of the canyon here for longer than any of us have lived. There are legends surrounding the source of the spring from the Ute Indian tribes that were once the human guardians of this land. Laurel, in her own words, came to believe that, "*A great and mighty spirit dwells here.*"

Laurel was a teacher, author, adventurer and joyful student of life. At an early age her innate understanding that it is love at the center of all life, led her to question a specific paradigm of religious belief where God was seen as a vengeful, punishing judge of humanity. Feeling that there must be a different answer, she dedicated her journey towards the exploration and articulation of the realization of divinity in human life. Throughout her quest, she encountered teachers from numerous ethnicities and faiths. Her path of service led her to write 13 books and countless booklets on sacred humanism. She founded the Order of the Fransisters: a multi-faith organization dedicated to bringing alive St Francis' prayer in the modern world. The Sprucetree cabin and adjoining All Faiths' Chapel were created by The Fransisters as a 'Restorium' – a place where people full of cares and fears could come and take time in silence in the mountains, connecting to creation and restoring themselves before entering back into their lives with renewed energy and faith in Spirit. Laurel wrote of this ethos in her autobiography *Sundial*:[23]

> 'Living is a moment-to-moment process. We live one moment at a time, NOW. We have the power to choose how we shall live this one moment. As we decide the quality to give this moment (hope or despair, love or hate, optimism or gloom) we make a pattern for the next moment and all of our future! When we realize this we become masters of our lives instead of slaves to circumstance. When we choose to live each one moment with God, the future can become ideal and divine. It is not our purpose to go out and do things but to go in and become one with the divine ideal. Then, to carry the peace and joy experienced in our quiet moments into our daily living, to give encouragement and peace to others by our example.'

She has been, and continues to be, a powerful role model to me and in many ways has become a beloved spiritual friend, long after her death in 1983. I have discovered more about myself and my unique story through the barely visible divine threads of her wisdom left embedded in this magical place. Every time I return to Sprucetree Restorium, there is another clue, another teaching waiting for me. It is as if she is now able to speak through the fabric of the universe itself. I could feel her presence and wisdom all around me in this mountain retreat as I arrived and reached out in silent thanks. She is part of the force of this place, more alive now than ever. As I wandered from room to room on that precious day, I knew I had come back to my own place of refuge and sanctity. I was being welcomed home into the silence.

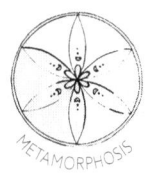

I woke early the next morning. Looking at the gentle glow from the sky, I realized that it was still just before dawn. Climbing slowly down the bed's ladder, I threw some warm clothes on, made myself a mug of tea and quietly opened the back door of the cabin that led right out onto the mountainside. Getting my bearings, I set out to the right of the trees, past the old wooden outhouse, and found the path through the wildflowers that I knew would be there. It had been many, many years since I had last walked this way. I was struck yet again at the beauty of the early morning sun that had just started to kiss the bark of the trees. Dew covered long mountain grasses, awakening them like a lover turns to their beloved in bed to welcome them to the new day. I climbed steadily up the steepening slope, carefully placing each foot with deliberate intention to make sure I didn't slip. The path was indistinct in many places and looked like it had not been walked for some time.

Working on a combination of intuition and memory I wandered to the left sensing where I wanted to go. Over the next ridge, I saw an opening in the trees. This was it – I knew it. After scrabbling over some fallen branches and soaking my jeans up to the knee in the morning dew, I found myself standing in front of a natural archway formed by the branches of the pine trees. A wide smile spread across my face as I beheld a sight that had existed in my imagination for many years.

Opening out before me was a small grassy clearing. Pyramid Mountain framed the sky off to the south-east, covered in dark pines and illuminated from behind by the rising sun. I took a deep breath and inhaled the scent of earth, pine resin and summer flowers. Closing my eyes I moved into the middle of the meadow and sank into a semi-trance state. I could feel the swirl of the canyon energy all around me and synchronized my own energy field into it, merging in frequency and dancing with nature itself. Swaying in harmony with the vibrations, I sent a loving greeting out to all the spirits of nature, beaming my delight at their breathtaking creations and thanking them for maintaining and caretaking this sacred place. I had finally made it back after all the years of longing and felt as though I had been allowed to come only after I had learned the lessons I needed to; through the significant initiation into my soul that I had undertaken.

I started to breathe in time with the movements of my body, raising my arms above my head and dropping them in prayer through my heart center in silent worship of life. I celebrated the fierce joy of being alive and one with all that is. For this is the true purpose of the Sprucetree Restorium and All Faiths' Chapel: to be in silent communion with the source of all life. To know yourself as one with this force and to revel in the peace and tranquility that results from this awareness. This was Laurel's intention and the focus of her work.

After a few moments I felt the warmth in the air increase and stopped with my arms outstretched above my head. A beam of warm sunlight touched the center of my forehead and I gasped with the bliss that flooded through my being: the Sun. Opening my eyes, I allowed the sun's rays to penetrate right through to the core of my being, burning away any residual pain that still remained from the long years of separation.

> I CELEBRATED THE FIERCE JOY OF BEING ALIVE
> AND ONE WITH ALL THAT IS.

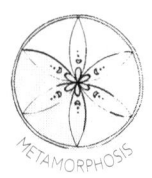

That night, after an evening spent in joyful reunion with my godparents who were still the caretakers of this place, I walked slowly down their driveway back towards the cabin and looked up at the bright starlit mountain sky. I now understood utterly the words that T S Eliot wrote over half a century ago: 'To come full circle and return to a place knowing it truly for the first time.'[24] I quietly knew that this was such a moment for me. To have come full circle through the years of a human story and to return to the place of my birth, knowing it truly for the first time. I would not have been able to reach this point if I had not chosen to experience ALL of the events of my life. I would not have been able to love this place so deeply if I had not had the benefit of the years of physical separation. That is the way of things. We are given the lessons we most need to learn and often fight them every step of the way as I had done. Yet the only reason we are resisting is because we can rarely see where the path through the dark forest of our experiences will lead us. Without the darkness there is no contrasting light.

> WE ARE GIVEN THE LESSONS WE MOST NEED TO LEARN
> AND OFTEN FIGHT THEM EVERY STEP OF THE WAY.

For a moment, I stopped walking and stood listening to the crickets and the small nighttime animals going about their ordinary magical lives. My gaze rested on the shadowy forms of the Sprucetree Restorium and, further back in the trees, All Faiths' Chapel that stood cloaked in the velvet of night. Emerging from the darkness, I saw a little girl in my mind's eye sobbing in her cold, gray English bedroom, longing for the light and life of these very mountains. Back through the years, I imagined I could beam love and comfort to her. I sent her the glittering seed of knowing that one day in her future she would stand in the very place she longed for, as a grown woman, finally knowing her own power and innate ability to create freedom. I told her gently that the seed would slowly start to sprout in the years to come and eventually would grow into a majestic tree of wisdom. For a moment, I thought I could see the hint of a smile on her face through the tears, as my gift was received into her heart. Into my heart. That girl would always be a part of me.

As I walked the last few steps across the footbridge, I could swear I felt Laurel's warm arm encircle my shoulders and I shed a soft tear of appreciation as I opened the front door to the cabin and made my way softly to bed. I wanted to dream with the spirits of this place; I wanted to listen to their stories, to ask them how I could be of service in the world now that I had returned to the gifts of a new life. My spark had been restored.

METAMORPHOSIS JOURNEY

ARE YOU READY TO TRANSFORM THE STORY OF YOUR LIFE FOR GOOD?

When I first did the journeying exercise that I offer to you below, I cried tears of recognition and shame, as I acknowledged the values that had influenced and created the main threads of my life story. Freedom, love, fun and divinity were at the top of my list and from these flowed a very simple expression of my purpose in life. Sometimes, we human beings make things so complicated – we become 'human doings' instead. The more preoccupied we become with the story of achieving and succeeding, the less we pay attention to what really matters to us. I had spent years choosing values other than those that were truly meaningful to me, all in the name of 'success', and it had made me miserable. It was time to let go so I could let in more of what really mattered to me.

Find a quiet space where you will be alone and can spend some time in meditation and self-reflection. An hour or so will do but if you have longer, take longer. Start off by creating a comfortable, cocoon-like environment. You may want to create a den of some kind with blankets, music and nourishing food. Nurture your caterpillar and reassure it that everything will be okay.

Grab a notepad or sketchbook and some pens. Close your eyes and spend a few moments breathing in and out of your heart. Imagine you can connect to your imaginal cells and that the deepest part of your soul will start to speak to you as you write or draw. Take as long here as you need to relax and listen.

When you are ready, start to write or draw the values that lie deep within your heart and answer some or all of these questions:

1. What values have guided your choices and decisions in life up until now?

2. What qualities do you hold most sacred and valuable?

3. What are the most important feelings that you strive to achieve?

4. If you could be remembered for being a certain kind of person in the world or for a certain quality, what would this be?

Spend as long as you want on this exercise writing down everything that comes to mind. It may be a lot or it may be a little. Then focus on the top five values that most resonate with you. These are the qualities that form your essence. Your values are your guiding stars, your core story threads, and the gifts that you bring to the world. They are your imaginal cells that will activate in the darkness of your cocoon as you transform into the butterfly of your true being.

Once you have become aware of them, take a moment every day, or as often as you can, to reflect on how they manifest in your life and where they are being blocked. How can you bring these values more and more into your lived experiences? How do you know when you have violated them and are heading off track? The more you pay attention to your core values, the more they will come alive in your life.

THE GIFTS

HOW CAN I GIVE AND RECEIVE THE GIFTS OF LIFE?

Eventually, we come to a point when we have been given all the clues we need. This is a moment of great responsibility. It is the point when we must stop simply wandering along the trails of life and begin to carve one through the world for ourselves, using our intentions. For the first time in our journey, we shift our focus from an inward path of 'me' to one of outwardly dynamic giving, or 'gifting'.

Through the process of remembering our stories' authentic threads, we have by now reconnected with the spark of unique genius that was born in our hearts when we came into this world. Through the alchemical fire of our testing times, we have discovered our individual strengths and have started to use them to create a life beyond the norm. Our experiences of the darkness and the light have begun to provide us with our healing crises (in their various forms) and we emerge from them with stronger mental, emotional and spiritual immune systems. By the time we reach the Gifts Stage, we have ventured home to our true self in a more mature form, having stripped away many of the layers of identity and programing that we accumulated in our younger years.

Following on from the Metamorphosis Stage, most of us will have experienced a death of our adolescent identity and be coming out of our cocoon into a wider world. Yet at this stage, our wings are still drying and our imminent flight is not just for the simple joy of being airborne, as it might have been at a less mature stage of our consciousness. With the gift of metamorphosis comes an almost instantaneous craving to share this magic with others, for the benefit of the wider community in whatever form this takes. This heavy nudge is the universe's way of ensuring that our growing creative power is used appropriately. We are only gifted with universal awareness and the ability to use our unique magic once we are willing to place them in service of something more than just our self. Following our metamorphosis, we naturally start to transition from a personal journey of finding the real 'me', into a more collective narrative of 'we'. In giving our gifts, we start to see how we are connected to, interact with and influence the wider ecosystem of life.

At the Gifts Stage of the Restory Cycle, we are reunited with our ancestors.

One of the gifts of the cocoon is our innate ability to be able to combine the lessons of our past with the seeds of our future. Once we have released our attachment to an old story, we are able to see it anew with fresh eyes, and notice the blessings it brings. In addition to our personal story, we also may begin to see with mythic awareness – the collective myths and echoes of our ancestors – something that is often forgotten in the western world. Wherever we come from on earth, that place holds layers of ancient social narratives relating to the people and the land, but due to the mobile nature of humanity these days, many of us were uprooted at an early age, moving once or multiple times to different places. We often lost our connection to our heritage when we were very young. At the Gifts Stage of the Restory Cycle, we are reunited with our ancestors. Whether this is a reconnection to the land of our birth and the stories that it holds, or to the narrative of our ancient bloodline, we often find ourselves being given the opportunity to be rooted within history once more. This sense of growing roots into our distant past, like a tree, gives us the stability from which to start to grow upwards and outwards into the world. We are able to share our gifts and experiences from a place of wisdom, connection and belonging, due to the inherent stability we discover.

Because of the nature of modern globalization, we may not find ourselves living physically in our ancestral places and spaces but we recognize the strength and wisdom that the path behind us gives to our forward momentum. Instead of misappropriating the cultural heritage of other peoples and lands, we ground into our own and discover our place in ancient community once again.

> RECOGNIZE THE STRENGTH AND WISDOM THAT THE PATH BEHIND US GIVES TO OUR FORWARD MOMENTUM.

Gifting becomes a two-way process in that we are both giving to and receiving from and through life in a continuous flow. Our acts of service do not always manifest in the ways we expect them to and often our greatest gifts are given in the small daily interactions with the world around us. This is one of the core areas where the Restory Cycle differs from the hero's journey. Our power stems less from the dramatic magnificence of the hero within us and more from the grace of our daily living in integrity and interconnection with the earth. We move beyond the traditional idea of being of service and our gifts are given in terms of our presence, love and appreciation of our human and more-than-human families – and less in the grand heroics of leadership. This doesn't mean that we won't be called into wider action on behalf of our communities, but that we no longer need *heroics* in our lives to feel recognized, validated and aligned to our deeper story. We let go of the collective human shadow of the special one/hero/leader/messiah and step into the unique grace of our own natural human beauty. As my grandfather[25] used to say, "The quality of the individual is based on their contribution to the whole."

> OFTEN OUR GREATEST GIFTS ARE GIVEN IN THE SMALL DAILY INTERACTIONS WITH THE WORLD AROUND US.

When we are able to hold a simultaneous awareness of how our personal story is constantly interacting and merging with the wider human narrative and mythology of life on earth, we enter into a state of grace where we are both being guided and we are guiding the course of our lives. Anthropologist and ecologist Gregory Bateson[26] spoke of grace as being, 'Our human way of re-accessing the sacred: of balancing our conscious purpose with the emerging purpose of the wider ecosystem of life.' Every moment becomes an opportunity to give and receive the gifts of our presence and we are asked to truly walk our talk to the best of our ability. No matter how big or small, tangible or intangible our gifting cycles appear to be, they all create ripples back into the cosmic dance of life.

> EVERY MOMENT BECOMES AN OPPORTUNITY TO GIVE
> AND RECEIVE THE GIFTS OF OUR PRESENCE.

Many native cultures have the idea of gifting as central to their stories and social systems, where happiness, success and satisfaction are obtained through giving back to one's community and ecosystem. Charles Eisenstein[27] suggests that one of the main causes of sickness in the modern economic system is that of commoditization: what were once our sacred gifts to be given freely to our communities have become products and services and are now sold, bringing in the energy of exchange and greed. How many of us as healers, visionaries (aka entrepreneurs), story makers and artists feel a sense of guilt when we charge for our services? How many people working within business, government, healthcare and education systems become frustrated when they are held back from doing the right thing because 'it doesn't make financial sense'? I have been beset by this conflict multiple times in my life and I know countless others who grapple with the same challenges on a daily basis.

So, as a balm to the wound of commoditization, I offer the concept of 'The Gift'. When we come to this stage of our journey and gain clarity of our unique magic, then we are given the opportunity to gift it, to give freely and without attachment to reciprocation or exchange in any way. Give just because we can. As many of you reading this will know and have experienced, when we give from this place of abundance, joy and freedom, we are gifted in return in multiple ways. The more we are able to give from a healthy place, living authentically in the world, the more the world offers us opportunities to dance our story into vibrant life. Looking back, the majority of the opportunities I have had to share my gifts in the world have come from the spark of me gifting them for free, initially at least. The adventures, the friendships, the teachers, the lovers, the ecstatic encounters of soul; precisely none of these came from an invoice, though all of them led to bountiful abundance, some of which was financial. This is the real gift of life, a constant flow of giving and receiving.

>GIVE FREELY AND WITHOUT ATTACHMENT
>TO RECIPROCATION OR EXCHANGE.

This stage of gifting is an invitation to tap into a larger sense of security, purpose and abundance in the universe. It is an invitation to put all that we have learned into practice and dance alive our story into the world in small and grand ways. We move out of the pure realm of imagination, dreams and visions and take these threads into our human experiences. It is a time of grounded vision where our definition of our 'work in the world' expands exponentially. We become potent and responsible in our play and every moment becomes a gift. The only appropriate response to life's events becomes *"Thank you."*

Emergency Happiness

>Daydreams are future visions
>Waiting to be danced alive
>Take the risk, make the jump
>Allow your gifts to thrive

It was late July and I was standing rather uncertainly in high heels and a neat cobalt blue office dress in the middle of a cricket pitch in south London. After my divorce, I lost a lot of weight and had discovered meditation and yoga. I was taking pride in my healthy appearance once again and it felt good to be alive.

As I looked around, appreciating the warm, sun-drenched day, I noticed an odd juxtaposition of life: council estate housing and graffiti-lined dirty railway sidings were in stark contrast to the crisply-mown, lush green grass carpet on which I was standing. Cricket for Change,[28] the charity I was visiting, also embodied this odd mix of vibes. They somehow managed to combine an archetypal English gentleman's game (cricket) with young people who came from tough backgrounds and faced a whole host of modern social challenges such as disability, gang culture and poverty. It was a mix that seemed to work against all the odds. Everyone who encountered the bright souls running this organization, myself included, fell in love with their spirit and humor in the face of adversity.

"*Okay, so I'm going to blindfold you,*" Andy said laughing. "*Do you trust me?*"

Giggling, I allowed him to tie a piece of cloth around my eyes. "*I wouldn't if I didn't know you were blind too,*" I replied.

My friend Andy was the Operations Director of the charity. He had developed a rare eye disorder at the age of 20 and was now almost completely blind. Since that time, he had played on the England Blind Cricket Team, helped set up the charity and coached thousands of young people across the world who also had visual disabilities. He had become so accustomed to his lack of sight that his other senses had kicked in to compensate. It was very difficult for those who didn't know him to realize he couldn't see. Such is the developmental growth we can access when we choose to see our potential weaknesses as our greatest strengths. He is one of the most humble and inspiring people I have ever met – someone I still look to when I need my own life challenges putting into a wider context.

"*So, in a moment, I want you to head towards the sound of clapping in the distance,*" he instructed me.

"*Okay...I may trust you but that doesn't mean that I trust him!*" I said jokingly, referring to the third member of our clan, also called Andy.

Laughing, he said, "*I'll watch him for you and make sure he doesn't pull one of his usual tricks.*"

Andy Number Two was the CEO of the charity and the longtime friend and partner of Andy Number One. I had met 'the Andys' a year prior to this meeting and had liked them in an instant. I hadn't met a CEO before who so loved playing the game of life like an ever-curious child. He was one of the only people I knew who could switch in an instant from serious and businesslike to ridiculous and childlike. It was a good skill to have (in my book) as it meant he didn't take life's dramas too seriously. I had been developing my own gift of 'potent playfulness' off the back of meeting these two.

Clap, clap, clap.

"*Off you go,*" Andy said.

'Okay,' I thought, '*just move towards the sound.*' It proved to be much easier said than done. Trust is a very big thing when your primary sense has just been taken away. I hesitated. I knew I was safe, as I had the Andys watching every move I made and yet there was still a small part of me that stalled. It was the part of me (and in all of us) that didn't want to look stupid if, in my disorientation, I fell in my high heels and dress and screwed it up. I took one small step forward, empathizing instantly with my friend next to me who had lost his sight and had to deal with facing the world in near darkness on a daily basis. I took another step into the unknown, thinking to myself that this must be how so many of the young people that these guys worked with feel every single day.

"*Come on Gen, you can run,*" I heard him say behind my right ear. "*Just trust your instinct.*"

'He's right,' I thought as I threw pride over my shoulder and started to run in my high heels across the grass towards the clapping sound, secretly entreating the angels to make sure I didn't fall and break an ankle. In darkness I ran forwards feeling the earth beneath my shoes and the wind rushing past my skin. Senses that were normally in the background came into sharp focus. They were somehow thrust into the limelight and given their chance to lead the show. '*This is actually kinda cool,*' I thought, as I started to forget my reliance on my eyes. I felt exhilarated and free, doing something that in theory I shouldn't be safe doing – running blind. I remember smiling, for this was exactly what I had spent most of my life doing in so many metaphorical ways.

JUST TRUST YOUR INSTINCT.

"*Whoa there, wild stallion!*" said the warm voice of the man behind the clapping hands. I felt his hands close around my shoulders and I realized that it was safe to stop running. Smiling as I took off the blindfold and blinking my eyes to adjust to the sudden brightness, I wondered how many other lost souls he had said those words to in some form over the years; how many people he had made feel infinitely better just by his playful smile.

"*Gen, have you ever thought about leaving the corporate world and doing your own thing?*" Andy asked this with a cheeky smile as the three of us walked leisurely around the cricket pitch.

"*Yes actually,*" I replied, surprised that he had tuned in to my daydreams. "*I guess it's a pretty common dream for those of us working crazy hours for someone else. The thing is, I am not really sure what I would do,*" I said.

"*What, you, the visionary, not sure what you would do? Come on girl, I know you better than that.*" He was half joking and yet there was definitely a trail of considered thought leading us somewhere new in the conversation.

I paused to think. "*Well, I know I would love to work with young people like you guys do and find a way to use all the psychology and leadership stuff I have been playing with. I am just not sure how I would pay the bills,*" I said, voicing the core concern that stops most people from jumping off the cliff into meaningful self-employment.

There was another pause and then he asked, "*What if I was to say to you that we would open the doors of our charity and help you to apply for funding for a program all of your own?*"

Silence. I waited for a moment whilst I digested what he had said. "*Wow...well I guess I would jump at that chance. I mean, I can't *imagine anything more fun than working with you both and learning the ropes of the charity sector."* (I recognized a small, scared part of me inside couldn't believe the words that had just tumbled out of my mouth. I silenced the fear).

"Wonderful, then it's decided! You can come and work up a new program with us and find your own message in the process. Look Gen, you will inevitably fall on your feet in some ways and completely screw things up in others. That's the nature of the game. But if, in the process, you will be able to start earning a living doing something more meaningful, then it will be worth the risk, right?" He looked at me right in the eyes waiting for my response.

"You're right," I said hesitantly, feeling the angels surrounding us in the sunlight. *"Give me a couple of days to think it through okay?"*

"Deal," he said. *"Now let's talk about how we are going to pull off the trip with the kids to Jamaica."*

Later that week, Euan and I were in a pub somewhere in Berkshire, glasses of wine in hand, batting around the idea of starting a business. For me, it was still squarely in the 'daydream' category, but with his analytical mind, Euan had already started doing what so many great men do when their women come to them with a challenge – he had started to 'solutionize' the whole thing.

"So, we can afford to take a hit on your salary for a while whilst you build your network."

They were words that made the independent woman archetype in my personality choke on her wine in fear.

"You pretty much just need to get out there and get a couple of good case studies under your belt. From there, you'll have people

coming to you and we'll be laughing. Who knows, in a few years I may even come and join you."

The last bit of his speech sounded great, but my mind and emotions were caught in the full flow of panic around the thought of being a 'kept woman' even for a short time.

"*What's wrong?*" he asked picking up on my mood change.

"*Nothing really,*" I said, trying to find the words that would explain the inner turmoil I was feeling. "*It's really just my independent rebel streak playing up. You know, the one that swore that she wouldn't let anyone look after her or that she would ever 'need' anyone to survive.*" Like throwing up, I felt a little better for purging my craziness.

"*Look, I see this as a trade-off,*" he replied. "*I can do this for you right now and then when you make millions in the future, you can keep me in the manner to which I have become accustomed.*"

Another jab of fear shot through my insides. "*I hate to be negative in any way, babe,*" I started, "*but let's just say on the complete off chance that I don't end up making millions, you know, just in case, no matter how improbable, what then?*" I stammered, partially joking, mostly not.

"*Well then, you will have to make it up to me some other way, won't you?*" he said laughing. "*Seriously, babe,*" he said taking my face in his hands, "*I am here to help you shine. No matter what happens, I want to do it.*"

I breathed out, releasing some of the tension I had been holding in my lungs. "*Okay...well, if you're sure?*" I said.

"*Where you are concerned, I am sure,*" he said giving me a gift that only he could. I had passed the inner test of receiving it.

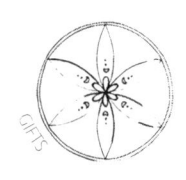

Fast-forward six months and I found myself driving down a deserted country road in South Africa with Euan at the wheel of our tiny, tin can of a hire car. We had come here on a weeklong break to get some winter sunshine on our skin and sleep off the hectic Christmas work period. I was sitting in the passenger seat, my eyes lazily half-lidded from the heat of the day and the exhaustion of our morning surf session. As I reached an arm up to flick a salt encrusted lock of my hair out of my face, I found myself shoved forwards in my seat as Euan slammed the breaks of the car on suddenly. A jab of fear ricocheted through my insides in expectation of some incident that would have caused the sudden stop. Looking up I saw no reason for why the car had halted.

"*Babe*," I started in a concerned tone before being interrupted by his excited voice.

"*That's it! It's there. That's the name of it.*"

"*The name of what?*' I asked, trying to hide a mild annoyance that my peace had been so abruptly shattered.

"*The name of your consultancy – look!*" he said grabbing my face and turning it to the left so I could see.

I found myself looking toward a row of ragged, aging shops. After a few moments of scanning to see what was catching his eye, I saw a small, bleached knick-knack shop. The white paint was fraying off the wooden walls. It appeared to be selling an array of 'tat' that no one in the world would ever need or use, yet it was the name of the shop that was now making me smile. I grinned and turned back to him, all my annoyance forgotten. "*You're right, that's it! What an awesome name.*"

Leaning over he gave me a tender kiss on the lips and whispered, "*That's what you do to the world when you are in it.*"

Returning his kiss, I felt a warm sensation in my chest, like universal confirmation. We had accurately named one of my gifts. The name painted on the front of the shop read 'Emergency Happiness' and thus my first business was born, kick-starting a journey that would see me trade in the raw ambition of the corporate world for the driving aspiration of service. In the following years, I would venture into the charity and business landscapes, offering programs that brought these two often disparate worlds together. I would learn how to thrive at the very edge of my personal comfort zone and trust the flow of universal inspiration and abundance in picking my clients and partners. Prisons, boardrooms and forests would become my office on a weekly basis. The gift of living for a cause greater than myself had begun.

CHANGING GIFTS FOR GOOD

CAN YOU EVOLVE YOUR CONCEPT OF GIVING AND RECEIVING?

I will always remember the moment that Euan and I sat down with our kids and asked them what gifts for Christmas would be truly memorable and meaningful. We quickly discovered that more things and new stuff was far less interesting than exciting adventures and experiences that we could share as a family. From that moment onwards, we have gifted each other experiences instead of things.

Me – Play with giving different kinds of gifts as presents for birthdays, holidays or celebrations; such as the gift of time, loving attention, appreciation, service, volunteering, listening, cooking or your complete and utter presence to another. Watch how you and the person you are gifting to feel when you enter into this altered reality of giving and receiving that which really matters in life.

We – Spend some time with friends and family exploring what gifts in life would really matter to them if they were to receive them. Perhaps make some new agreements around traditional holidays to give and receive different kinds of gifts that would really enhance and enrich other people's lives as well as your own.

Often the main story in the way of us entering fully and freely into the gifting cycle goes something along the lines of, *"What have I got that is of value?"* or *"I don't have enough time, money or ability to give them what they need."* In redefining our concept of what gifting means, we are able to step into this energy in a completely new way and open the floodgates to new experiences, abundance and flow in our lives.

Beings of light

> Beings of light, shining in the starry night
> Bringing us love and memory
> Dare we accept their gifts
> And open the doors to our own?

When our cosmology and our innate knowing of how the world works expands, occasionally we can open the doors to an experience that is so beyond the realms of the current human reality, it is hard to find words that can describe it. This story is somewhat like that. I will do my very best to convey my experience to you but please accept that sometimes language is far too clumsy, especially when it comes to describing the nature of our spirit and its adventures beyond this third dimensional reality. I invite you to engage your imagination and feel into the energy that lies beyond the words you are reading on the page. After all, there are many more ways of communicating than just what we can read; many more ways to tell a story than to speak it.

LANGUAGE IS FAR TOO CLUMSY WHEN IT COMES TO DESCRIBING THE NATURE OF OUR SPIRIT.

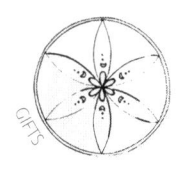

"So, the doctor told us that the baby has been in breech for a while and that it's likely her waters have already broken. It could be any hour now that she goes into labor."

My mother's voice was deliberately positive over the phone, but I knew she was trying to hide her underlying concern. I took a deep breath, tuning in to see what my inner guidance was on this one: still a 'no'.

My little sister was nearing the end of her first pregnancy, which had been uncomplicated up until this point. Now that she was about to go into labor, every aspect of my big sister heart wanted to pack my things and run to her side, but it wasn't quite so simple. Euan had taken a new job in Germany and we were about to fly to Munich the next day to start flat hunting. The plan was that I would 'hold the fort' in the UK, continuing to work on my fledgling business and we would fly back and forth at weekends, dependent on whether we had the kids with us or not. It was a big move and a big thing for our relationship. As with any new change, we both felt a little uncertain and a lot excited.

"*Do you think I should cancel the flights and come?*" I asked my mother, hoping her intuition would give me a different answer to my own.

A pause. "*Honey, I don't think so. I really feel like everything will be okay without you this time.*"

Ouch. A wrenching in my stomach. Up until now, and ever since I had been young, I had been the one to ride into whatever family challenge was occurring and to make everything okay. The one who pulled the different sides together and brought everyone back to common ground. It was my thing. My gift. Even though my intuition agreed completely with my mother's it was a super-large, jagged pill to swallow. My ego's story of being the savior was taking a hit.

"*You're right,*" I said reluctantly. "*I will call Cate and make sure she knows I will be with her in spirit.*" Learning to let people travel through their lessons solo was so hard. I said my, "*I love yous*" and hung up. They will be fine, I reassured myself as I tapped my little sister's number into my phone.

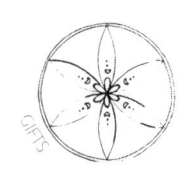

Munich is a beautiful city. It was October and the sky was a crisp late autumn blue. The trees had released their leaves, leaving plenty along the sides of the well-kept pavements to kick through in my boots. Being in the south of Germany, the city had been too far away from the English army in WWII for it to be a bombing target and as a result, most of the tall town buildings from the 1800s were still intact. They were cleanly painted in bright colors and richly decorated with ornate panels, interspersed with beautiful balconies and roof terraces. Post-war Bavaria had become the economic powerhouse of the country and the city had been developed in recent decades to take on a cosmopolitan sleekness that blended well with its history. It was full of beautiful people going about their beautiful lives.

That evening, Euan and I found ourselves drinking possibly the best margaritas I have ever had and tucking into a large plate of enchiladas and green chili. A new Mexican restaurant had just opened on the edge of the main marketplace and we had managed to squeeze ourselves in, sitting at the bar that overlooked the kitchen with three round and friendly Mexican chefs to amuse us.

"*I like it here*," I declared after my third margarita, much to the amusement of the chefs who, having taken a shine to us, were feeding us freebies and tasters from their favorite dishes. A few drinks later, we found ourselves rolling into our hotel bed, more than a little drunk. As my head hit the pillow, my eyes closed, hoping that the spinning of the room would stop as soon as I sank into sleep. Thankfully, relief was almost immediate.

It was dark and my left eye opened a crack. After a moment, I started to realize what had awakened me. The whole room was humming strongly enough to have brought me back to consciousness. Gradually as my eyesight adjusted, I realized that it must still be the middle of the night. My questing hand found my phone that was on the bedside table beside me. Turning it over I saw that almost one hour, give or take a few moments, had passed since I had gone to sleep. '*Strange,*' I thought. I felt no trace of the margarita-induced drunkenness and instead my whole body was buzzing with energy.

'*Okay,*' I thought as I turned over onto my back quietly so as not to wake Euan who was fast asleep. I allowed my brain to quiet in meditation while my energetic body expanded. Over the previous couple of years I had become accustomed to being awakened by energetic waves in the middle of the night and I wasn't perturbed or surprised when I felt my energy grow and blossom wide, moving upwards beyond the physical confines of the hotel room and outward into the night sky.

I felt myself expand, growing wider, deeper, fuller and upwards. Beyond the clouds, beyond the upper atmosphere and out into the universe. Gradually, I came to rest and found myself floating in the cosmos, looking down at the beautiful earth. I could see her pulsing with the same vibrations that had called me out from my hotel room. Such beauty and magnificence. I meditated there in silent awe of our beautiful planet, whilst still being fully aware of the duality of my experience. I could feel my human body lying on a bed somewhere in Munich whilst my consciousness was free and expanding in multiple directions and dimensions simultaneously. I was experiencing a part of everyone and everything and yet was still somehow also confined to the boundaries of individuality as Genevieve. A strange dichotomy.

As I hung out there with the stars, I noticed that another being had joined me. Condensing my awareness back into the larger energetic signature that could still be described as 'me' I found myself in front of a vast being of white light. To say that I was looking at him (for it felt distinctly masculine in nature to me) would be incorrect, as I didn't feel as if I had eyes in the human sense, yet I could perceive him in front of and all around me. His energy was powerful and yet light and dynamic. There was no hint of a threat, only the frequency of wisdom and timelessness. I sensed a voice coming from him that communicated a question to me; it was beyond words even, yet I understood.

"*Are you ready to hold more light?*" he asked.

Without pausing, I responded with a similar pulse of confirmation from my being: "*Yes.*"

Then he communicated, *"Good, then step into my body."* Actually, the word 'body' isn't really what he meant but it's the closest translation I can come to in our language. Without hesitation, I moved forwards into the form of this being and as I did so I found myself enveloped in the purest white light I could ever recall experiencing. Beyond white, beyond light – pure vibration. Two strong pulses of this energy moved through me and I felt a flash at my temple points (or what would have been my temples if I had been in human form). A second one immediately followed the first. In an instant I was rocketed back into my body and I found myself lying on the bed in the hotel room once again. Feeling completely comfortable, I registered what happened for a split second before my eyes closed. As I slipped into unconsciousness, I could feel the angels around me working to help me assimilate the vast amount of energy that I had just absorbed. I sank into a deep and dreamless sleep.

Are you ready to hold more light?

The next morning, I woke up hangover-free and feeling good, apart from an odd feeling in the middle of my chest. I pushed myself up on the bed, rearranging my pillow so I could sit upright and drink some of the water next to me on the table. Euan leaned over and gave me an absent-minded kiss, staring down into his iPad.

"*How long have you been awake?*" I asked, yawning sleepily.

"*Only an hour or so,*" he responded through an email haze.

"*Babe, it's Saturday morning,*" I reminded him with a smile as I pushed myself up to go into the bathroom.

"*Yep, I'm emailing the landlady of the flat you decided we are going to live in to tell her we'll take it.*"

"*Fair enough,*" I laughed weakly. The weird feeling in my chest flared up again. *'Just breathe Gen,'* I reminded myself.

As I stood in the shower I started to pay more attention to what was going on physically. I felt as though my heart was missing a beat. Thump, thump, thump, in a regular rhythm and then just as I would start to relax thinking everything was normal again, I would feel it pause for a second, and then a larger than normal beat, THUMP, as my heart kicked back into rhythm again.

"*Babe,*" I shouted from the bathroom, "*I think my heart is beating erratically.*"

"*It's because you're around me,*" he responded. "*That happens to all the girls.*"

Pause and then THUMP again. My sense of humor started to depart. "*Seriously, it's not funny, I really mean it,*" I said with an edge in my usually calm voice.

"*Relax. It's probably just the margaritas,*" he said.

'*Doesn't feel like a hangover to me,*' I thought.

Over breakfast I became too preoccupied with the sound of my erratic heartbeat to notice anything that was going on around me. The angels were a calming presence and yet (as is the way when fear starts to creep into our thoughts and feelings) even their reassuring voices started to drift away and become faint. I knew when I consulted my intuition that what I was experiencing was a result of the massive energy surge the previous night and yet the voice of fear was taking over my awareness, chanting, '*It was too much and now you will pay for it.*'

Looking up from my inner turmoil my eyes met Euan's as I took a gulp of my orange juice. "*What's wrong with your eye?*" he asked nonchalantly looking towards the right-hand side of my face.

"*What do you mean?*" I said, placing my hand up to my temple and rubbing, half expecting to see makeup coming off on my fingertips.

"*There's a red line next to your eye,*" Euan said. "*Go to the bathroom and take a look.*"

"*Are you sure it's not eye shadow?*" I asked momentarily distracted from worrying about my heartbeat.

Licking the tip of his finger he reached out and gave me a spit-wash. "*Nope, still there,*" he said.

Puzzled, I stood up and made my way through the busy breakfast room towards the ladies' toilets. Heading for the mirror that reflected the most light from the ceiling spots, I tilted my head to the side to see exactly what Euan had described. Next to my right eye was a thin red line that started at the corner of my eye and moved across my temple to the edge of my hairline. There it seemed to stop. I wet my finger under the cold-water tap and rubbed at it. Nothing, still there. *'What the...?'*

Before I could finish my question I felt myself ricocheted back into my experience the previous night, at exactly the moment when the two waves of white light had shot through my temples. *'Holy shit!'* I thought, my skeptical programed human mind in shock at the physical validation my body was providing. I realized that on one level I had already started to archive my experience in the 'make believe' or 'meditational vision' files. I was now having to rethink my internal filing system, making a whole new section called 'multidimensional weirdness'.

Walking back out in the restaurant, I felt the THUMP of my heart miss another beat. I gathered myself together to tell Euan what had happened. He had just sat down with another cup of coffee as I returned to our table.

"*See, I told you,*" he said, motioning to my eye.

"*Yep, babe I need to tell you something,*" and I began.

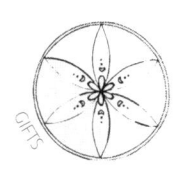

I was subdued as we wandered the cold gray winter streets of Munich. It was a new place and so usually I would have been excited, bouncing around new corners and exploring new places, yet I felt heavy with everything that I was experiencing. Euan had listened intently that morning and accepted my story even though he couldn't mentally understand what had happened to me. He was amazing in this way; believing my experiences and encouraging me to accept them for myself. I also found my mind wandering to my little sister a lot. She must be almost ready to give birth by now. I was excited to welcome a new soul into our lives and yet concerned that I was not physically there by her side. Truthfully, I felt guilty that I was away sorting my own life out rather than being with her if she needed me. The guilt weighed down on me like a lead coat around my shoulders, adding to the general heaviness that I was feeling. To ease it, I texted my mother to see if there was a status update. Almost immediately I received a message back reading, *'You and your intuition. They went into the hospital this morning and she is doing well. It shouldn't be long now.'* I took a really long, deep breath and handed my phone to Euan so he could see what was going on. Closing my eyes in the middle of the busy street I beamed out rays of loving support to my sister and her partner, imagining the energy moving across the geographical distance to enfold them both in a cocoon of positivity.

Later that day, we found ourselves back at our hotel room. Euan was taking a nap on the bed and I had grabbed my book to read, but set it down again as soon as I realized I had re-read the same paragraph three times and become distracted on every round. I could feel a pull on my consciousness from somewhere. Closing my eyes I found myself immediately transported to a hospital room. I became aware of the concerned face of my sister's partner looking down at me. Framed around him were the walls of a surgery room and masked nurses and doctors. There was a surgical covering over my belly and legs. Somewhere in the back of mind I realized that I was seeing out of my sister's eyes. The baby was about to be born by caesarean section. The vibrations were calm and yet tense. Not exactly worried, but somewhat stressed trying to deal with a situation that had not been expected to unfold like this, I started to take deep, yogic breaths synchronizing with my sister's. Breathing in beaming light and holding a space of love took over my consciousness for the next few moments. I became lost in waves of energy flowing between, around and through everyone present and involved. I became the energy itself, ebbing and pulsing: the spark of life.

I BECAME THE ENERGY ITSELF, EBBING AND PULSING: THE SPARK OF LIFE.

Then, I seemed to crystallize back into my own form of 'me', Genevieve, hovering in a dark space with tiny glittering lights everywhere I looked. In front of me a being came into my awareness. She (because it definitely was a 'she') was made up of a vast array of rainbow light. Joy and love sparkled from her and I felt both a sense of recognition as well as exuberant excitement being in her presence. Wordlessly we greeted each other. I became vaguely aware that my physical body back in Munich was crying tears of joy, overcome with the emotion of welcoming this rainbow being back into our lives. I watched as her energy started to condense and spiral into tighter and tighter rings of light like DNA. The spirals were moving downwards through levels of energy. The angels were directing her towards a single point of light below us. Tracking the process, I followed her movement and the scene around me shifted back to the hospital room. The rainbow spirals flowed into the light, which was expanding, gradually becoming a physical body. I heard from somewhere in the background the crying of a newborn baby and observed the light pulse one last time before fully absorbing itself into the form of a baby that was being enfolded in my sister's arms. My niece had arrived.

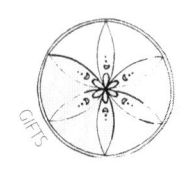

Pause...THUMP. I felt a wave of fear wash over me once again and breathed deeply, clutching Euan's arm tightly for a moment. He looked at me, searching my face for a clue as to what he could do to help. I knew he found nothing.

"*Do you want to go back to the hotel babe?*" he asked. I paused, about to say yes, but instead found myself looking up at the massive structure of the Frauenkirche Cathedral in front of me and felt instantly drawn towards it for a reason I couldn't explain.

"*Not yet,*" I replied, motioning towards the door. "*Let's go in there.*"

Looking at me for a moment in disbelief, he agreed. His arm folded around me in support as we walked up the steps. I understood his confusion. It wasn't exactly a normal habit for me to want to go in churches.

Opening the heavy door, we walked into the impressive space inside. Vaulted stone ceilings lined the main passage towards the altar at the far end of the church. To the left glittered a stand of votive candles fairly typical of Catholic churches. I felt powerfully drawn towards the tiny flickering flames and without saying a word, I started to move towards them. As I made my way forwards I suddenly felt a wave of nausea rise up my body from the tips of my toes through my legs, upwards into my chest. Not having control over my movements, I instinctively paused over the candle display and reached out, my hands gripping the front edge of the flaming shelves. The feeling of sickness was moving upwards at a pace and I had no choice but to open my mouth and allow a '*whoahhhhhh-hhh*' of breath and energy to escape my body and energy field. As I watched, I saw a wave of heavy, thick energy move out and away from me, dissipating in the cold air. Instinctively I looked upwards, entreating an explanation from a higher source and wondering what the hell was happening. As soon as my eyes rested on what was hovering above me, I had to smile. Above the candle display that I was now clinging to for support was a large statue of Mother Mary herself. She wore a welcoming smile of loving compassion and was staring down at me reassuringly. I felt instantly better.

Taking a deep breath, I loosened my grip on the candle stand and felt Euan's presence by my side. Ever the strong protector, he pretty much picked me up, allowing me to lean into his warm shoulder and walked me over to the closest pew. Without a word, he scanned my face to make sure I was okay and then left me to my inner process in an act of deep understanding and love. I had no hope of verbalizing what was going on and he knew it was better to let me work it through. My body was still shaking with the aftereffects of my energetic purge and my heartbeat was still erratic. However, instead of fear, I had started to feel a deepening curiosity building in my chest. The compassion of Mother Mary had touched me and, for the moment at least, had taken away all my fear. Raising my head, I found myself looking at the large statue of Jesus hanging on the cross over the final archway leading to the high altar.

'*Please,*' I found myself saying inside, '*I don't know what is happening to me or what gifts I have been called into. I placed myself in service of all beings a long, long time ago and yet...I just need a little help to understand and assimilate.*'

I felt my prayer (for that's what it was) beam out beyond the walls and arches of the Cathedral and into the universe. Almost immediately a golden light started to grow underneath the statue of Jesus. I recognized the golden being that appeared immediately and was filled with joy and, quite frankly, relief at his arrival. The glowing powerful presence filled me inside and out, holding me in a gentle embrace of unconditional love and truth. I breathed out a sigh. My entire being relaxed into this embrace, much like I can imagine a newborn baby relaxes in the arms of its mother.

'*Dear one,*' I felt the golden voice vibrating all around me, '*you are perfectly where you need to be. Do not fear. You are always loved, always supported, always on track. You have all the help around you that you need.*'

His presence held me for a few moments and then started to fade into particles of vibration. By the time he was gone, I was feeling completely refreshed, loved and knowing that everything was perfect. Looking up, I saw Euan drawing up to my side and reaching out his hand towards me. I took it and smiled, seeing that it was covered in shimmering light. Looking upwards I gazed into his eyes.

'*You okay?*' they asked wordlessly.

'*Everything is okay now and always,*' I smiled back. Laughing with relief, we turned, arm in arm, to walk back out onto the winter streets of Munich.

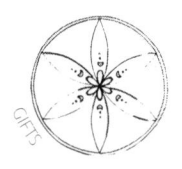

My experience with the energy being taught me many powerful lessons, some of which are still percolating today. I learned discernment; about the value of 'looking before you leap' into another's energy space no matter how benevolent it may seem. Despite the powerful being offering assistance with love, his frequency was so high that it has taken me years since to acclimatize my own system to fully integrate the light I absorbed that night. Being a 'light bearer' can have dramatic and uncomfortable repercussions in your life. It's not all blissful and harmonious. With every gift comes a responsibility to learn how to use it wisely. My heartbeat has not returned to normal since that night.

> WITH EVERY GIFT COMES A RESPONSIBILITY
> TO LEARN HOW TO USE IT WISELY.

I have since had several beautiful experiences with the rainbow soul who is, in this lifetime, my niece. She continues to teach me, and many others, important life lessons in her own unique way. I learned through her birthing experience that sometimes we can be of more service and help when we gift our energy in non-physical ways. To this day we share a deep connection that goes far beyond time, space and language. Mostly, we play!

INTENTIONALITY

ARE YOU READY TO BECOME THE CONSCIOUS CREATOR OF YOUR STORY?

Me – Practice setting clear intentions at the start of each day that are aligned to your unique gifts. Play with the breadth and depth of your intentions to experience different levels of the gifting cycle. For example, set an intention to see every interaction with another as a gift (breadth) or intend to focus on one gift in particular (such as your ability to listen) and see how many different ways in which you can give this (depth).

We – Make time for a regular check-in with the people you love to share the gifts you give and receive in your daily lives. The more you start to become aware and tell the new story of the gift of life itself, the more your perspective will shift and the closer you will become with your community.

Many of the 'mishaps' and stumbles along the journey through the gifting stage are experienced because we have yet to step fully into our power and ability as a conscious creator. We leap before looking, move too fast and often don't stop to consider the consequences of our well-intended actions. These lessons are here to teach us discernment and discrimination.

Heyoka

> Medicine wheel, spinning through time
> What secrets do you have to show me?
> How does our life become our art?
> How does our work become our play?

Descending down through the woods to the Sprucetree cabin, I grabbed my yoga mat and made my way over to the octagonal wooden platform at the side of All Faiths' Chapel. The rising sunlight was lighting up the plants and trees with a delightful golden halo, reflecting rainbow fractals off the morning dew. Flicking my mat open, I looked up and took a deep breath full of the universe, filling my lungs with gratitude for simply being alive in the moment. Stretching my arms upwards, I began my practice and dedicated it to the cathedral of nature that surrounded me. Each breath I took was filled with sacrament because it was being breathed once again in the place that I had longed to be for so many years. Each movement and posture became a celebration of being alive. My gratitude became a gift to all the beings that surrounded me. This was my place and now that I was here again, every moment was filled with beauty and rejoicing.

Breathing deeply into my belly, I slowly rose up into warrior pose, elongating my arms, lifting my spine and fixing my gaze over my left arm and fingers. As I continued to breathe, sinking deeper into meditation, my unfocused eyes gradually noticed a spinning circle of energy about the size of a large Frisbee appear three feet in front of my hand. Curious and yet calm, I asked the symbol to slow its spinning and reveal its form to me. I continued to breathe and wait, even though my legs were starting to burn from holding the posture for this long. Gradually it responded to my request and the images within started to clarify. I received the impression into my third eye (ajna chakra) that I was looking at a medicine wheel. I could make out the four quadrants, a circle in the center and small points of light all the way around its diameter. As I watched and waited, the medicine wheel stayed for another 30 seconds or so, then slowly faded away. I was left wondering what it was trying to tell me.

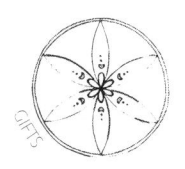

I took another sip of my coffee, carefully placing it back into the cup holder of the SUV I was driving along Highway 6. It was early in the morning and I found myself taking the scenic route to Estes Park for a conference I was attending. I had no idea what to expect. My

Energetic NLP teacher, Art Giser,[29] was running sessions here and I had jumped at the chance to come and support him. Driving up the winding canyon roads towards the high mountains, I found myself wondering what adventures lay ahead. By now I had started to know that when I was drawn to a place there was usually a reason, whether a 'chance' meeting, the introduction of a new lesson that I needed to incorporate on my journey, or a gift I was here to give. I found myself intrigued as to how the next chapter would unfold.

"*Darling, you live your life through a constant stream of inspiration and divine guidance,*" my grandmother had said to me the day before, as we had shared our customary tea.

Finding the entrance to the conference center I signaled to turn right into the driveway. A huge elk walked majestically out across the road. Smiling, I looked at him and he looked right back at me, both of us oblivious to the oncoming traffic. After a few moments of silent exchange I had the sense he approved of my being here and with a slight nod of his huge head, he wandered off into the woods. 'Passed the first test,' I thought, smiling to myself.

LIVE YOUR LIFE THROUGH A CONSTANT STREAM
OF INSPIRATION AND DIVINE GUIDANCE.

It was a beautiful location with log cabins and meeting halls built on a high mountain meadow, framed 360 degrees by the snow-capped Rocky Mountains. At 7,500 feet, the air was light, fresh and full of energy as I breathed it deep into my lungs. After signing in, I wandered over to say hello to a group that I recognized from one of the trainings I had attended in London. Smiles, hugs and mutual excitement passed between us as we reveled in our location.

After lunch, I wandered away from the others to explore my surroundings and came across a beautiful grove of Ponderosa pines. Greeting the trees, I sat down with my back against one of their tall trunks facing outwards to the mountains. Taking the conference schedule from my bag, I scanned down the list of sessions watching for any that jumped out at me. Absently picking up a pinecone and holding it in my hand, my eyes rested on one name and stopped: 'Heyoka Merryfield will screen his new film *Sundancing The Muse*' it read. Intrigued, I decided I would have to go along and see it.

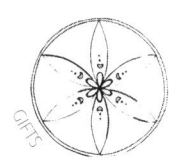

Reaching my arms up high into the mountain air I stretched and yawned as I walked away from the breakfast room. The conference had so far been an eclectic mix of mysticism, energy work and spiritual teachings. It was interesting and full of good people, but nothing had blown my mind...yet. Looking at the schedule I noticed I wouldn't be needed to teach any sessions that morning and so I scanned down to see what I might spend my free time doing. *Sundancing the Muse* jumped off the page at me once again and, smiling, I started to make my way over towards the room where it was being screened.

It took me a while to find it, winding my way upstairs and back down again searching for the room number on my conference agenda. Just as I was about to try and find someone to ask, I noticed a pale glow coming from the end of the hallway in which I was standing like a lost tourist. Following my instinct, I walked forwards. Rounding the corner of the door I came into an empty room with a film projector set up. Sitting causally with his feet up on another chair was a man I recognized from the opening event of the conference a few days earlier. He was wearing faded jeans tucked into his cowboy boots and a beautifully worked leather waistcoat over an ornate white shirt that looked like something out of a renaissance fair. His long graying hair was pulled back into a low ponytail that ran down his back. Around his neck was a beautiful blue amulet that had the face of a white eagle sparkling at me.

On seeing me enter, his face lit up with a warm welcoming expression. There was a twinkle of mischief in his eyes.

"*Hi,*" I said walking right over to where he was sitting and dropping myself into the chair next to his.

I noticed a slight smile tweak the corners of his mouth, as if he found my boldness amusing. "*Hi,*" he responded, "*I'm Heyoka.*"

I reached my hand out to grasp his and immediately felt a current of energy pass between us. "*I'm Gen.*"

Adopting a similar relaxed position on my chair, I noticed how comfortable I already felt in this man's presence. Turning my head so I could look at him while I spoke, I started to tell him the story of why I was here at the conference and what had led me to come and see *Sundancing the Muse.*[30]

"*Where do you live?*" he asked me as I paused to take breath.

"*When I'm not traveling, mostly in the UK, kinda close to Henley-on-Thames,*" I replied. During this period of our lives, Euan and I were splitting our time between Munich and England.

"*Strange,*" he said, "*I knew I had to pay attention to who came to see the movie this morning. I used to spend a lot of time there. I was good friends with George Harrison. I made a lot of jewelry for him and his wife.*"

"*You're kidding!*" I replied, excited. "*The house where he used to live is gorgeous. I drive past it all the time.*"

We smiled at each other in silence for a moment, both entering in the game of the universe and appreciating the gifting cycle that was opening up between us. I suddenly felt compelled to tell my new friend about the medicine wheel image that had appeared to me but just as I opened my mouth to speak, another person found their way into the room, breaking the exchange. As we started to do introductions and Heyoka stood to play the movie, I bit my tongue. 'There will be enough time,' I thought to myself as the lights dimmed and we sat in companionable silence watching the movie that told the story of Heyoka's life.

If you ever have the time to watch *Sundancing the Muse*, I recommend you do. As I watched scene after scene unfold, and listened to him articulate the painful and yet exquisitely beautiful path of walking his unique story, I was filled with a sense of recognition for my own journey. As one person vulnerably tells their story, those who hear it (and I mean REALLY hear it) immediately get the gift of seeing their own face reflected back through our shared human narrative. The words 'me too' create a sense of connection with the storyteller and create a magical space of safety; compelling anyone who is ready to voice their own human longings, joys, fears, insecurities and aspirations. In many ways, we are all the same.

As the credits finished, Heyoka stood up and put the lights on once again. I found myself lost for words and yet full of sentiment. Our colleague stood up to go to her next session leaving Heyoka and I alone once more.

"*That was achingly beautiful,*" I said.

"*Well thank you,*" he smiled back in return. Just as I was about to share, Heyoka continued to speak into the space between us. "*You know, my Lakota friend Susan and I are planning on creating a medicine wheel ceremony on Thursday night. Would you like to come?*"

I gasped, amazed that he had tuned in so completely to the question I had been about to ask. Channeling my amazement into my smile, I beamed back at him: "*Of course, I am honored that you would invite me.*"

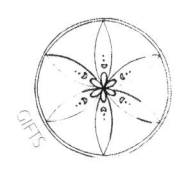

"*Time to go,*" my friend said. She had kindly offered to let me stay in her room for a night so I could attend the medicine wheel ceremony and not have to worry about driving the hour and a half back to Sprucetree afterwards. Walking out of the lodge, I looked up at the sky and saw dark black thunder clouds moving in from the west.

"*Looks like Mother Nature might add some of her own music to our ceremony tonight,*" I remarked to her as we walked. As we made our way towards the ceremonial space, I saw Heyoka silhouetted in shadow at the doorway, eagle feathers in one hand and a stick of sage in the other. Smiling warmly as we approached, he came over to us, and one at a time, making sweeping motions with the feathers he was carrying he allowed the sacred smoke of the sage to cover our bodies, clearing the space surrounding us. I could feel my own energy respond in recognition to this ancient ritual cleansing and breathed the 'smudge' deeply into my lungs, feeling it swirl along the meridians of my energetic body. Opening my eyes, I found Heyoka looking at and through me to a deeper space beyond the human. I looked right back and honored him in the same way.

Inside, people were gathering in a circle, with Susan Powell[31] organizing us like children at their first formal ceremony – which is exactly what most of us were – instructing us all gently yet authoritatively. We gathered, naturally making space for others who arrived and passed through Heyoka's smoke. There was an electricity growing in the air around us and I wondered to myself how much was a product of the storm growing outside versus the storm inside. Then, as Heyoka closed the door gently behind him, the ceremony began.

Susan looked around the circle at each one of us in turn, fixing us with the same deep gaze that we had encountered from Heyoka at the door.

"*Welcome friends,*" she said. "*Because we have all traveled different paths to come here tonight and have different stories of what a medicine wheel is and means, I will start with this: the essence. Then we will all create our wheel and journey within and without together.*"

My body shivered with more than the chill in the night air and I could feel a warm energy rising from the base of my spine up towards my head. She began to weave the story – her story – the story of ancient peoples on earth and the universal story within which our modern lives twist and turn. I felt dizzy and yet completely at ease as I listened, losing track of time and the space around me. I closed my eyes to become part of her narrative, dancing and twisting my own tale within the energy of the myth.

I eventually felt myself being pulled back into my body and realized that the group had fallen into silence. Opening my eyes I seemed to look directly into hers. She smiled and said, "*It is time to build the medicine wheel. Gen, would you lay the stone that will be at the center of our wheel? The core of the universe.*" She was indicating that I should stand and take the large stone in front of her feet.

Smiling and feeling deeply honored, I walked slowly over to her and with great reverence picked up the raw piece of white quartz that had been born in the very mountains beneath our feet. It sparkled with flecks of mica and streaks of red from the iron-rich soil. I moved intuitively, speaking silently to the spirit of the stone in my hands and asking it to show me where it needed to be placed in order for it to anchor and direct the energy of our wheel. I stopped when I felt compelled to do so by the stone being I held in my hands and, bending down, I gently placed the quartz on the wooden floor of the cabin allowing it to settle itself into the perfect place. White of the heavens and red of the earth, married together to represent the union of life. Looking over at Susan she nodded and smiled, releasing me to return to my space in the circle.

Stone by stone our small community created our medicine wheel; each rock being laid in a ceremonial way by a different member of the group. The four directions drew outwards: East, South, West and North from the central stone. Then the inner circle was formed, representing the inner world held within each of us. We then completed the outer circle, each of us offering the stone friend that we had brought, representing the steps along the human journey through life. Breathing deeply of the sage smoke, I felt the space within the wheel come to life with an energy of its own as the last stone was laid. It pulsed and hummed like the portal I had seen at Sprucetree, alive with its own wisdom and frequency.

Susan and Heyoka started to beat the drum and rattle, adding sound vibration to the wheel. Closing my eyes, my journey began. Spinning, I drifted beyond the boundaries of this world and into the swirling darkness of the places in between. I was familiar with these spirit roads from my travels in the dream state, and so was not afraid. I felt myself being pulled inwards and down until I was hovering above the central stone of the medicine wheel that I had laid with my human hands moments before. The quartz, now in its energetic form, was a glowing portal of dark light. Magnetic, iridescent and yet peaceful, I was brought into its orbit and settled into a rhythm; spinning and yet stable. It wanted to show me something. I saw a dark green and blue crystal energy forming around me, full of geometric shapes. The tendrils of my energy that had once been somewhat like hands and feet could reach far and wide beyond the confines of the earth and even the universe. I felt my crystal form expanding into vast dimensions beyond space and time. Like so many of these experiences, I was fully myself and fully one with all creation concurrently. Vast and small in one breath, one twirl of my cosmic dance; consciously consumed in the creative forces of life.

> I WAS FULLY MYSELF AND FULLY ONE
> WITH ALL CREATION CONCURRENTLY.

Gradually my crystal dancing slowed and I felt myself expand to grow wings. At first, I became the form of a human woman flying amongst currents of energy between dimensions. Then came a beak and feathers. I opened my mouth and felt the exquisite cry of the eagle I had become echo out across the worlds. I shivered with a more than human joy at my form and my experience. More embodied than my last dance, I noticed that my feathers were iridescent rainbows that exuded trails of light wherever I flew. My beak was shining gold and my eyes were blue and clear.

Then after some time, the magnetic pull of the medicine wheel caught me in its embrace and I followed its invitation, recognizing the circle I had built with friends. Swooping down and hovering above my human form sitting still in the circle, I noticed my talons were holding something. As I felt the pull of my body magnetizing the eagle form into its energy field, I looked at the object I had brought back with me from eternity: a green turquoise medicine amulet lay shimmering in my grasp.

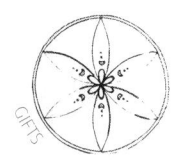

The bright glow of the sunshine peaked in through the gap in the curtains of my friend's room, reaching me where I was sleeping in her spare bed. Stretching and quietly rising, I crept to the bathroom so as not to wake my sleeping companion. I had one thing on my mind – I needed to find Heyoka. Passing by the breakfast room, I headed right up to the cabin where the exhibitors' stands were set up. An intuitive hunch told me to go there first and as I entered through the doorway and saw him sitting behind his table polishing one of the necklaces from the display case, I knew my inner needle had pointed correctly.

"*Good morning,*" he said cheerfully, catching my eye and smiling as if he had expected me to arrive right when I did.

"*Good morning,*" I smiled in return, not really knowing where to start with my story. "*Heyoka,*" I began, "*have you ever had any experiences with a rainbow eagle?*"

Laughing, he put down the necklace and said, "*I thought I felt another eagle in the room last night.*"

I smiled, feeling the power of my medicine wheel journey building up inside my chest and moving up to my throat to be spoken. I shared my story with him, or at least as much of it as I could find the words for.

After I had finished, he sat in silence for a moment, then said, "*Well, it sounds like it's time to make you a medicine necklace.*"

"*I was hoping you would say that,*" I laughed, feeling as if I was about to leap off another metaphorical cliff.

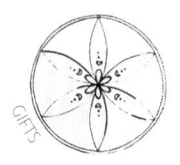

I would come to respect and honor Heyoka deeply in the years to come as our relationship grew. The Temple of Earth and Sky,[32] his house and studio in Stevensville, Montana, is one of the most magical places I have ever visited on the face of this earth. It remains a pilgrimage place for me to this day. His sacred art is an expression of the magic and unifying human mythology in our changing world; each piece a unique physical manifestation of a sacred dream, vision or story that he has been given to create. In the years since that first medicine wheel ceremony I have been able to open the door for many others to access Heyoka's gifts and creations. It is a great honor to share another's unique magic with the world.

"*We are not led to each other by accident,*" I found myself saying to him on a chilly spring morning, a few years later as we shared cacao over his breakfast table.

"*No, we are not,*" he smiled back. "*Come on, let's go for that hike. I want to show you my favorite place in the mountains to meditate.*"

And with that we set out on another journey, walking side-by-side, grateful for the gift of our friendship.

WE ARE NOT LED TO EACH OTHER BY ACCIDENT.

Vision quest

> One foot in front of the other
> We cry for the vision of our life
> Ancient voices whisper truth
> And ask us to be brave enough to hear it

Sitting in the early morning sunlight of Denver airport, swirling the remnants of tea around in my paper cup, I reflected. Since leaping off the cliff into a new relationship and vocation I had spent the previous seven years wandering and exploring the world with a sense of freedom and reckless adventure that had scared most people in my life, including myself at times. Butterfly-like, I had followed the different flowers of my career, relationships and my life. I had been blessed with many gifts and lessons along the way, yet something was missing, something important.

Once again, I found myself in a dark place (these cycles seem to go in sevens). Not emotional darkness, like depression, but the sort of darkness that descends upon you when you realize that you are ready to step your life up a notch. I had begun to feel increasingly out of place in the world I had constructed and the 'gypsy' identity I had been wearing had started to get itchy. As friends, clients and project ideas started to drop away or fall flat, I felt a great deal of fear. I couldn't see what was around the next bend in my life's road and began to steel myself, trusting the process of emergence (having lived through it several times already). Something was building. It was time to recycle my life.

TRUST THE PROCESS OF EMERGENCE.

One gray afternoon when the emotional stress of 'letting go' of yet another client became too much, I found myself retreating to the sanctity of my meditation room. Blissfully quiet and serene, the couch beckoned to me. I sat down gratefully, pulling my old childhood blanket over my knees as a comfort mechanism. Gradually, I allowed the anxiety created by the loss of a work contract to flow out of my body and into the earth through the soles of my feet. After a few moments I looked up. My eyes fastened on a particular book resting on the middle shelf of the bookcase. It caught my attention so completely that it appeared to be glowing at me across the room. Smiling as I recognized this 'sign' from the universe, I rose and crossed the room to gently take the object of my attention into my hands. Turning it over to look at the front cover I recognized it as a book I had bought in Glastonbury years before but hadn't found the time to read. *Soulcraft*[33] by Bill Plotkin invited me to open its pages and find an answer. Flicking through the pages, my fingers stopped automatically and I opened the book to see the words 'Vision Quest' staring back at me. I sighed with an intuitive knowing. A journey I had dreamed about for years was finally ready to be embarked on.

The practice of vision questing is a core part of many cultures across the world and something that I had known, since childhood, I would enter into when the time was right. I was ready to drop my human chattering and enter into silence and communion with the earth. I longed to speak with my ancestors and the chance to retreat to the wilderness and listen was precisely what I needed. Devouring Bill's book, I discovered that his organization, The Animas Valley Institute,[34] ran quests in my home state of Colorado. It was the perfect set up.

In the months leading up to my quest, as recommended, I entered into a deep preparation – mentally, emotionally and physically. I altered my diet and began to fast one day a week, preparing myself for the four-day fast that was a key part of my upcoming journey. On the fast days I felt clean and clear in a way I hadn't experienced before. It was as if the lack of physical food in my body allowed the veils of the world to become transparent and I received many insights into the transition that was underway.

I wandered as often as possible in nature, learning to become comfortable with being lost; a practice that has since taught me a lot about how to be okay with 'not knowing' where we are going and trusting that we will find our way out of the woods. Prompted by Bill's book and with Cuan's full support as my life partner, I wrapped up many loose ends in my life, speaking words of gratitude and closure to old lovers, family members and friends. I let aspects of my work slip through my fingers with trembles of trepidation. It was a cleansing, a stripping bare and I had already started to feel lighter.

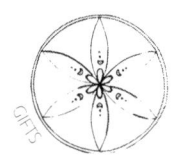

When the time to quest finally arrived, I found myself in a group of 13 fellow seekers. We had arrived one by one in a beautiful valley on the edge of the ancient Anasazi lands in the southwestern tip of Colorado, close to the border of Utah. I was immediately enchanted by the landscape of my birth and ran joyfully into its embrace at every opportunity I had. In the day, the dry heat bounced off vibrant red, yellow and orange sandstone mesas. At night, we were enveloped in the deep dark of the desert, watched over by a million bright stars. I entered the process of coming home to the land, to my story and to my gifts.

One hot, arid afternoon, at the invitation of our guides, I set out to wander the land in search of answers. I was seeking a deeper truth and, like a hunter, I tuned my senses into the signs of tracks. Something in me knew that if I were to be considered worthy of finding the object of my search then I would have to prove to the universe that I had learned how to listen, see and feel my way beyond the boundaries of this reality. My lessons during the Clues Stage of my journey would serve me well.

I found myself following invisible energy lines that wove their way across the landscape into the distance – 'spirit paths' or 'fairy roads' my mother had called them when I was a little girl. Somehow, the memory of this inner GPS system had returned in full strength since coming back to Colorado. As I had known subconsciously as a child here, if you know what to look for and how to listen, the land, its creatures and the air itself will leave you clues as to your path forwards. The spark of my childhood gifts was being fanned back into a more mature flame.

THE SPARK OF MY CHILDHOOD GIFTS WAS BEING FANNED BACK INTO A MORE MATURE FLAME.

A large desert yucca beckoned me, grabbing my attention to show me the place where I was to leave the main path and make my way through sage and Indian paintbrush plants towards a large, red rock ledge. Reaching its base, I saw that my stone friend had brought me to a place on his back where it was easy to find footholds. I climbed up to the ledge that, in my eyes, was sparkling with more than just the sun. Carefully, I scrambled up. On arriving at the top, I saw with a small gasp of surprise a covered door into the rock with the top rungs of a wooden ladder peeking out. My heart started to beat faster as my intuition received information regarding the nature of the space I was being led to. Slowly, using all my strength to pull back the heavy corrugated metal cover, I revealed the entrance and held my breath as old stale air escaped through the black hole at my feet. My breath caught in my throat in excited anticipation. I hadn't been into an 'earth womb' since I was a small child and never alone.

Before my mind could convince me otherwise, I swung my backpack over my shoulder and tested the first rung of the ladder that led down into the darkness. It seemed steady and firm enough underfoot. Slowly and carefully so as not to fall, I descended into the black. I was gradually cloaked in cool, dark air that contrasted sharply with the hot desert wind above. I closed my eyes for a moment to allow them to adjust to the reduced light. When I opened them again, I was able to make out the smooth circular walls of the underground chamber I had been led to: the kiva, a place sacred to the indigenous peoples of this land, where we can speak to the voices beyond time.

As I asked permission to enter this sacred space, I thought I heard the whispered voices of the ancestors in my ears and had the impression of a welcome. Sitting down on the dusty dirt floor, I took a moment to prepare myself, contemplating the spiders' webs and faded paintings on the walls. I could hear the hum of the earth like an intense pressure in my ears. I calmed and focused, the sound gradually clarifying into a regular rhythm. Consciously entwining my energy with the place I found myself in, my own heartbeat slowed and synchronized to match that of the earth. I was in her belly and I had a question. There was no need to ask it aloud; she could hear my heart.

> ONCE A CHANNEL TO THE SPIRIT WORLD HAS BEEN CREATED, IT IS STRENGTHENED WITH EACH RECONNECTION.

Energy started to swirl around me in the darkness and I felt the air grow heavy with the essence of ceremonies that had been conducted in this place coming alive once more. Once a channel to the spirit world has been created, it is strengthened with each reconnection. I was here, now, tapping into centuries of focused ritual intention. The portal opened up quickly and a rising pulse started to move in the center of my body. The energy whirled around me faster and faster, making me dizzy with its power. As I began to lose my ability to think clearly or attempt to control the course of events, I surrendered to the process. I felt safe and suspected that my question had been heard and received. After a moment, I started to wordlessly speak:

'I have come in humility. I have come for an answer to the question that has lain within my breast since before this life began. The eternal question that all human beings are designed to awaken to: Who am I?'

Thum, thum, thum, thum. The pounding increased to a crescendo pummeling my nerves. Then, softly, a female voice that was deeply familiar to me broke through the earth orchestra and spoke:

'Star Seed. You are a Star Seed. It's time to remember. It is time to move beyond all human stories.'

I exhaled. At first my mind couldn't believe what it had heard but I knew the words were for me. My ego tried hard to tell me I was imagining things, but still, I knew the words were for me. My heart beamed out gratitude for the answer I had been given.

I now had a new question – one that may well take a lifetime to answer.

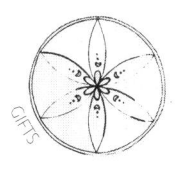

"One foot in front of another is the best way to start a journey," a companion whispered in my ear. We had stopped to observe the awe-inspiring vista that was revealed before us. The sheer beauty of the raw wilderness of the sandstone canyons made my breath catch. My throat tightened with the years of suppressed sadness I held having grown up away from the land I loved. *'How much I have missed you, earth mother!'* I silently prayed.

Further down the steep rocky trail, our group paused to conduct a ceremony. I found myself being called to a large, flat rock a short distance off the path. He (for the rock felt masculine) invited me to sit in his lap. Falling silent in his sun-warmed arms, I looked out at the community of pine trees surrounding me. They seemed to want to join me in the moment of gratitude. I sank into the deep place of bliss beyond human 'doings' and merged into the landscape.

Feeling complete and seeing other members of my group heading back to resume our trek, I hopped down from the rock, stroking it with thanks. I happened to glance down at the ground. To my amazement, a foot or so away, I saw a small movement in the mountain grasses and looking closer beheld the entwined forms of two slim, earth-colored snakes. I couldn't tell where one ended and the other began, so close were they in their loving embrace. I felt deeply grateful at the magic of witnessing these two beings. It humbled me and I bowed low before them as they stared back at me with an acknowledgment equal to my own. I had no words for the gift and omen given to me by my earth mother. In the potency of the moment, the metaphor of the snake shedding her skin was not lost on me. Nor was the idea of the merging of the masculine and feminine energies of earth. When we commune with the earth her voice begins to speak to us loud and clear. This is natural magic; our birthright.

The metaphor of the snake shedding her skin was not lost one me.

We had been in the canyon for little more than a day when the synchronicity of my snake encounter deepened. I was preparing to search for the place of my solo fast when our guide approached me with a glint in her eyes. Tossing her head to the west, she smiled and said, "*You know, beyond the confluence of two rivers lies Snake Lovers' Canyon.*" Smiling at the universe speaking loud and clear, I acknowledged her guidance and knew where I would go for my fast.

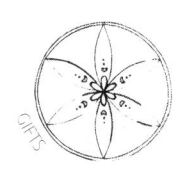

I awoke before dawn listening to the soft sounds of birds and animals calling forth and preparing for a new day. Stretching out in my sleeping bag, I noticed how quickly I had become comfortable sleeping on a thin mat on the ground. This canyon was fast becoming 'home' in my heart, as do all lands when we know how to speak to them and become a part of their living ecosystem.

The previous day, I had found the perfect sacred space for my solo fast: a beautiful sun dappled clearing by a creek, watched over by an enormously ancient grandmother Ponderosa pine. The tree rested against a tall canyon rock wall and there was a soft blanket of pine needles covering its floor. I knew it was 'my place' the instant I had wandered into its serene container. I packed my things with a shiver of anticipation, and after a swift farewell ritual, headed down the trail with my heart glowing.

My path meandered between the two rivers to the confluence where they merged. Here, I branched left and followed the dry creek bed. Listening to the song of the canyon, I greeted the communities of beings that I met along the way. Chipmunks scrambled from limb to limb above my head, rock people lined the path, guiding me forward, and the winged ones sang a chorus of welcome. Just as I began to wonder if I had lost my bearings somewhere along the unseen path, I saw a glimpse of bright blue through the trees and recognized the bandana that I had tied to the branch of grandmother Ponderosa the day before. I had arrived.

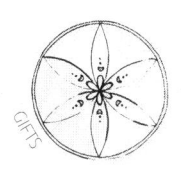

The sun was setting over the canyon walls, bringing them to life in scarlet, amber and golden hues and I found myself absently playing with some juniper berries that had fallen to the ground from the tree next to me. I picked them up and dropped them again, over and over. Each time they repeatedly fell back to a configuration of three in a row, just like Orion's Belt. Smiling at this mental connection to my childhood loves, I wondered at its relevance to the next part of my quest.

As I continued to ponder the threads of my story, thunder rolled in the distance. Its ominous tone reminded me of my task this night. I had spent a week preparing for my 'death lodge ceremony' – a core part of most vision quest journeys. It was to be an honoring of my old story and a celebration of the new person I was becoming.

Arising from my perch, I left the juniper berries where they lay and walked slowly and purposefully towards the large and imposing group of rocks that I felt would be a good place to die. Receiving their permission to begin (a warm feeling in my belly), I laid down and stared up at the darkening sky. My surroundings within the rocks were tomb-like and yet as I attempted to start my death ceremony I felt disconnected and distracted. *'Something isn't right,'* I thought. Glancing up at the rock face behind me, barely visible in the twilight I saw what I thought was a small human size hole in the side of the rock. *"Oh no,"* I muttered under my breath as I realized the invitation that I was being given. '*Spiders!*' was the thought that quickly followed, with a shudder of fear following quickly behind. A struggle ensued for a moment between my rational mind (and its ideas of physical safety) versus the deeper call beckoning me forwards once again. Breathing deeply to calm the butterflies that had taken over my stomach, I surrendered to the process of transformation for the hundredth time since this journey had begun and started to carefully climb up the rock face in the deepening darkness.

Three days without food had made me weak and I was more than aware that at any moment I could slip and fall, seriously hurting myself miles from any help. I filed these thoughts under 'not useful' in my head and proceeded to take my time with each hand and foothold. When I finally arrived, gasping in gulps of air, I saw that the hole was perfectly sized to fit my body into, much smaller than my survival instinct would have liked. Shining my flashlight into its interior I saw, just as expected, multiple spider webs. My hunch that it would be occupied was confirmed. With a shudder, I entreated the occupants that they host me for my ceremony. I asked that we could cohabit and be at peace with each other and in return, I would try to make as little lasting impression on their home as I could. Then I waited, listening to see if I could sense a response. I found a sense of inevitability and peace washing over me. '*I'll take that as a yes*,' I thought, almost wishing that the response had been different.

Fighting back my fears once more, I gradually, inch by inch, wedged myself into the hole; my sense of anxiety increasing with each centimeter that I moved. The reality that I could die here, bitten by one of the cave's inhabitants, created the perfect environment for my death ceremony. Prompted by the very real sense of danger, I began to cry. The catalyst of my physical vulnerability opened the door to a wider sense of the beauty of my human life. I knew that I wasn't quite ready for its story to end. Through the tears, my journey across many lifetimes flashed before my eyes in fragments, evoking the tastes, smells and visions of the things that had been both intensely beautiful and painful at times. As I traveled consciously down the pathways of my life it became so clear to me that we cannot live fully without life's polarities being experienced and merged. Light and dark, fear and love – they are just two sides of the same coin. I realized that I felt no regret, no anger, no resentment; just deep gratitude for the experiences I had shared with others on this amazing planet. And for the multitude of gifts I had been given.

> WE CANNOT LIVE FULLY WITHOUT LIFE'S POLARITIES
> BEING EXPERIENCED AND MERGED.

Forgetting time, I sank into the darkness of the void, in between stories, preparing to be reborn as a universal servant. Quietly, vigilantly, the spiders watched on and spun new webs.

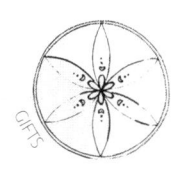

The previous night's 'death' had taken its toll on my fading energy; a state heightened by a lack of food and a sleep broken by dreams. I felt weak, yet calmer and clearer than ever before. As I sat naked in the sun under grandmother Ponderosa she was teaching me to create a representation of my destiny from the kiva for my final ceremony in Snake Lovers' Canyon. With the permission of the creek, I had gathered the slender branches of water reeds and was weaving a four-pointed star. I hung a pinecone from my grandmother in the center, entwined with some of my human hair.

After spending most of the day in a trance-like state weaving my sculpture, it was with some surprise that I realized dusk was speeding its path across the horizon. *'It won't be long before the guests arrive,'* I thought to myself and wandered over to my camp to find some clothes for the ceremony. One by one my family and friends appeared in the night sky, sparkling their welcome and their love. I made my way in the growing darkness over to a beloved rock in the shape of a broken heart and carefully climbed up to stand with one foot either side of the gaping crack down its center. Gazing up at the sky I was filled with wonder and awe at the beauty of the Milky Way. Billions of my invited guests beamed their joyful attendance across eons of time and space. Holding my 'star seed' aloft I called out, to the universe above, below, within and around me:

"I have listened. I surrender to my gifts. I inspire and illuminate soul stories into germination, giving them the courage to walk their true path. I place myself in the service of moving beyond our human stories into a vaster universal cosmology. I enter into harmony with the creation of a new story on earth."

> I PLACE MYSELF IN THE SERVICE OF MOVING BEYOND OUR
> HUMAN STORIES INTO A VASTER UNIVERSAL COSMOLOGY.

Across the horizon, a fiery shooting star arced wide across the night sky. With a gasp of delight, I knew that I had been seen, heard and witnessed by the cosmos. A shiver passed down my spine and rocked my body as I started to sense the extent of the prayer I had just made.

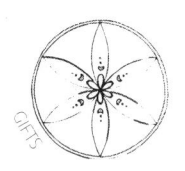

The time had come to return. Walking slowly back along the creek bed, towards my human tribe, I contemplated my experiences. I was humming with new life and energy. In my weakened state I was looking at the ground carefully as I walked, to ensure that I didn't misplace a step. As I did so, my gaze was caught by a flash of white amongst the pine needles. Bending down carefully, so the pack on my back didn't topple me over, I realized that the object of my attention was a broken eggshell. I looked closer. Spiraling trails led away from its empty husk. This was no bird egg. It was a recently hatched egg of a snake. For the hundredth time since beginning my journey, I was awed by the voice of the earth speaking so clearly to me. A powerful omen for my return – like a snake, I had shed my human skin and had been reborn.

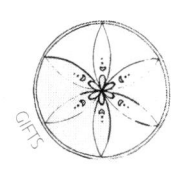

That night at dusk I made my way down to the creek with the same friend who had whispered in my ear at the start of our journey, to witness the nighttime galactic show. He and I had become closely linked during our quests and we felt utterly comfortable in each other's presence. We lay down together on the bank, enfolded in our sleeping bags, feeling like children enjoying a spectacular firework display. As I looked up towards the blanket of stars, I once again saw a shooting star blaze across the sky. It was so bright and close that I could almost feel its fire on my face as it flew. Then another and another! The sky was suddenly ablaze with stellar light that was reflected in our own bodies. So much joy. So much love. I have no words that come close to describing it.

Just as I started to wonder if my small human body could hold so much heaven, a powerful current of energy began to move inside me, beginning at the base of my spine, and then moving in waves of energy up towards the crown of my head. I felt as though 'I' was simultaneously melting and expanding into a much larger sense of self. Looking at the gleam of my companion's eyes shining in the darkness, I saw that he too was experiencing the same merging with the bliss of the cosmos that I was. Waves of ecstasy crashed through the cells of my body and I felt as if, for the first time, my physical form was opening to accommodate the hugeness of my soul.

The awareness of my mind started to fade, yet my intuition and senses were heightened. I felt my companion's hands reach out for mine and as our palms connected, I merged completely with him, the earth and all of life. Surrendering to the movement of energy flowing between us, we unified, falling into transcendence. Our eyes closed in bliss but we did not slumber. As our kundalini life force energy merged, we entered a liminal place between waking and sleep, sinking into the essence of all things living and dying. We melted into the love that lays beyond all form. We lay suspended like this until dawn. We are truly children of the earth with our feet in the ground and our souls in the stars.

As the golden sun crept over the canyon walls, I opened my eyes and saw that my brother and I were still laid in our sleeping bags on the creek bed, forehead to forehead and feet to feet. My human consciousness solidified, individuating once again and I became aware of our physical situation. Laying as we were, from above we looked just like the snakes I had seen on my initial descent into the canyon; masculine and feminine in total harmony and balance. A reflection of life itself in total harmony. A breathtaking celebration of a journey well traveled.

> WE ARE TRULY CHILDREN OF THE EARTH WITH OUR FEET
> IN THE GROUND AND OUR SOULS IN THE STARS.

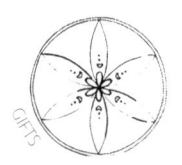

It felt really strange to be driving a car again after only knowing the weight of my pack on my shoulders and the sounds of my earth family in my ears for weeks. It felt even stranger to be walking through the front door of my grandmother's home in the suburbs of Denver, but when I saw her beautiful face, I could do nothing other than hug her for the longest time.

"*Darling, what has happened to you? You look just like a wild thing,*" she exclaimed after I finally let her go.

Making us both tea, I settled in to tell her about my journey. Seeing her face light up encouraged and nourished me. It reassured my mind that it was safe to speak of sacred things to others who have not yet traveled these paths, perhaps even laying the seeds that will eventually tempt them to their own journeys.

After a few pleasurable hours spent in my grandmother's grounding energy, I made my way up the mountain to the Sprucetree chapel, where 34 years earlier I had been held by Laurel herself and declared a child of the stars. Crossing the threshold, I smelled the familiar scent of aging wood and the dust of an old building rarely entered by people.

I was struck by the extent of the journey I had lived to come back full circle once again to this place. I raised my head and looked up at the crystal hanging from the ceiling in the same place where I imagined it had been the day of my christening. The vast beauty and gift of my life passed through my awareness and I experienced the ultimate perfection of each and every moment that had led me to here and now. Soon I would have to leave this beloved place once again. This time, however, I would leave having placed my life in service of something far greater than myself. This time I would leave with a heart cracked wide open to the adventure of life.

Reluctantly I made my way towards the door of the chapel, reaching into my pocket to find the old key with which to lock its box of treasures and memories safely away until I returned once again. Closing the door softly behind me, I felt Laurel smiling proudly. One foot in front of the other, I set out to walk a new path with the universe as my guide.

> I WOULD LEAVE WITH A HEART CRACKED WIDE OPEN
> TO THE ADVENTURE OF LIFE.

Sacred marriage

> Our coming together is determined
> By our ability to forgive and evolve
> When we see with the eyes of love
> Our walls simply dissolve

The locals say the Big Island is a challenging place to visit. Stories tell us of the goddess Pele, who dwells in the island, as the mistress of divine passion, manifestation and of the eternal cycles of birth, death and rebirth. Life is constantly in motion here just like the new land that is born through the lava beneath your feet. All I know is that there is no other place like it on earth where we are called to intensely face, surrender and heal our inner shadows and fear.

These narrative threads were all running through my mind as we sat on the small plane coming in to land on the Big Island of Hawaii. Four years previously, I had seen and experienced this exact moment playing out to the tiniest detail in a vision: Euan and I sitting in a small plane, looking out at the storm-gray thunderclouds surrounding Big Island, as we come in to land. As I had now experienced my premeditation in real time, I knew what we had come here for.

We had been on quite a journey together to come to this moment in time. The ripple-effects of my recent vision quest had simultaneously brought us closer together and yet cracked us wide apart through our socially programmed fear of what my experiences might mean for us as a couple. We had been moving through deep and murky relationship territory ever since.

For him, it had been agony to hear of the depth and erotic intimacy of my experiences with my human and more than human companions, especially given that he wasn't the one there to share them with me. His masculine story of wanting to be my hero was hurt by the realization that I could love other beings as deeply, yet differently, as I loved him. Patterns stemming from past pain, betrayal and social narratives about what monogamous love and relationships are, had all arisen to be faced, discussed honestly and untangled.

For me, it had been a tough trial to simply share my journey from a place of complete and utter honesty. I had encountered my old adolescent fear of 'it's not safe to tell the truth' and had to gulp back my compulsion to 'white lie' in order to save his hurt feelings. It had been horrible to watch my truthful words cut open old wounds in us both, yet I knew this was an important part of us evolving individually and together as a partnership. There had been moments where I had to face the fear of losing him if he couldn't or wouldn't understand the depth of divine love I had cracked open to. There were also moments where I wondered whether he actually believed my experiences, because the facts didn't fit with the common human story of love. The depth of magic and love that my time in the canyon had awakened in me is rarely spoken about in our society. Yet to honor the gifts I had been given required complete integrity and I knew in my heart that they would be taken away again if I wasn't strong enough to hold them.

Over the previous weeks we had passed through the alchemical fire repeatedly and had been purified together. From the vantage point of my cosmic experience, 'who' the masculine being had been was of no particular relevance. However, for Euan, the thought of me merging with a man other than himself was hard to swallow in a culture of western monogamy. He was encountering issues of betrayal, ownership and exclusivity. I was trying to make sense of an experience of universal merging, for which there are few words available!

We surrendered to our shared fear of losing each other, our families and the security of being a 'couple' in favor of speaking and living our truth. It had taken us both to the point of being willing to walk away from each other and the people we loved the most to maintain our integrity. In doing so, we had repeatedly been able to come back to each other stronger in our authenticity. We had moved beyond co-dependency in favor of an honest relating that had healed us both. Such is the challenge for anyone who undertakes the building of a sacred and lasting relationship in our times, where the old accepted stories of marriage and partnership are undergoing radical evolution. We are in uncharted territory and we only have the truth that lies in our hearts to turn to in order to guide us.

TOUGH BLISS

After sailing through stormy seas together we were now on the Big Island to complete our process. We had decided to speak sacred vows that would join our two lives into one for as long as we loved, lived and walked together.

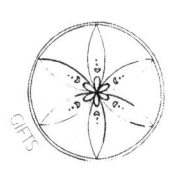

On the night we landed in Hawaii I had a dream.

> I find myself sitting on the shores of a wide river,
> surrounded by a community of different people.
> Some are familiar to me and some are not.
>
> I walk over to a man who reaches his hand out
> and invites me to step into a boat resting at the edge
> of the water. As I accept, he pulls me into his arms
> in an embrace and hands me a piece of paper on which
> are written six steps to sacred relationships.
>
> I look at them one by one and feel them
> absorb into my heart.

1. Spark of recognition
2. Run or stay
3. If you stay, BE fully present
4. Walk together
5. Merge and separate gracefully
6. Unify

I wake to the darkness of dawn and know I have been given a powerful relational teaching.

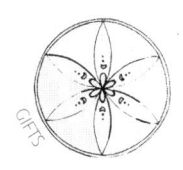

Euan and I were driving up the coast to Pu'uhonua O Honaunau, an ancient Hawaiian place of healing. In the past times it had been the home of royalty and a place of refuge for defeated warriors who had violated 'kapu': the sacred laws. If a person committed kapu, they would be given a chance to swim through shark-infested waters towards the shores of Pu'uhonua O Honaunau. Should they reach it without being eaten or speared by the King's guards who awaited them on the coast, then their kapu was forgiven and they could live. It is a place where you can make peace with the past and ask for forgiveness: where the spirits of the ancients still powerfully dwell.

We were both consumed by the restful, divine energy of the place. Walking slowly, hand in hand across the white sand amongst the reconstructed houses and temples we followed an intuitive path, heading for a platform of lava rock that stretched like Pele's hair out into the sea. In silence we removed our shoes and walked across the warm lava stone barefoot. I felt the energy of Pele pulsing through my feet with a sweet sense of tranquility: harmony and love washing gently upon the shore from mother ocean.

We stood apart for a few moments, each of us having our own personal dialogue with the ancestors, asking for release and forgiveness in our own ways. When I sensed that our individual prayers were complete, I walked over and crouched by him at the lava edge where the small waves kissed our toes. Gently, he reached over and scooped some of the warm water over my feet, washing them clean of the dust of our journey. My breath caught in my throat. The simple act of washing my feet with such care spoke more to me of the strength of our bond than a thousand kisses. Looking at him, the moment stretched into what seemed like a timeless eternity. I savored his face, his energy, the essence of who he is as a man.

If only we could take the time to really look at each other this way. To see beyond our projection of who we 'think' our partners are, into the depths of their souls. If only we could awaken to how much love magic is present in the small acts of life as well as the large ones. It is a practice we have continued ever since.

I knew in this moment that we were ready for our vows.

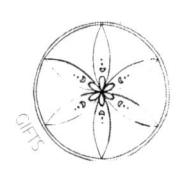

We arrived in the heart of Volcano National Park just before sunset. As we got out of the car and prepared to hike back to the spot we had chosen, I found my thoughts oddly silent. I had no expectations and therefore no resulting nervousness. I was simply witnessing what was unfolding and listening to the world around me. It was a quiet form of bliss.

Euan finished packing our things into our green rucksack and in the space of 'not thinking', I reached up to push the truck closed. As it shut, I felt his energy spin next to me and turned to see him looking in horror.

"*You didn't just do that? The keys are in there*!"

My pulse started to beat a little faster and I gasped in surprise. Whether it was the lack of food for two days (we had been fasting to prepare for our ceremony) or that I was mindlessly blissed-out, the fact remained that I had 'just done that' and we were now locked out of our car. Silence fell as we both chose how to respond.

It would have been very easy to decide, from a story of fear or superstition, that 'something' was trying to stop us saying our vows and completing our process. It would have also been easy to call the whole thing off and panic, or for an argument to break out. Instead, after a pause, I laughed. Euan smiled and then started laughing too. My practical brain kicked back in and I asked him if he had his phone. Relieved when he said, *"Yes"*, I found him the number and he calmly called the hire car people to arrange for Triple A to come out and save us. We had at least 90 minutes before they arrived to hike out and complete our ceremony.

"You still wanna do this?" I asked, testing him.

"More than ever," he replied with a smile.

I was proud of us both as we slowly walked up the trail towards the volcano in silence. I too was sure of the 'rightness' of this decision. To say sacred vows of love and commitment in front of Pele was not something undertaken easily or lightly, nor was it something that either of us would break or disregard. Our preparation and testing process over the previous weeks, months, even years since we had come together was the most difficult process I had ever walked through in a relationship. It had also been the most awesome and blissful. There had been moments when I had wanted to run away, moments when I had been tempted to blame him for my struggles and moments when I had wondered what I had ever done to deserve this wonderful man's love in my life. It was the latter that had allowed me to keep walking the path of love by his side. There was an innate understanding that had built between us – neither one of us wanted to take the easy route and run away this time. The strong foundation of our relationship was strengthened every time that we helped each other to accept and heal both our darkness and our light.

As we cleared the jungle forest and walked out onto the volcanic plain around the crater we saw the perfect sunset in motion. It was clear as far as our eyes could see, a miracle in itself given it had been raining only an hour before. The sky was washed with pinks and crimsons, the distant peak of Mauna Loa standing tall and wise as our witness. It was the first time I had seen the mountain summit in all her glory and, in the years since, I have never seen her as clearly as I did that night. Blown away by such a perfect setting for our ceremony, I smile-cried in appreciation of the vast beauty of the earth, and for the magic of our human lives. Looking over at Euan, I saw he was doing the same. Pele wanted us here, despite the obstacles that we had to jump and the challenges that we had faced. We had made it, together.

As we sat down on the lava hair of Pele, the air was pregnant with anticipation. Smoke gently puffed from Kilauea's crater. Euan, a natural poet, had written the most beautiful vows I had ever heard and as I received them, I had the distinct sense that I, like the lava, was glowing brighter and brighter with every word. I felt fully seen for who I was as a human, a star and a soul for perhaps the first time in my life. When he was finished, I just looked at him. Drinking in the moment before letting it go.

Then it was my turn. I was clean and clear like the air high at the top of a mountain. I had come through the trees of the forest and could see all around me in every direction. I knew who I was and who I wanted to spend my life with and he was sitting right here beside me. My vows had come from a deep place beyond me and I had not thought about a single sentence as I had written them. The words had come through my heart, yet the eloquence of the language was my soul's touch. I tasted each one as it left my lips, noticing how delicious it was to speak complete and utter truth and love to the universe as it was reflected in his eyes. I was speaking these vows to every place and every time; to every being in the universe.

> HOW DELICIOUS IT WAS TO SPEAK COMPLETE
> AND UTTER TRUTH AND LOVE TO THE UNIVERSE.

When I had finished, I looked up at the crater in the distance. The reddish glow that had been faint when we arrived was growing brighter in the gathering dusk. Pele again, witnessing. Euan held me tightly and we didn't speak for the longest time. In moments like these there really is no need to talk. You both know exactly what is happening inside the other without moving a muscle or thinking a thought. These are the moments we live for, we long for and we know will come eventually when we have done our healing and embraced our fears. But they only come if we pay attention. If we listen to the beat of our story and don't go back to sleep. Ever present, allowing the universe to dream itself alive through us.

Saying goodbye to Pele and full of the deepest source of gratitude, we walked back to our car to wait for the Triple A man. It was getting cold now the sun had departed and I thanked the angels that we had grabbed our hoodies before I had shut the trunk. We huddled together for warmth, sitting on the bonnet of our car.

As I looked up at the carpet of shining star-friends cascading across the night sky, I felt them looking back at me, proud. Beaming love to my star family, I wondered for a moment if they could see and hear me. After a short time, a star shot across the horizon and I smiled. They had heard.

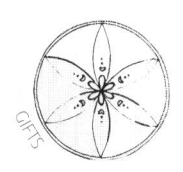

A few days after returning to England we awoke before dawn into the silence of our Avebury home. Instead of trying in vain to sleep through jetlag, we got up and settled into the living room with early morning cups of tea. Lazily, I started to check my emails, but was caught instead by an intuitive thought to see whether there had been any crop circles appearing in the Wiltshire landscape whilst we had been away. With the rainy start to the year, the crops had been later than usual and no patterns had yet been spotted to my knowledge. I punched in a Google search and felt my pulse quicken. The results confirmed that the first crop circle of the season had appeared in a field, just a few miles from our house and on my birthday. Holding my breath as I waited for the image to load onto my screen, I was convinced that whatever appeared would hold special significance for me, given the events of the previous months. Nothing could have prepared me for what I saw when it appeared.

My heart started to beat, not fast, but strong; so strong that I could feel destiny pulsing through my veins. I gasped and grabbed Euan's arm over the sofa to get his attention. The image on the screen was of a perfect four-pointed star, etched into a field of golden rapeseed. In the middle of the star, the bright yellow flowers had been compressed to form what could only be described as a diamond/pyramid- shaped seed. It was almost an exact replica of the star-seed sculpture I had created in the canyon on my vision quest.

For a moment I couldn't speak, so taken aback by the universe's blatant message was I. When I recovered myself, I turned to Euan and said, "*I feel a new tattoo coming on.*"

Laughing he replied, "*The only thing that surprises me is that this kind of stuff still surprises you!*"

Re-dreaming

Restore
Reenergize
Reignite
Remember

I am naked, sitting on a white wooden chair in a room the same color. Looking down at my body I see words appearing all over my skin as if they are tattooed. All the words begin with 're'.

Restore
Reinvigorate
Reenergize
Remember
Relight
Renovate
Reignite
Reconnect

I am confused and look up. My grandfather is sitting next to me with a warm, amused and knowing smile on his face. He looks just how I remember him when I was five or six years old. Seeing my confusion, he leans in close and asks me, "Genne, do you really not remember why you know all these things?" I know I should remember but the knowledge feels far away, buried, hidden.

Looking up I see the wall of the room falling away to reveal a cosmos filled with a million stars all greeting me with love. Walking towards me are a man and a woman who I recognize immediately. As they draw close, the man holds back, allowing her to approach me, holding out her hands in welcome. I stand, naked and covered in words, moving forwards into her soft embrace. In my ear she whispers: "It's time to give your gifts."

I wake up.

GIFTS JOURNEY

ARE YOU READY TO STEP FULLY INTO THE ABUNDANCE OF LIFE?

Often when I am working with people on their gifting cycles, the first barrier that comes up is the challenge of finding the time to give. Undoubtedly, many of us have 'reality issues' of work, family and personal responsibilities that will affect how much and how often we can dedicate focused time to giving our innate gifts. However, I would like instead to offer an alternative between 'daily living time' and 'gifting time'. Instead of seeing these from the old story of separation, I instead offer you a different narrative based on unity.

What if, in your daily life, you were presented with multiple opportunities to give your gifts as you work, care for your family and earn a living? What if, instead of carving out a few precious moments here and there whenever the chaos of life subsides, to share your talents, you found ways of incorporating them into your daily schedule so they become a part of who you are and how you live in each and every moment? For the story of 'time as a gift' to embed itself, all that is needed is awareness and intentionality. To switch your senses, intuition and soul from 'off' to 'on' and to notice how the small acts of life are actually enormous opportunities to give your gifts to the world.

If you would like to play with this, find some time and grab your journal. Tune into this stage of your Restory Cycle and start to write a list of all of the gifts that you have been given on your journey so far. These can be everything from the tangible 'how to write and deliver kick-ass project plans' through to the more ethereal, yet equally important, 'sharing random acts of kindness with others' or 'encountering angels'. Your list should include a range of both 'small' and 'big' gifts to embrace the breadth of your life as a cycle of both giving and receiving.

Next, review each gift on your list and start to notice where you can give this through your daily life to others. Where are you already exercising these talents and how could you do more of what is already there?

Take a moment to feel into, and write down a commitment to, the universe that encapsulates your wish to gift your talents to the world in an increasing and expanding form. Write this in your journal and then say it out loud at least three times until it feels natural and coherent in your body. If you feel ready, speak your intention out loud to people around you. You may be surprised by how fast your life starts to present you with opportunities to share your gifts from here on in.

Something magical starts to happen when we not only set an intention but we are willing to share it publically with others and the world. We start to become responsible and accountable for creating new stories, not just for dreaming them. Connect to the seed of your gift, write its story, speak the story to others and act out that story with every opportunity that is given to you for the good of all. This is the real process of magic.

UNITY

HOW AM I INTERCONNECTED WITH THE UNIVERSE?

'First you have to let go,
Only then can you truly surrender
Only then can you truly trust,
And only then can you truly have faith.
When you have faith you can enter the 'Gateway'
And when you enter the Gateway you stop living life
And life starts living you
And then you dance
That's all that's left to do!'

—The Gateway by Lawrence Bloom[35]

Unity is one of those words that can mean many things and hide many secrets. We come to it when we are ready and not before, although its sweet aroma stalks us every day of our lives. The Unity Stage in the Restory Cycle is by its very nature hard to describe in words. Many teachers, saints and laymen and women have attempted to do so, each with a unique voice. And yet, like every story, these accounts feel incomplete. Unity is something we must discover ourselves.

In its largest sense, unity represents a realization and conscious merging of our individual story into the vaster mythology of the cosmos. In true unity, our questions, our seeking and our hunger all fall silent in the face of the truth that all of life and its events are interconnected. This is the place where we step beyond our narratives, identities and beliefs into the fertile ground of an unknown and vast territory.

Having gone through the death, rebirth and metamorphosis stages, we begin to know ourselves as divine beings in human form; as something greater than a sack of bones and skin that exists to survive and grow in a world driven by power, control, status and possessions. We are asked increasingly to merge our personal agenda with the will of life itself, moving beyond all judgments and polarities. This is the death of the individual self and rebirth of the universal self.[36] In order for this to occur, a deep surrender is required. As Joseph Campbell[37] reminds us, 'The hero is the master of self-achieved submission.' Our submission is an act of devotion to the greater good of all beings. This is where 'me' becomes indistinguishable from 'we'.

We have by now been on a long undulating journey between separation and unity, at a minimum for many years and perhaps even many lifetimes. Splintering and reforming again and again in an alchemical process of purification. In coming to the sixth and final stage, we inevitably come full circle back to its beginning. Elements of the Spark Stage that we were born into are assimilated and understood for the first time in new ways, facilitated by our journey through the rest of the cycle. The connection with life that we experienced as a young child comes fully back to us now in adult form. We find an expanded sense of agency within the myth of unity. It is the ultimate act of self-responsibility and the moment in time when we transcend the victim narrative completely. When we unify with life, there are no more excuses. We become a part of creation itself.

The process of surrender is about trust. Trust in a higher form of creative intelligence in the universe than that of our human intellect that guides us. Trust in the deeper currents of personal destiny that move through our lives from birth to death, whether we can see them or not. Trust that we have a vital part to play in the emerging modern mythology of interconnection and human beingness. This kind of trust is something easy to say and not so easy to act out on a daily basis. This is why trust is one of the master practices that we only reach when we are ready. There are so many things that appear to threaten us, separate us and distract us that it can be hard to continually trust there is a force at work in the universe that guides and protects us. A force that exists within us, as well as within all living things and is precise and perfect in everything it does. This kind of trust takes some work.

I have learned over the years that trust is something that you must 'feel' and repeatedly enact again and again to ingrain that feeling in your bones. It is the feeling that comes when we enter into a dynamic partnership with life instead of trying to control or manipulate it. This doesn't mean that we give in (or give up) on life, handing our free will over to faith and fate, letting go of any responsibility; quite the opposite. We stop striving and trying to make things happen, relaxing into a form of action that comes from a place beyond 'me'.

'Surrender' is also a curious word. It has different connotations for many of us and I feel it's important to define my meaning of it here. In my native language of English, it is often viewed as a negative or subservient response to a conflict of some kind. We think of 'surrendering to our enemies' or 'giving in/giving up' in the face of life's challenges. It is regularly used to imply weakness and failure. In many Christian traditions the act of 'surrendering to God' is meant to gain you peace by putting your life into more capable, divine hands. In Arabic, the word 'Islam' can be translated as 'surrender or submission'; however, if you look at the root word, it is 'salam' which means 'peace and safety'. I tend to experience the act of surrender more in line with the principle of 'salam'. When I surrender my human story over to the pulse of the greater universal story, I am surrendering to the intuition, synchronicity and guidance that comes to me in unexpected and magical ways. I walk the knife-edge between logic and instinct; both skills feeding a balanced response to the options I am presented with in the world. I hold self-responsibility for my choices whilst still considering whether they are in service of the greater good.

In coming into connection and communion with the universe around us in this way, I find we are able to act with more authority and agency than we ever did when our human ego was trying to run the show. Our lives become a dance of magic and radiance, at the same time as leading us into ever more challenging circumstances and difficult relationships. Things definitely don't get easier the further into unity we travel but they absolutely get more beautiful and ecstatic.

We learn to release the compulsion to 'make things better', 'heal people' or 'save the world' by simply accepting things as they show up. We are asked on a daily basis to dance between individual sovereignty and collective service; to walk between many different worlds as cultural translators, sharing our gifts of service with whomever, wherever we are brought into connection. We fall in love and make love to life as a continual process. It is the delicate art of balancing persistence with desistence.

> UNITY IS THE DELICATE ART
> OF BALANCING PERSISTENCE WITH DESISTENCE.

This stage has manifested itself for me in certain repeatable patterns, behaviors and experiences:

1. Taking action towards something that feels right even though I can't see how it will be successful in the long term.

2. Realizing that there is nothing inherently wrong with me or the world. That my life experiences are catalysts to prompt me into action on behalf of 'we' instead of 'me'.

3. Being guided by magical, synchronistic events and 'lucky' opportunities.

4. Living mythically by witnessing potential plotlines, archetypal influences and quests as they appear in your life and the wider world.

5 Developing the ability to be creatively in discomfort, challenge, conflict and chaos: holding both dark and light without judging them as right or wrong.

6 Entering a heightened sense of interconnection and communion with the all human and non-human beings.

7 Love (in all its forms) becoming the core driver for our decisions.

8 Experiencing 'God' as a verb rather than a noun.

The stage of unification with the bigger universal story could also be described as a form of alchemy: the ancient art of transforming base metals to gold, or lower forms of consciousness to higher forms. For me, this alchemy is hard to put into words or a (simple) step-by-step process. Each of us experiences alchemy in our own unique way, dependent on our soul's vision, mission and story. Essentially, the Restory Cycle is an alchemical journey. It takes our essential self or our *prima materia* from Spark Stage, through a process of *separation* where we experience ourselves as isolated and individual (Tests Stage), to one of *conjunction* where the elements of our story start to join together in a deeper pattern, pointing the way towards our personal mythology (Clues Stage). From here the elements of our soul story undergo a *fermentation* process where the imaginal cells of our narrative fuse into a new form of person (Metamorphosis Stage). This leads to the eventual *distillation* of our true self and story (Gifts Stage) and the final stage of *coagulation* of the purified essence of our self and life where spirit descends fully into the matter of our physical human form. It is during this final Unity Stage we realize that everything in our external life stems from our internal levels of consciousness. Indeed, the nature of true unity dictates that there is nothing outside of ourselves. 'Me' merges completely with 'we' and we start to reach the stages of non-dual awareness where the story of interconnection comes alive in the cells of our being.

The Restory Cycle is an alchemical journey.

The practical process of alchemy becomes a daily choice – to consciously breathe into and let go of anything that we have outgrown, creating space for new understanding, experiences and opportunities to emerge. We surrender to the 'gold' of our soul story, which in turn grows and expands at the rate that our courage facilitates. It takes constant bravery to live in an interconnected world, where there is no one or no-thing to hide behind when life becomes challenging. We understand that 'magic' is our innate ability to co-create with the natural forces of life.

When we reach this stage of the journey, we return to the beginning once again, fully embodying the energy of our spark. We come home 'within' and know ourselves as a human aspect of the universe for the first time. We rest content for a while in this stage, but only long enough to gather our energy, assimilate our wisdom and begin another cycle of the journey. Our spark has expanded to fill our lives and we are subsequently ready for new tests, new clues and another metamorphosis. Our soul story continues to evolve within in the eternal spiral of life.

I believe we can witness the human pulse towards unity emerging powerfully across our beautiful planet. From synchronized global events, to indigenous activism galvanizing multicultural community support; the heartbeat of unity is growing stronger. With the digital revolution we are able to connect, commune and synergize with the human and more than human communities on earth like never before. It is an inspiring time to be alive.

We can witness the human pulse towards unity emerging powerfully across our beautiful planet.

The memories I share with you here are some of the pivotal threads from my own soul story as it has emerged in the unity phase of the cycle. At the time of writing I am only just beginning to fully see and feel the power of unity in my own life. In many ways, I had to reach this place in order to be able to write this book. I share these stories with you with the intention for you to see, feel and know how this stage manifests itself in all of our human challenges and blessings, so that you too will know the flavor and sound of this stage when it enters into your own beautiful life story. Here by way of tempting your mythic taste buds, are my own adventures into the state and Unity Stage.

I'm holding out my hand to you: come with me. Let's play.

The land of alchemy and light

> Alchemy in the land
> Transmutation in the light
> Ancient and new becomings
> Emerge in love from the darkness of the desert night

I had fought coming to this place. I mean, I had *really* fought it, mentally and emotionally. I had tried to find countless reasons to justify why I shouldn't, couldn't or didn't need to be in Egypt but the magnetic pull of my story brought me here nonetheless. I have come to realize that when we are facing a choice in our lives that will take us way beyond our comfort zones, the defense mechanisms that activate to keep us within the safe confines of our existing world are persuasive. Mine have become increasingly tricky over the years, evolving into a complex system of security measures, increasing in subtlety and challenge the further I go into the process of transformation. With each step made towards surrendering to the uncontrollable flow of my story, my ego inevitably has to release its hold over the habits of my life and take a back seat in the journey.

In this case, Level One of my ego's defense mechanism was to throw up practical concerns such as not having enough money, time or freedom. Of course, this was a flimsy argument and one that I quickly saw off with the truth (I had plentiful time and resources if

I chose to allocate them here). With this hurdle negotiated, Level Two kicked in. My friends and family started to sing various songs of doom and danger. *"You can't go to Egypt! It's not safe. It's a war zone. You'll be killed or kidnapped or mugged."* These stories came in multiple forms from multiple mouths. I watched them buzz around my consciousness like those annoying flies that refuse to fly out of the open window offered to them. There were moments when the projected fears of those around me infiltrated my inner world and I felt like abandoning the whole journey. Yet somehow, the quiet calm voice of my soul would return to assure me that it was both safe and necessary that I go. At this stage of my restory journey, my soul almost always wins. Underneath the surface games of tension, I knew I was going.

At this stage of my restory journey, my soul almost always wins.

My adventures in this alchemical land have been numerous in recent years and perhaps there will come a time when they become a book in themselves. Once I mustered the courage to visit there in person, I have been called back again and again on multiple mythic adventures. Egypt is awakening to its own modern myth and I have a feeling that it may want to be told in new voices and new settings. For now, I share with you some of the essence of my early journeys in this land and the nature of the alchemy that I tasted. If you have not visited, I hope that one day you may find yourself led back to this ancient place too. If you are called, I pray you will have the courage to go.

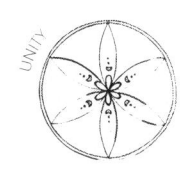

The gray and black Egyptian crows cawed above my head, insistently grabbing my attention as if they were trying to tell me something important. Beyond the lush oasis garden where I sat in the early morning light, I heard the car horns and braying donkeys of the awakening east bank of Luxor overlaid with the musical prayer songs broadcast from the city mosques.

I had been in Egypt for little more than a week, having found myself on an adventure led by my friend and gifted astrologer Tom Kaypacha Lescher.[38] Each day, as we traveled down the Nile by sailboat, I found myself surrendering more and more into the energy of the journey and the deep companionship and love offered by my traveling companions. Our boat of international adventurers quickly settled into a rhythm and cadence together, dropping our masks and emotional protection patterns faster than usual and slipping into the easy, intimate friendships of adopted family. As stories were shared and the 'me too' moments accumulated, we forgot our perceived differences and became siblings by choice. All of us in some way had reached an impasse in our social, spiritual and psychological lives and had been drawn together by variations on a single question: How can we fulfill our destiny in this lifetime? It was the question that united us.

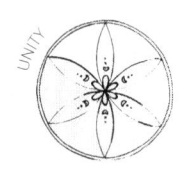

I was standing at the gates of the temple of Hathor at Dendara, a powerful place dedicated to the divine feminine in all her forms. The morning sun blistered down, shimmering in waves of heat over the arched gates of the temple and I wrapped my light, silver scarf around my head to shield it from the sun and hot desert air. I couldn't help but notice the growing feeling of recognition that this temple was evoking inside me. I was sure I had been here before and yet was tempted to dismiss it as 'wishful thinking'. As a storyteller by trade, I am more than aware of our ability to become lost within a story of our mind's making and yet, equally, I have repeatedly experienced the power of a deeper mythology speaking to me in visions and dreams. Here, in Egypt, I was being called to utilize both my logical, deductive brain and my visionary, intuitive senses to determine what was real from what was romantic illusion; a challenging task in a land where I have found that whatever beliefs we hold deeply in our being have a habit of manifesting physically for us to see and heal. Here things manifest fast!

I followed my group at a distance into the great entrance hall. Arching backwards like a gymnast, I stared up at the hieroglyphs engraved across the ceiling. I drew a breath in appreciation at the vibrant colors that had recently been restored by teams of archaeologists. Narratives of gods and goddesses, humans and star beings wove together into a vast creation story above my head. Aware of the tourist groups around me, I carefully allowed my energy field to expand and feel into the morphic fields of the temple. (A morphic field is a phrase coined by British scientist Rupert Sheldrake[39] to describe fields of memory and organizing information held in nature and the wider universe.) It was the memory of the temple itself that I was attempting to access and after a short period, visions began to flash into my mind's eye. Some of them felt connected to my personal relationship with this place and others were more universal, taken from the residual energy of the collective experiences of the initiates who had inhabited and cared for the temple over millennia.

Without thinking, I followed a pull towards the back of the temple, finding myself at the underground entrance to the crypt. Glancing briefly for permission to enter from the temple guard standing at the top of the stairs, I took his proffered hand and stepped down into the gaping hole in the floor onto an old wooden ladder that led into the darkness of an underground chamber. Coming to the base of the steps, I slid my body snake-like under a low hanging stone ledge, beyond which lay a five-chambered room in the earth under the main temple. My fingers traced patterns along the figures and exquisite hieroglyphs on the walls. It felt achingly familiar.

My body, moving instinctively, walked to the right and came to a halt at the end of the chamber. Kneeling down on the floor, ignoring the dust that had been down here for centuries, I bowed forwards in front of the image that was engraved into the wall above me. Two queens, sat back to back on thrones, adorned with the symbols of royalty and divinity. I laid my forehead, my third eye, on the ground, ignoring the small voice that called for cleanliness, and uttered my own words of power in a prayer: "*I surrender my life to serving the new human story on earth. May my thoughts, words, actions and essence serve all life.*" My head started to spin with the waves of energy that spiraled around me and I had to breathe deeply to remind myself I was still kneeling in a human body. Humming and beating, the heartbeat of the temple came alive in my body. I was vaguely aware of other people coming to join me in the chamber but felt no call to move from where I was kneeling.

A masculine voice started to chant and I recognized it as coming from the mouth of my friend Daniel. In response and without thinking, my own feminine voice rose to meet his, entwining like a serpent seeking union with her mate. We sang alive our ancient and modern oaths. It was as if the sound was being sung 'through us', from a place beyond our current lifetimes. Ancient memories rose to the surface of my mind's eye and I watched them play out across the screen of my consciousness. I was overcome by a feeling that I had lived, loved and learned in this temple a long time ago.

> I HAD LIVED, LOVED AND LEARNED
> IN THIS TEMPLE A LONG TIME AGO.

Then as spontaneously as it had begun, it was over. Leaving the chamber with a hug from Daniel, I crawled once more under the ledge that led up towards the ladder. I was suddenly hungry for fresh air and the light of the sun. Waiting for me at the top with a strong hand and a grin was Hassan, our Egyptian guide and protector for the journey. Hassan[40] and his family have run tours across Egypt for decades and he has the unique ability to create a bubble of safety and peace around those who are in his care. He is tall and strong in his body and energy, reminding me of the ancient temple guards in the mythology books I had devoured as a child.

Pulling me up and out of the staircase with ease, he said with wide brown eyes, *"Sister, you have brought the light with you. You are glowing!"* Before I could open my mouth to give an explanation, he held a gentle finger over my lips and said, *"Shhhh, breathe deeply and go outside into the sun,"* gesturing for me to exit through a side door. Marveling at the emotional intelligence of my new Egyptian friend, I walked outside to find a quiet place in the garden where I could pull myself back together.

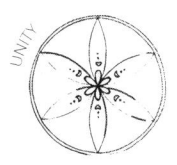

'Who is he?' I wondered as I stepped off the plane into the early morning heat of Luxor airport. Breathing in the warm desert air, I slowly allowed my breath to pass my lips, feeling my whole body relax with the release. Egypt: I had returned.

It was my fourth trip here in a year. The land had awakened me to a whole new level of connection with the universe. With each journey here, the process of natural alchemy cleansed and healed something else in my ancient memories. Whether you believe in reincarnation or not does not really matter. Egypt, both ancient and modern, has the ability, for those who are ready, to pull out of the depths of our human memory banks any and all of our fears, shame, guilt and hurts. I believe it does this so that we may acknowledge the parts of ourselves that have remained in shadow and see that they hold the keys to our liberation. It is the things we are most ashamed of that hold the key to our greatest gifts but these can only be given to us if we are willing to face and claim them. Just as in the process of physical alchemy, first the alchemist must purify the essence of the elements they are working with. Once distilled, the elements are prepared for transformation and finally metamorphosed into new expanded forms. My mind, body and emotions were being purified and prepared.

> IT IS THE THINGS WE ARE MOST ASHAMED OF
> THAT HOLD THE KEY TO OUR GREATEST GIFTS.

I could feel Hassan waiting for me at the exit to the airport. Ever since we had begun to dream walk together (have the same dreams on the same night), he had become an ever present part of my consciousness. Dream-walking is something that is common in many indigenous societies, often linked to shamanism. It happens spontaneously when we meet souls that we have known in previous lives and existences.

My relationship with Hassan was different to Euan. With Euan, the charge of Eros and a deep human love was our connecting force. With Hassan, it was more ancient and felt like family. I suspected we had lived lifetimes as siblings, parents, lovers and friends, all of these roles blending into one eternal relationship. I had no mental models to explain the magic held between us and nor did I want any. If we needed to provide some reason for the connection I felt it would be lessened somehow.

After he had enfolded me in one of his huge bear hugs and we had escaped the chaos of the airport, we sat in the sunshine, smiling with the simple joy of being together again. After some moments, he said, *"Love for nothing, sister. It is the deepest form of love that we can ever wish for in this life. It never dies and never gets complicated by sex. This is what I have for you. It will never grow old."* I smiled, agreeing with his explanation. Outside the western world, the understanding of love and all its varieties and flavors is alive and multifaceted. Greek, Italian and Arabic to name a few are all languages where there are multiple words describing the essence of this universal force of creation.

'Love for nothing' is a love that lies beyond carnal, sexual attraction yet can also occasionally encompass this. It is the unattached, unconditional love that we aspire to with our friends and family, yet rarely achieve in practice. It transcends the traditional cultural laws that govern love between male/female, old/young, married/unmarried. It also asks us difficult questions. Can we continue to love someone beyond our physical desire to make love with them? Can we move beyond sexual attraction and into an unknown space of true eroticism as creativity? I believe that we can, but to do so requires radical honesty: first with ourselves in order to acknowledge our real desires and longings for intimacy and second the ability to speak honestly and without restraint to 'the beloved' who shows up. There are a million ways we can love each other and the beings of the world around us, most of which are untainted by the guilt and shame that naturally accompany the predominant story of 'The One'.

The myth of The One drives its subtle hooks into our psyche in the form of our eternal search for our true purpose (implying that we only have one true purpose in each lifetime), our true home (suggesting that there is only one place in the world that will make us happy) and our true selves (as if we can reduce the complexity of a human to one face). Coming to Egypt has taught me many things, but mainly how to love without guilt.

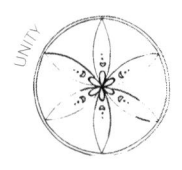

Following the trail of synchronistic clues being laid out before us, Hassan and I had decided to return to Abydos to sink into the silence of the desert and listen to the myths of life and death that it holds. We had shared many dreams of this temple and wanted to go there in person to see what it had to tell us. The energy of this ancient Temple of Osiris is one that cannot really be described, or done justice to with words alone. For me, this space is pervaded by a sense of deep, dark peace, the type that comes only when someone has surrendered their life completely to a higher destiny. When you are ready to let go and move with the flow of the universe then you will find yourself in Abydos. Of course, as this book has hopefully made clear, first you have to lose yourself completely in order to be found here.

Once we had arrived and spent some time in the temple, we made our way to the cool interior of The Flower of Life Guesthouse.[41] Elder Ameer Kareem who has lived in Abydos all of his life is one of those unique and humble teachers who has the ability to look through your eyes and into the core of your soul. That night he took me to the rooftop of the guesthouse to meditate and tune in to the messages of my dreams. Anointed with sacred oils and with the sweet, musky incense smoke filling my lungs, he placed warm hands on my temples and began to mutter under his breath as he read the story of my soul. I felt the threads and wefts of narratives flowing from my heart through the skin of his fingertips and into his consciousness. After a long silence, his soft voice broke through the sounds of the night:

"You must start to believe the messages you receive from Spirit. Believe them and speak them regardless of the consequences. You will speak these things and some will listen. Those who do not, will in time come to see the truth. Speak with clarity and do not fear."

Thus is the magic of Egypt. Whatever we carry in our heart comes to life. Whatever our soul wishes to be made known to us, will be spoken. Few come here until they are ready to take responsibility for giving birth to their soul story. To force entry is to pay a steep price. To come before one is ready to 'die', will invite chaos and pain. Yet once arrived, depths of bliss are available to all who invite it in with an open heart and surrendered mind. In the years since meeting, Hassan and I have hosted many alchemical journeys in this land and the magic between us continues to deepen. I believe we reunite with the key characters in our story at precisely the right time. The universe always knows when and why. We must become adept at listening.

The universe always knows when and why.
We must become adept at listening.

On the eve of my sixth journey to this land, a friend of mine Giles Hutchins[42] wrote to me. To this day his words are one of the most accurate and eloquent descriptions of the essence of Egypt that I have ever heard:

'The journey has begun for you. Be prepared Genevieve – the ancient wisdom ways of esoteric Egypt are powerful and quite merciless at times. Be prepared to walk the razor's edge and to go through not just a 'dark night of the soul' but a few of them, as the spirals twist you down and around...There will be depression, but that will lead to deeper 'knowing' and deeper 'self' – beyond our human stories...You will be going far beyond any story of 'I' or for that matter 'we' and into waters without charts...and so on the one hand, be prepared, on the other, nothing can prepare you, only faith, trust, courage and of course love, the very thing you are exploring.'

The next day whilst driving back to Luxor along parched desert roads, Hassan turned to me. Gently laying his hand on top of mine he asked, "*Sister, where do you go next on your travels?*"

Giving his hand a squeeze I smiled and said, "*I head back to the United States, dear one. I am going home to see my family in Colorado.*"

A rare flash of concern passed over his typically jovial face. With worry in his voice he asked, "*But sister, isn't it dangerous there? I mean you could get kidnapped, raped or killed. We hear of this happening to women all the time in America.*"

I had to smother a giggle as the multitude of European voices that had warned me of the same dangers in Egypt came ringing back in my ears.

"*Don't worry Habibi, I will be careful. After all, it's my home too and it will care for me just like you protect me here.*"

As we drove on in companionable silence, I had to marvel internally. I guess humans really do share the same stories about the things we fear.

UNITY

HUMANS REALLY DO SHARE THE SAME STORIES
ABOUT THE THINGS WE FEAR.

THE MIRROR

CAN YOU SEE YOURSELF REFLECTED IN THE EYES OF OTHERS?

We – It can be hard and humbling to face our shadows. One of the most transformative practices is to work with the principle of the 'sacred mirror'. Ask someone close to you to tell you where, when and with whom they witness you exerting a need to control, where they see you forcing strong opinions/judgments or where you seem to be trying too hard to influence the natural course of life's events. If you can hear and receive their feedback, the output will provide you with rich material with which to alchemize.

In a world experienced through the story of unity, we really are connected to everyone and everything around us. Fully accepting this can be a challenge at first, especially when we have been taught to believe the opposite and to project our innermost desires, judgments and beliefs onto the people and places in our lives. One of the fastest ways to become aware of our projected fears and judgments is to invite them into our awareness so they can be claimed, worked with and dissolved.

Chief Black Spotted Horse

> Our true family waits for us
> As we travel the pathways of our soul
> Joining the dots between past and future
> Reminding us to come home

I felt the plane start to drop and looked up to see the Black Hills of South Dakota stretching out across the frozen winter landscape. I was landing in Rapid City for a meeting with Chief Black Spotted Horse[43] of the Lakota Sioux. He and I had been introduced to each other via email by a mutual friend who had heard him speaking of the Star Nations. I knew instantly that we must meet each other. Once again I was following the call to adventure, leading me off on a trail that I had no idea where it would end. It was simultaneously scary and exhilarating.

Grabbing my bag and the keys to a brand new white jeep from the tiny airport terminal, I pressed the green call button on my US cell phone.

"*Gen*!" I heard his deep, musical voice greet me from the other end of the phone. "*I am at the hotel already – see you soon my friend.*"

I gulped. I could feel my ego starting to throw up its habitual protection barriers to keep me safely confined within my comfort zone. These 'chance' meetings never happened by accident and always led me into new adventures. I firmly reminded myself that my soul was in charge. After all – it had never led me astray.

The automatic doors slid open for me as I walked into the brightly lit reception of the Best Western hotel in Rapid City. Both the sofas in front of me were empty and the only person who appeared to be there was the brightly smiling receptionist who beamed at me as I looked around. Then my attention pulled to the left and I noticed a man sitting in one of the voluminous armchairs sipping coffee from a large paper MacDonald's cup. I knew immediately it was him. He grinned at me and stood up, coming over to enfold me in a big bear hug. Without saying a word, he turned me gently towards a glass cabinet towards the back of the room that displayed the full regalia of a Lakota Chief in his ceremonial eagle feather bonnet and buckskin robes.

"*See this*?" he said. "*This is me, Chief Black Spotted Horse.*"

I smiled. This was my first meeting with Izzy Zephier: nephew of Lame Deer and descendant of Black Elk and Chief Iron Wing who rode with Crazy Horse. He is one of the wisest and most humble men I have ever met.

Later that evening after we had settled, I found myself sitting cross-legged in front of him. He took up a position opposite on a chair by a window where we could see dusk falling. After saying a blessing and brushing me lightly with his eagle feather bonnet, he began. He started with the stories of his youth. Growing up on the South Dakota reservations hadn't been easy and it was a world that had been the cause of much anger, guilt and personal pain for me as a white American. Ever since I was a little girl, every time we drove through the native reservations I would cry for the injustices committed against a people submitted to mass genocide and suffering. I knew that this horror had been repeated the world over many times, but for some reason the agony of the North American native peoples has touched me the deepest.

My own ancestral heritage is 98% European, something that I have struggled to connect with for many years due to the vast amount of horror inflicted on the world stemming from the politics, economics and social structures of these lands. However, our stories are determined by the temporal and spatial lens through which we tell them. If we go far enough back, or change our context, then we find a new perspective on even the darkest elements of our history. I know amazing souls who have, through forgiveness and surrender, found the love in their hearts to absolve horrific acts of abuse, war and violence. In a time when increasing numbers of people are discovering our shared human heritage through DNA testing and ancestry studies, I sense we have a unique opportunity to create a modern mythology based on interconnection and global human responsibility. In my work across the world, I have increasingly found myself surrendering to the larger narratives of earth time, which reminds us that as a species, we are simply a tiny speck on the timeline of our planet.

However, as Laurel once reminded me, *"We are born in certain places and lands for a reason,"* and I felt a deep connection to the indigenous peoples of the northern US. Their pain had been like an open wound to me throughout the years and I had repeatedly tried to bury it, hiding from what it might mean to my story. Now, sitting here in front of Izzy, I had no other choice but to confront it head on. As I listened to him telling me story after story of death, torture and his path to the way of the true warrior I allowed my tears to fall. If he noticed he didn't say. After a brief pause of silence, his storytelling shifted tempo and sensing my readiness, he began to tell me about the end of days and his vision of our human future:

"The people of earth have strayed too far off the path set by Wakan Tanka, the Creator. The mess that has been created by the white man will have to be cleansed so that we can start again. This time that clearance will come in the form of fire and earth changes. A long time ago, I had a vision sent to me from Crazy Horse himself. In my vision, a white horse came and took me out into the stars. In the Spirit world there are four horses: the black, the red, the yellow and the white. The Creator sent the black horse first, bringing the original instruction of how to live on this sacred place. Then the red and yellow horses traveled together: they brought all the song and ceremonies for humankind. But soon after, humankind decided to go the other way into the material world. So now people have gone too far, and we are in a time of wars, disease and chaos. The Creator is telling us to stop and come back to the original instruction. If you look at where we are, then you will see that everything is out of balance because the Creator didn't say to go this way. Everything has to be undone. If humankind doesn't do this soon, then the Creator will release the white horse of destruction to reset us back to the original instruction.

"It is time for us to learn the original ways from the elders, for those who remember to take up the ancient laws and walk once again on the true path. It is my job to create a place of safety and sanctuary for peoples of all colors and nations who would come as they are called. The Star Nations have told me more of this in the sweat lodge ceremonies. This sacred land will be somewhere in the Black Hills."

We had been sitting for hours and my back was aching. So was my heart.

"Why must it be this way, Izzy?" I asked him, heavy with sadness for the upcoming times of trouble if his visions came to pass. He sat there for a moment before taking off his bandana and wiping eyes that had become as tearful as mine during his narrative.

"Because we have strayed too far from the path set out for us by the Creator. Because we have forgotten the sacred laws that keep balance with all of life. Because we need to begin anew from a place where all the nations of earth can live in unity together with our brothers and sisters on earth."

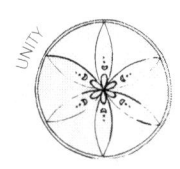

My body involuntarily shivered with delight as Izzy sat in the passenger seat next to me and started to sing a traditional Lakota song. It was hauntingly beautiful and achingly sad. We were headed to Bear Butte: an ancient sacred place on the edge of the Black Hills, renowned for vision quests and visitations from the Star Nations (angelic beings and extraterrestrials). Bear Butte stood tall and imposing against the pale yellow grasses of the plains. We drove past the tourist car park and headed down a small track to the side of the ranger station, one reserved for the native peoples. As we parked the car, I looked up and saw the willow bark skeletons of several sweat lodges perched on its slopes. I was experiencing a strong humming vibration within my body. Izzy handed me a bundle of things that included a tobacco pouch and a large blanket. Shivering at the icy wind that whipped all around us, we carefully made our way across the snow-laden bridge towards the lowest sweat lodge. I sensed the presence of the star beings here and watched Izzy to see if he had also tuned into them. If he did, he made no sign of it.

We reached the sweat lodge and he turned around, wrapping me gently in the blanket like a loving grandfather. The humming grew louder and as if the information had been placed in my head, I suddenly knew that it was coming from the Butte itself. I had been shown these places before in meditation: vortices where it is easy for our star friends to traverse down the dimensional levels in order to do their work on earth.

Izzy started to sing. It was a powerful song of calling. "*Wakan Tanka, grandfathers, witness this woman Genevieve. She has come for your blessing. She has come to dedicate her life to the giving of her gifts on the earth and in the stars. She asks for your help.*"

He turned to me. Moving me gently forwards into the place where he had been standing, he said, "*You too can say a prayer.*"

Taking a moment to gather my thoughts and feelings so I could adequately express the waves of energy wanting to be spoken through me, I took a deep breath and then said to the ancestors: "*Wakan Tanka, my brothers and sisters on earth and in the cosmos, I surrender my life in service of all beings. In service of life. In service of the love that binds us. I ask for your help and guidance. Take me to places and people who need me the most. Show me how to awaken their memories of who they truly are. How to live lives that are in unity with life and the laws of creation.*"

I turned to Izzy who was smiling his approval. Reaching into my pocket, I took out a bright blue crystal that I had found mysteriously in there a few days before. I couldn't remember where I had got it from but knew that now was the time to offer it. It sparkled brightly in the late afternoon winter sun as I turned to lay it on the altar space in front of the sweat lodge. Silently I thanked the beings that were gathered for their work, balancing the energies of earth and the cosmos; work that goes unnoticed by the majority of people on earth.

Standing up, I faced Izzy. He reached out to hand me something. I saw with a gasp of surprise that it was the red cloth that had been hanging at the door of the sweat lodge in front of which we were standing.

"*This is a waluta,*" he said, handing me the bundle. It seemed to crackle in my hands with energy as I took it reverently. "*We use these to protect us as we enter into ceremony. It will also protect you as you journey from this place. Smudge it every day at dawn and repeat your prayer to Wakan Tanka. It will keep you safe.*"

I felt so honored. It must have shown in my face because Izzy cracked a smile. He stood next to me and wrapped us both in the blanket. The late afternoon sunlight took on a deep golden hue and the air sparkled with the presence of our wider family who stood there with us witnessing life unfolding.

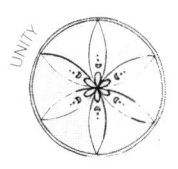

Our third day together had dawned bright and cold. After another beautiful evening of storytelling we had both risen early, shared a simple breakfast of oatmeal and toast before jumping in my jeep and heading out to a favorite place of his wife Nora, who had passed away some years ago. As we drove along the curving canyon roads, I was stunned by the beauty of the narrow, deep rock walls and the winding creek that had cut them over the millennia: intoxicated by the beauty of the country of my birth.

Izzy asked me to pull over in a lay-by on the side of the road and we got out, taking with us a few ceremonial things we had prepared. Instead of the songs and prayers I was becoming accustomed to, Izzy started to talk with her, giving her the news and telling her how well their boys were doing. I was deeply touched. When he had finished we threw a piece of gray Saracen stone that I had brought all the way from Avebury as an offering down into the creek. He turned to me saying, *"You can speak with her too."*

As he headed back to the jeep, I turned to face the tree and could almost feel Nora's spirit surrounded by other grandmothers. Taking a deep breath, I surrendered my mind and allowed my heart to speak through me.

"Nora," I started, *"Grandmothers. All my life I have been surrounded by the Warriors. By men. I know how to heal them; how to love them and care for their souls. But I sense such a great need in* the women now. I ask that you teach me the women's ways so that I can also play a part in awakening the women. Your help would be received with much gratitude."

I sensed an approval in the request from the gathering of spirits on the other side of the creek.

With one more bow of my head in honor of them, I turned and made my way back to the car where Izzy waited. Climbing in without a word, I started the engine and pulled out, heading back the way we had come. After a few bends of the road, Izzy turned to me and said, "*Nora said what you asked back there was good. That they will help you.*"

I felt relieved that my heartfelt prayer had been heard and wondered what adventures would await me in fulfilling it. After a few miles driving in silence he turned to me and said quietly, "*You are not who I thought you were, Genevieve.*"

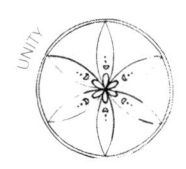

I was zipping up my case as I heard a gentle knocking at the door. Smiling, I knew it would be him. I went over and opened the door to let Izzy in. It was early and I was packing for my flight back to Denver. He came in, gave me a hug and sat down at the table. I finished what I was doing and realizing that I had a few moments before having to leave, sat down beside him. We just looked at each other in silence for a few moments, acknowledging without words all that had passed between us.

"*I will be back, uncle,*" I said, breaking the silence.

He looked at me long and hard and then started to rearrange a few items that were on the table in a curving line. "*Look here,*" he said tapping the table to ensure he had my attention. He pointed at the first object that happened to be a pepper shaker. "*Whatever is ours, we will catch up to in time. Don't try and go too fast, you might miss a step."* He illustrated this by moving his finger from the pepper, past the salt and onto the napkin holder. Going back to the salt, he continued: *"Don't try to take what is not yours, you will regret it."* He moved from the salt off the table and towards a flyer that was lying next to the TV. *"Just keep putting one foot in front of the other and if you are true to your path then everything that is yours...everything...you will catch up to in time."*

JUST KEEP PUTTING ONE FOOT IN FRONT OF THE OTHER.

I reached out a hand and squeezed his in gratitude, his words ringing directly into my heart. *"This is your home Gen,"* he said. *"You have been away for too long. I don't like the thought of you being out in the world in the times that will come. Here I can protect you. Here I can keep you safe."*

I started to cry and stood up, giving him a big hug. As I was enfolded into his arms, I heard him say, *"I love you. Come home soon."*

Wiping my eyes and standing up, I looked at the warrior in front of me and said, *"When the time is right uncle, I will come back. I will come home."* I was reminded of the six-year-old girl who had sworn a similar oath on a plane to England all those years ago.

The shadow of sickness

> Can we really know life
> Without knowing death?
> Can we face our mortality
> And see the beauty that lies in every breath?

What is it about the human mind that forgets so quickly? It seems to me that in many ways we live our lives in ever repeating cycles of forgetting and remembering, forgetting and remembering. We move in and out of our stories in fractal patterns of resolution, our focus at any point determining the breadth, color and tone of the version of reality that unfolds around us.

What is it about the human mind that forgets so quickly?

One of the most dramatic cycles of remembering usually occurs when we are faced with our own mortality, or that of people close to us. In the modern western mythology we have very few stories that help us to make meaning and come to terms mentally and emotionally with death. This problem is perpetuated by our obsession with remaining forever young, vibrant and healthy. We rarely honor the process of aging. Most of us arrive at the door to greet death unprepared and often fearful of our own annihilation. The biological fact that a part of us will cease to exist at the moment of our physical passing is flavored by our particular cosmological belief system, but is an inescapable truth nonetheless. Which part of us dies is the subject of much debate and your answer to this narrative question will often determine the sorts of death lessons that you are faced with as you progress through your journey. Yet facing it is inevitable for us all. Perhaps it is the final ultimate act of unification?

Having danced around the story of death at various points in my life, it was not one that scared me anymore. Or so I thought. My parents are both relatively healthy individuals and my sisters and I had managed largely to escape our childhood years with only a handful of breaks, bumps and standard childhood illnesses between us. I therefore found myself unjustifiably confident and with my head fully buried in the sand when the time came for my personal lesson with this powerful creative force.

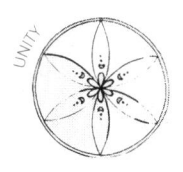

Something had been nipping at the edge of my awareness like a mosquito buzzing in the darkness whilst we are trying to sleep. A month or so prior to this, a good friend of mine had become sick. Really sick, really fast. At the startlingly young age of 32, she had discovered (after several rounds of misdiagnosis) that she had a highly aggressive form of myxoid liposarcoma cancer. Intuitively, I knew something was wrong before I had sent the text message and received her distraught reply. Little did I realize just how connected we were to be in this journey until the pain started. Perhaps it was all the sand in my eyes and ears from having buried myself in a cultural belief of physical immortality. Or perhaps it was just that my old story of invincible health was now starting to wear thin and ragged around the edges. Either way, the pains were now reaching a level where I could no longer ignore them.

    I clutched the steering wheel as another agonizing cramp rippled through the left side of my lower abdomen. I was attempting to drive to the airport for a week of client work in Germany and had started to wonder if that was a good idea after all. Cold waves of fear washed over my belly, swamping my rational mind. *'Don't be ridiculous,'* I said to myself. *'You are just imagining it.'* I had been oscillating between these different excuses to normalize things for a week or so now and the ragged stories of attempted self-comfort were all crumbling. There was a growing shadow of fear taking over my consciousness inch-by-inch, moment-by-moment. Like gray clouds that move slowly across the horizon, I knew they would eventually obscure any sun of optimism that I was trying valiantly to maintain.

    "You're fine," Euan would say confidently whenever I spoke to him about it. I wanted really badly to believe him and part of me did.

I trusted his intuition like I trusted my own which emphatically told me that this was a lesson of some kind. The trick is to discover specifically what the lesson is before we rip ourselves in two with anxiety.

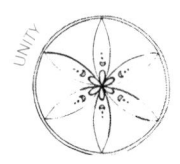

"*Ouch,*" I gasped as quietly as I could under my breath as another stab of pain hit me.

"*You okay?*" Euan asked.

"*Not really,*" I said through gritted teeth. *"It feels as though there is something swelling inside my right ovary."*

I tried to breathe through the cocktail of panic and physical anguish. Three people we knew in the last few months alone had contracted cancer; one had already died. No matter how many times I had meditated, called in healing energy, and breathed through it, the situation had not improved. In fact, it had steadily worsened.

"*Drink some water, we are almost there,*" Euan said from the driver's seat, passing me the bottle. We were heading down to Devon to go camping. Euan, being generally averse to roughing-it, had as usual opted for the 'glamping' end of this spectrum. We were driving towards a luxury eco pod.

Half an hour later, we pulled up the driveway to a cute little farm. Wood was piled up against the side of the old farmhouse and I could see several solar panel blocks standing by a small paved stone path. It cut its way through a long, lush green field of grass that led to one of the most impressive 'tents' I have ever seen. Standing a good 15 feet high was the large hexagonal structure of an eco pod. The frame was made out of a honeycomb structure of metal scaffolding, fitted together perfectly to look just like a giant pollen spore. Over this, forming the outer skin was a white tarpaulin that became transparent at the front end to create a large, panoramic window. Peering inside, I gasped with amazement as I saw a large double bed strewn with pillows and throw rugs, a dining room table, sofa, two chairs and a large movie projector hung from the ceiling. The pod itself was positioned on a wide wooden platform, overlooking green fields full of sheep and cows peacefully grazing as if they knew that their home was paradise on earth.

"Well, you certainly know how to do camping, darling," I said with a wide grin as Euan carried our bags up the path.

Later that evening, I laid stretched out in the double bed, my tummy full of great food and my legs curled comfortably over Euan's as he read next to me. We had enjoyed a wonderful dinner at a local pub and had spent the evening laughing and loving. I found myself looking out of the wide panoramic window up at the rising moon above the cows' field, my mind returning again to ponder the lessons that I was learning.

I had done all the usual precautionary checks with the doctor and they couldn't find anything wrong with me. I had even gone to the hospital for a scan which had also turned up nothing. Yet the growing pain in my abdomen didn't stem from nothing. I couldn't work this one out rationally, so the only choice I had left was to submit to the process. Surrender to my pain and my fear to see where it would lead me. As my eyes started to close, I had an image of a teacher of mine, saying *"Ask fear what it has to tell you."*[44] My breathing deepened and my head became heavy on my pillow as I fell into dreams.

ASK FEAR WHAT IT HAS TO TELL YOU.

In the inky black darkness of night, I became aware of a snapping noise from somewhere close. As I listened, my mental catalogue managed to identify it as the sound of plastic against metal. Wind was whipping around the frame of the pod and stirring the outer skin into a frenzied hammering. Even though I was safely tucked up in our warm bed, I was now fully awake and aware of a deep sense of discomfort and anxiety. My heart was pounding and my diaphragm was tight with tension. I was afraid. I let out a sigh laden with exhaustion. I was so sick and tired of being scared of an unknown threat.

'Okay, enough's enough,' I said to myself internally, followed by 'Jesus, Gen, get a grip would you.' I breathed deeply and decided to get up so as not to wake Euan. Climbing slowly out of bed in the darkness, I managed to grab his hoody from the sofa where it had been thrown a few hours before. Pulling it on over my head, I shivered as the cold cotton met my fevered skin. Groping around using the bed frame as a guide, I moved into the center of the rug that was thrown across the middle of the floor and sat down, pulling the hem of the hoodie over my knees and to the floor so I was cocooned in it. For a while I just rocked backwards and forwards in the dark, listening to the wind and acknowledging the ever present pain on the right side of my abdomen.

Then, giving in, I started to cry. At first a few tears trickled silently down my cheeks but they quickly developed into sobs that came from the bottom of my heart and ripped through my body. Sobs that felt as though they came from other places and other times in my life. I let them come. I let them tear me apart. I let them escape and ricochet out into the night, calling in the spirit of fear and death to attend on me. After a time, I felt my voice rising in my belly and whispered to the darkness.

"Come on, let's do this.
Show me what you are trying to teach me.

"Let's assume that I am going to die in the next six months.
Let's assume I have cancer that hasn't been caught.
What do you want to show me, fear?"

Silence. The wind howling. The snapping of the skin of our pod in the dark. And then...an image started to present itself to me in the darkness. I saw myself dying. I saw the faces of doctors and the tears of my family. I saw Euan and the kids trying to put a brave face on things and crying quietly at night into their pillows. Then I saw something that I didn't expect: my smiling face staring up at the bright sunshine. Me, bent over a laptop writing. Writing this book. Me, enfolded within the strength of Euan's arms. I felt joy. I felt love. I felt exhilaration in experiencing the things and people that are most important to me in this life.

>Euan's kiss
>The mountains drenched in sunlight
>Playing with my stepchildren
>The laughter of my sisters
>The proud look on my mother's face
>My father calling me 'kiddo'
>My book, finished and bound on the table
>The sun
>The moon
>The damp summer grass
>The Nile at dawn
>Stars wheeling above my head
>The smell of a kiva

These were the things that life was really made for experiencing. These were the important things. I smiled back at fear in the dark and reached out to embrace it as a part of me. I was complete. I knew what it had been trying to tell me:

>Pay attention
>Stay focused
>Love
>Write
>Love some more
>Be grateful for each and every day you have on this beautiful earth
>Merge fully with the process of life
>Unify with death

I now knew what my fear had been trying to tell me.

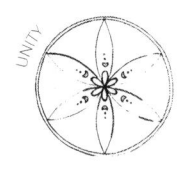

I felt a pinprick as my new homeopathic healer flicked an acupuncture needle out of my lower leg. Smiling, I looked up and marveled at how much he looked like Merlin the wizard. Trust the universe to deliver me to the archetypal energy healer!

"Well, I am very pleased with your progress indeed, Princess," he said, turning to consult his notes.

"*You should be*," I laughed back at him. "*You have not only managed to balance my hormones so that the pain is completely gone, but you have also regulated my heartbeat, cured my allergy of horses and sorted out my metabolism.*"

"I aim to serve, Princess. I aim to serve."

I guess sometimes all we are expected to do is make friends with our fear and everything changes. I had to move through the darkness in order to understand the full extent of my love for life.

A few weeks later I received a text from my friend that read: "*I am cancer free!*" Looking out of the window of the house I shared with Euan, I smiled and silently thanked the universe for the magic of interconnection. As one of us heals, so we hold a similar space of healing for those we love to come into. With deep gratitude to fear, I sat back down at my laptop and continued to write.

MY LEGACY

WILL YOU COMMIT TO LIVING YOUR BIGGEST STORY?

Me – Imagine that the universe is your boss and that you are being called to give a keynote speech telling the story of your legacy on earth. What would you say? What would you commit to? What can you do to make the most difference to the world whilst you are living? If you wish, find a place in nature and create a space where you can speak this dedication aloud to the universe. Ask yourself, once done, if what you did was powerful enough. Do you feel energized? Do you feel your oath in every atom of your being? If not, do this again and again until you do!

We – Making a public dedication is a powerful way to hold yourself accountable for bringing a new story of unity into your life. If you feel called to engage with the magic of manifestation in this way, create your declaration of service and speak it publically to your people, the earth and the cosmos. Make no mistake, you will be heard.

The difference between dreams and destiny is in one word: action. We must take action on the path of our destiny to bring it into form in our lives. The first step of turning a dream or a vision into reality is to commit to it, preferably publically, so you have a team of witnesses who can remind you of your story-making path. Then you have to find the discipline to act on this again and again and again.

Grandmother vine

Ancient teachers reside in the earth
In her plants, minerals and waters
They are waiting for us to listen
To speak their language and to remember

Tobacco smoke drifted past my nostrils in spiraling tendrils, weaving its dance through the darkened maloka. Outside I could hear the sounds of the jungle at night, awake and pulsing with life in myriad forms, weaving together in an orchestra of song. I was deep in the heart of the Peruvian rainforest on another adventure, this time in the safe hands of my friend, sister and plant medicine teacher, Rebekah Shaman.[45]

I hadn't intended to explore plant medicines but the universe had other ideas. Through a series of synchronistic events, I had been strongly 'advised' ('pushed' may have been a better word) to come here and I could think of no better guide than Rebekah, given her decades of experience having lived in the Amazon and been trained by an indigenous Peruvian shaman. She has a unique gift of weaving a container of love within which she catalyzes healing through unification with the earth and her plants.

Nothing prepares you for your first immersion in the Amazon rainforest. It is an ecosystem like none other on earth, an incredible experience of being dropped into the lungs of our living, breathing planet. So here I was, a humble student awaiting my teaching from the earth herself. I stretched out long on my mat, elongating my muscles like a cat, before settling back into a comfortable position and closing my eyes. The earthy, bitter taste of ayahuasca was still lingering on my tongue as I extended my consciousness outwards into the darkness, wondering what her gifts would be. It was the second of five ceremonies with this powerful plant medicine as my guide.

The previous night, I had been gifted with an incredible, blissful merging with the cosmos itself followed by the excruciating experience of becoming the living system of the jungle. To say it had been overwhelming would have been the understatement of the century. (You try becoming aware of every living being in the rainforest simultaneously!) I had also been shown the fractal nature of the cosmos, where the micro mirrors the macro, and every 'reality' is holographic in nature containing an element of everything else. My first journey with the grandmother vine (as Rebekah calls her) had been largely positive and I had been left feeling confident in my ability to ride her visions. Perhaps a little too confident.

Tonight, as I relaxed into the flow of the medicine, I felt cosmic arms enfold me once more and lift my consciousness upwards, traveling up along the energy lines of our universe. I was guided towards an immense library where vast archives of energetic codes began to access my soul's energy system, flowing in, through and around me in complex matrices and geometry.

I lost all sense of time and the external reality had left my human body lying on a mat in a dark room and moved in between worlds, submitting to the process. Gradually, the codes stopped and I became aware that I now stood alone on some kind of dark platform made of a substance that resembled black granite. In the distance, I could hear human crying and somewhere my mind registered that it was the sound of people next to my physical body. Suddenly the black platform that I was standing on shook so hard that I almost fell from it. Coming back into my human body with a jolt, I realized that my ears could hear someone close to me throwing up violently and several people sobbing. I was overcome with a need to try and help them and yet when I opened my eyes, the room was full of swirling colored patterns and I couldn't see normally. The thought that I was blind sent a wave of panic down my spine and I started to breathe faster and more deeply, to calm my racing heart.

Energy started to course through my body. Waves of fear and confusion washed through my cells. My body started to ache as if I had been beaten by sticks and I became aware of growing knots of pain in my heart and stomach that somehow weren't all my own. At first I assumed that I was tuning in to the pain of the people around me, but the agony quickly expanded and widened. It was as if I could physically feel the fear of all the people on earth crying out to be saved from their feelings of isolation and despair. Excruciating pain ripped its way down the front of my body and I felt as though I was being cut open with a razor blade. Somewhere amongst the experience, my mind noticed the corresponding adrenaline rush of my physical body responding to the experience and I wondered whether it was 'real'.

'*Okay Gen, calm down,*' my human self said, trying to regain some form of control over my experience – in vain. Instinctively, I reached out for my 'spiritual support crew', as I often did now when I was struggling, yet was alarmed to find that none of them appeared or answered. The angels had fallen silent. My fear ramped up another level with the thought that I might have to move through this alone. As I breathed deeply into my chest, I was shaken once more as though the ground beneath me buckled and I found myself falling into a deep blackness within my inner world. I was vaguely aware that my body reached out and pulled my blanket over my head, folding my body into the fetal position. I started to lose any sense of who I was or what was happening.

As I fell, everything I knew about 'me' started to melt away. First, my train of thoughts ceased and everything became silent. The silence brought with it relief from the fear and relative peace. Next, I realized that my sense of self and memories that went with 'me' were fading fast. This was accompanied by the question, *'Will I emerge from this experience or is this the end?'* Throughout all my wild and crazy experiences over the years, I have almost always maintained the knowing of who I was, managing to keep my little fingernail clinging to the cliff of my current identity no matter what was happening. This time, from somewhere deep inside, I knew I had to let even that go; to surrender utterly to dissolution and allow myself to be completely annihilated. I hesitated, balking at the challenge in front of me. *'What if I never return?'* a part of me wondered in the darkness. *'What if I die here in the void?'*

Time hung and stopped. Sensations (not entirely unpleasant) were still coursing through my body, shaking me with contractions as if a new being was about to be born.

'The baby doesn't cling to the womb,' I sensed. The caterpillar emerges from the cocoon. *'If I am to die, then let me die consciously,'* I said to the dark and with that, I let go. My fingernail slipped off the cliff edge and I let go of my self, my life. My breath became no-one. Utterly nothing. Falling into the darkness of every no-thing and every-thing.

Silence.

Stillness.

Pregnant death.

The void of destruction and creation.

Pulsing, vibrating frequencies.

Peace.

I. There was still an 'I' present and knowing itself.

Me. There was a sense of me. Some kind of separate self.

Puzzling.

Curious.

Gradually the 'I' that remained in the darkness began to realize that there was a sense of 'realizing'. There was something or someone puzzling in the nothingness. I felt a primal urge to give shape to the knowing 'I' and considered the best way to create that form. From a place beyond thought, I began to breathe. Then 'I' became aware that somewhere in the middle of the breathing was a heart. Then 'I' knew that from somewhere and some-when, there was a heart that could be expanded and followed.

A piercing white light appeared as a tiny spark within 'me' and grew rapidly, radiating its fine light like a prism into the blackness. A beating began somewhere deep within the dark and synchronized with the light. The throbbing umm, umm, umm reached out, radiating like a star being born. I concentrated on growing the light and it responded, taking on rainbow hues and flowing textures, soft like silken streams that glided outwards in all directions. The sensations in my body began once more and form and shape became apparent. 'It' was beautiful, and there was once again a sense of self to register the beauty.

Then a question came to me through the darkness as my light grew. It was not a voice or words *per se*, but the essence was registered in the light that was 'me' nonetheless. It asked me possibly the most difficult question I had ever heard:

'*Are you willing to surrender your soul?*'

The 'me' that had become aware of itself as light, hesitated. In soul form I was beautiful beyond compare. Immortal. Essential. Infinite. Could I surrender my eternal spark in order to unify completely with life? Could I give up my highest form in service of the plan of creation that I couldn't understand?

I hovered there in the eternal darkness, considering my answer. Yet there was really only ever one that I could or would choose to give. The choiceless choice of our highest unfolding.

My light beamed its answer.

'*Yes...I have surrendered everything else, why not this too?*'

All of a sudden from above me, a glowing white hand reached through the darkness. I reached out instinctively, grasping it whilst in the same moment noticing that I had a hand with which to grasp and by which to be pulled. I felt 'myself' being drawn upwards and enfolded in a warm embrace of soft white light. It was the light of pure love I had felt in this form only a few times in my life. I immediately recognized the being who was now holding me in his arms like a brother. It was the same being that I had seen years ago walking through the bright sunlit garden.

"Well done sister," he said. "*You had to prove to yourself that you could return unaided. Melt and reform. Find the light of your own soul in the darkness of creation and then surrender even that. Create your own form renewed as the Creator itself.*"

I was once again surrounded by familiar angels and guides who had come to witness my re-membering and I felt the light of a thousand kisses showered onto me from all dimensions. The infinite pain of the human world had led me through its center into the infinite bliss of the erotic life force itself that was beyond and inclusive of this pain. Without the pain of separation, we cannot know the bliss of reunion.

WITHOUT THE PAIN OF SEPARATION,
WE CANNOT KNOW THE BLISS OF REUNION.

Then, slowly, the scene shifted once more and a pulse of energy raced through me, shifting my form into that of an immense bird. My head tilted upwards to an azure blue sky whilst my arms lifted, becoming rainbow-hued wings. The piercing cry of the eagle burst through lips that became a delicately arched, razor sharp beak. I rose up, stretching my wings, and launched into the eternal sky. The eagle's cry broke my lips again and again. I was calling. I could feel the currents of energy guiding my avian body upwards beyond the earth. As I circled the earth, flying amongst the stars, I heard an answer in the distance and my sharp eyes saw what I was aching for: my golden brother. Intense joy welled up inside of me as we recognized each other and the balance our energy brought to the planet. We wheeled together and spun vibrant patterns in the cosmos in our joy of being embodied once more.

He and She
Form and Formlessness
Separate and Unified

Heading in opposite directions, he traveled west to east, close to the earth flying in spirals, shining his golden light of creation and focused form. I turned sun wise, spinning the container for all things, weaving life from the divine love of the universe, held within my rainbow wings. Around and around we flew until all of the earth was covered in our shared light. Our story, our family, our love for a world in the process of being reborn as we were. Meeting at the apex of our flight, we flew and merged into each other. Wing tip met wing tip. Body met body. As one we returned to our source. I melted into a bliss beyond anything I have ever known. A bliss that comes when we become the essence of the universe itself.

After a time, I opened my eyes and I became aware of myself as Genevieve lying on the floor in the middle of the Peruvian jungle. I felt as though eons had passed whilst I had journeyed, rather than just one night. Realizing that I had my mind back once again, I started to reflect on my journey and the initiations that I had passed through. I saw how pivotal my experience of the darkness had been in order to deliver me reborn into an understanding of light. How excruciating it had been to feel the pain of the world, believing that we are separate from each other so that I could then unite with my soul, truly becoming my rainbow form in order to weave a new story for the earth.

I felt the comforting closeness of my angel friends and merged with their consciousness wordlessly seeking their wisdom.

'Tough Bliss,' they said. *'This is your journey on earth.'*

With a shiver of recognition, I knew that they had just confirmed the title for the book you are now reading.

Deer Heart Woman

> Everything we encounter is here to teach us
> To help us re-member our unity
> To surrender to the forces of creation
> Allowing ease and joy to be our foundation

Email from Izzy Zephier, Chief Black Spotted Horse, 19th May, 2015.

Hey Gen. I have some time and want to tell you where your name comes from. A few years ago, I was out on a survival walk. It was a very beautiful and memorable time. I got to meet and visit with many of the relatives who live out there. Anyway, I was walking along the river bank when I came around the bend and there standing in front of me was this huge buck, a doe and a baby fawn. We proceeded to visit and he started to tell me some things. All the while, the baby was peeking around its mother, very shy. The mother and baby were standing behind the father. I was shown the beauty of the family and all that goes with it, so as I was thinking of you the other day suddenly the image of that time came and they told me that you have the heart of the mother deer. Love and kindness is all around you and then your name was given: Deer Heart Woman. These names are very powerful and very sacred. Very important is the responsibility that comes with the name. We have to carry the name and also live up to it. You are already doing it in many ways. The rest will come in short time as you continue on your journey. I will be here for you whenever you need me. Connections are very important no matter how big or how small. Sometimes the big are small and the small are big. I am happy, big connections small connections, they are all the same. It is what we do with them. Stay true on your path and then all answers will be there for you. We only have to stay alert and always awake of everything happening around us. Journey well DEER HEART WOMAN.

I had been given a new sacred name.

My mind was full of questions. What did this mean and why had she come to me now? Then, as I started to contemplate her energy, synchronicities occurred that led me deeper into the medicine at the heart of deer.

I found myself traveling with my friend, teacher and adopted aunt, Brooke Medicine Eagle,[46] to the Crow Reservation in Montana. Brooke and I had met when she was at Heyoka's place when I had arrived in the spring. We had fallen in love with each other immediately and knew that we had been matched by the Creator to do important work in the world. We have been friends ever since and she is one of the most special people in my life. It was Brooke who would hold space for me on my second vision quest and introduce me to a deeper level of my medicine.

I was being called to listen deeper than I have ever listened before, just as the deer listen with their large ears to the subtle sounds of the forest. By now, I had learned to recognize the sacred speech of the universe that draws us out of our comfort zones and deeper into the mystery. Its voice had been dancing in my heart for a while. When I mentioned to Brooke that I wanted to find some time on the land to tune into its voice, away from the distraction and noise of daily life she had smiled and said, "*I know just the place.*"

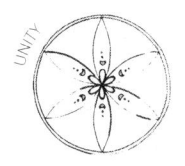

Sacred Ground International[47] was founded by Tanah Whitemore: an exquisite artist, wisdom keeper and global visionary. She was also to become a friend and elder sister to me. From the moment that I saw her and Brooke waving to me from the bottom of the escalator in Billings airport, my heart warmed. I knew we were destined to walk together in this life.

Sacred Ground is a 3,500-acre ranch on the Crow Reservation in Montana where Tanah has lived on and off for most of her life. One of her names, 'Buffalo Woman', was the omen that years later would call her back home after the collapse of her international clothing business. Today, she is the sacred mother for a herd of buffalo that grace the mountain slopes today. Held by the ancient Pryor mountain range with their crystal caves and powerful earth energy lines, Sacred Ground is a unique place on the planet. Its spring waters have been tested to be amongst the highest and purest quality on earth – once you drink of them, they catalyze powerful shifts in your vision and action. Angels, star beings, nature spirits of all kinds and the ancestors are as much residents of this land as the buffalo, bears, coyotes and humans. Their voices are clear and their invitation to step into a greater experience of who we really are is insistent.

"*Why have you come here?*" Tanah asked me as we sat opposite each other at the breakfast table, with the rising sun sending its rays through the wide living room windows to warm our bodies.

I sat in silence for a moment considering my answer. Finally, I surrendered the voice in my head to the one of my soul that I could feel bubbling up in my throat wanting to speak. "*I have come to learn about the universal laws. I have come to understand what it is that the Creator wants me to do in the world.*"

After a pause where she considered my words, Tanah smiled and replied, *"You have come to the right place. My life here is a constant practice of living the universal laws of the Creator, yet this isn't a path that you embark on with ease. This is a place where it is impossible to tell a lie. This is a place of absolute truth. You will leave here understanding who you are and 'why' you are here. Don't concern yourself so much with the 'what' or the 'how'."*

She rose and went into the small, neat kitchen to wash her coffee mug. After she had finished she turned and addressed me again. *"People often come here to find out who they really are. You will discover this and how the universal laws flow through you in a great cosmic story of unity."*

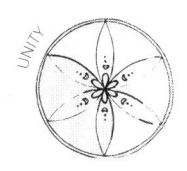

I was lying curled up like a baby, inviting the early morning sun to soak into my cold bones. My bed was a large patch of scented creeping juniper whose home was high up on the planes of the ranch. I had been invited to go out on the land to fast and seek a deepening of the visions that had been coming to me since I had arrived. My prayer, as I had left Tanah and Brooke that morning, had been 'to know myself as the Creator'. Tanah had said that it was a brave prayer.

The past few days had been full of blessings that only a group of women could share. We had cooked and shared delicious food and gone about our tasks on the ranch with presence and deep attention. We had followed the voice of the land, the ancestors and the nature spirits, engaging in activities such as clearing the sacred spring at the foot of the mountain until the water ran clear and steady once more. And all the while we shared our deepest pains and soul's longings in order for them to be held in the communal love and understanding that had built between us. Circles of women the world over engage in these practices to heal each other and the earth with their intentions and actions. It had been powerful work. And I had remembered the voice of the Creator.

All these years after my latent human gifts had begun to awaken, I had developed deep and loving relationships with a number of human and non-human teachers. The angels had become constant companions, the nature spirits danced through my life at differing levels of presence. Certain masters would show up from time to time to gently set me back on track. However, through all of this, somehow, it hadn't occurred to me to seek a direct level of contact with the Great Spirit itself. Perhaps I was still clinging to old paradigm programing around 'not being worthy' or 'not being able'. Or perhaps I simply hadn't reached the point in my journey where I was ready to go right to the source. Either way, I had been reminded out here in the silence of the land that the voice of the Creator is always there, waiting to be engaged with, waiting to be asked. So, I had set out with my prayer to deepen my knowing of my inherent connection with the force of life itself.

Drifting in and out of conscious awareness I was simultaneously aware of my body lying on the juniper with the morning breeze playfully teasing my hair whilst my soul traveled on inner planes. As I moved through the unseen energy pathways of the universe, I heard a voice address me with a direct question: *"So, daughter of the sun, do you want to do this the fast way or the slow way?"*

I paused and considered my answer, feeling that somehow neither of the options I was being presented with fitted with my prayer. After a moment, I replied, *"I want to do this the Creator's way."* Feeling a level of humorous approval from my questioner, the voice returned once more, this time with an instruction.

"Well then, get back on your horse and grow."

My eyes blinked open as I returned fully to my body contemplating the meaning of the statement. Stretching my body long on the ground, I realized that I had been dreaming for over an hour and that the sun was climbing in the sky growing with strength and warmth as it did so. Taking off my coat, I beamed a silent thanks to my solar companion for its life-giving light and made my way back down towards the aspen grove. Within it nestled Moon Rock Springs where crystal clear mountain water flowed out of the inner womb of the earth. Stopping to give thanks to the waters and scoop up a handful of the sacred water to drink, I remembered the five statements of human truth that Tanah had given to me the night before.

The five statements:[48]

1   I am the thoughts of God.

2   All resources are available to me.

3   I have the answer.

4   I am the miracle and everything in my life is a reflection of this.

5   I am enough.

I sat down with my back to one of the aspen trees and, giving thanks for her support, started to meditate on these statements. I realized that if I accepted these as 'my truth', then my life would shift in important ways, namely, I would stop worrying and stressing about 'how' things would happen and trust that if it was for my highest good and the good of others, then the creator in me would, well, create! I also reflected on how much of my time, energy and conscious awareness was currently being taken up by my human brain trying to work out the 'how'. If I started to trust that this process of creation would be taken care of, then I would be able to focus my attention on the 'why' and the 'who' I was choosing to become.

In trusting the inherent wisdom of the Creator to create, I would also begin to drop all judgments of whether the events in my life were 'good' or 'bad'. If I am the 'thoughts of Creator' I reasoned, then there is no good or bad – only creation. I contemplated the sheer amount of latent energy, time and inner resources currently being taken up by my anxieties that would be released were I simply to accept these statements into my world. The edges of my inner belief systems were emerging for transformation.

The edges of my inner belief systems were emerging for transformation.

Stripping off my clothes, I walked naked into the flow of the spring as it cascaded over rocks and tree roots towards the larger creek bed. The wind bathed my skin, blowing it clean of old beliefs and habits that I no longer needed. Reaching down, I anointed the energy centers of my body with the cold spring water, vowing that each one be fully opened and placed in service of the Creator who lived through me. I felt the ancestors gather in a circle around me to witness my ceremonial oath and in the sky above me I saw a young eagle circling low over the creek. I had been witnessed.

Later that day, I sat watching the sun arc down in the west, glowing golden across the pale grasses of the range. A small herd of buffalo were grazing in the distance under the watchful gaze of the mountain. Moments before, a coyote had trotted out of the chokecherry bushes, looking me directly in the eyes before heading off in search of dinner. I had become a resident of this land and its inhabitants were accepting of me as their neighbor.

Contented, I witnessed the deep levels of peace and grace that were flowing through my body, mind and soul as they integrated together in my heart center. Then, from across the creek from where I sat approached a female figure that I instantly recognized. Sitting down cross-legged in front of me so that her knees touched mine, White Buffalo Woman smiled knowingly at me.

"*Sister, you have prayed a powerful prayer today and you have been answered. This one prayer will encompass all other prayers that you have ever or will ever pray.*"

We sat in silence for a moment as the impact of her words sank into my soul. Rising slowly, she kissed the center of my forehead and said over her shoulder as she walked away, "*I will walk with you.*"

I sensed from her parting tone that I was going to need all the help I could get in order to live this prayer.

I will walk with you.

Just as I was about to begin worrying again about the magnitude of my oath or the potential direction that my life would take having given it, a familiar presence arrived and hunkered down next to me, reaching out a hand to take mine in his. I was starting to get to know this being that treated all as his brothers and sisters, and his presence was a comfort to me. Before I could voice my concern, he silenced me with his own golden words: *"You are trying to make this hard again. Why don't you instead make it easy? Let this be easy and let it be full of joy."*

I repeated his invitation in my heart. *'Let it be easy and let it be full of joy.'*

It sat well with me and brought instant relief against the machinations of my ego. Sighing deeply, I returned to the state of peace and sat companionably with him by my side until the sun sank below the horizon. Dusk fell, blissfully calm.

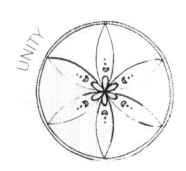

The time had come to leave Sacred Ground. I had finished packing Brooke's car and was hovering around the altar, saying my final goodbyes to the decorated buffalo skull that graced its center. Looking up as Tanah entered the room, she raised her eyebrow, enquiring into the nature of my prayers.

"*Oh, I was just thinking about the sacred name that my uncle Izzy gave me, and praying for clarity*," I responded. "*He had a dream where a mother deer came to him and told him I had the heart of a deer. My name is to be Deer Heart Woman*," I told her.

She smiled and then after a short pause, said softly, "*I am a Deer Warrior. I have a story that might help you to understand the nature of deer medicine.*" After a short pause where her eyes closed part way, allowing her to listen deeply, she continued.

"As the deer joyfully went up the mountain to see the Creator she had no fear anywhere in her being. This was because she knew deeply who she was and that she was a part of creation and life itself. Her heart was so full of excitement to see the Creator that she could only see a joyful outcome to her journey. As she stepped lightly up the mountain, she beheld a huge, dark, demon. When she saw this, she noticed that it must be in pain given it looked so full of anger and sorrow. With only love in her heart, she invited the demon to accompany her to see the Creator, insisting that it would make it feel better. The demon was so taken aback and confused that the deer showed no sign or acknowledgement of its ugly fearsomeness that it paused to question itself. Behind the 0darkness of its anger and sadness, it wanted the joy and peace it saw in deer's heart. It wanted to follow her. Together, they traveled back to the Creator and led all other creatures back home at the heart of the universe."

After she finished, we both stood in silence for a few moments appreciating our shared medicine and the growing love between us. We were sisters of the deer tribe, remembering how to lead all the beings of the earth back to the Creator through love.

Living with an open heart involves taking risks.

It would be trite to say that living with an open heart involves taking risks. It clearly does. The deeper realization for me is that love comes in many forms. It is both light and dark, separation and unity, anger and bliss. I believe that we cannot truly know one end of this scale without also knowing the other to some degree. Living as Deer Heart Woman involves trust. A massive and never ending trust; that the Creator and the universe is built from love and that this love is multifaceted and endless. I experience both the darkness and light of life, moving through both with my heart open wide to the love of creation. A heart that opens wider with every brave step up the mountain I take.

COMMUNION

ARE YOU READY TO EXPERIENCE THE QUIET BLISS OF UNITY?

Me – One of the most beautiful practices in unity that I often enter into is that of eye gazing with a human or nature being. It allows us to sink beyond the chatter of the mind and into a wordless space of witnessing our interconnection and unity with 'the other' in our partner. To do this, find a nature partner (this could be a tree, a flower, a patch of earth or anything else that connects with you) and gaze eye to eye for a minimum of five minutes. You can set a timer to allow you to be fully present with the experience. Notice your stream of thoughts gradually drops away as the time progresses and imagine that you can connect and merge your consciousness with that of your partner's.

We – Expand your communion practice and add narrative to it by finding a human partner. Repeat the exercise above, again for five minutes, minimum. Take a moment to share your experiences once your time is up and notice how the experience of unity is often vastly different and more varied than we would expect.

The experience and memory of unity sits around and within us in every single moment. However, it can be challenging to drown out the distractions and noise of the world around us to remember this. The good news is that you don't have to be a skilled meditator to find five minutes (or 10, or perhaps even 20) in your day to create connection with the universe. Try this practice for a quick fix of unity and notice how your daily stress falls away!

Coming home

Home
It calls for us to remember and rejoice
That we are creation in human form
That we are there in every moment we choose to love

Home is something that we all long for and very few ever find, truly. Some people have always known a place that they define as home. Others spend their entire lives searching for it. For me, the concept of home has expanded and now has multiple layers and textures.

Most importantly, there is the feeling of coming home to ourselves: of moving beyond the culturally constructed judgments and criticisms to a point where finally we are comfortable in our own skin. This feeling of being 'home in myself' is something that I am only now coming to embody in my late thirties.

As a small child, whilst I lived in my spark, I inhabited this sense of 'personal home' more than at any time in my life, before I learned to forget who I was and don the mask of social acceptability. Yet this forgetting is an important part of our tests. Unless we come to know the discomfort and alienation of being away from the home within, we wouldn't truly understand or appreciate finding it again when we return.

To feel at home in our bodies, minds and souls, I believe we need to have acknowledged the deep intelligence of our hearts that quietly tells us in every moment of every day that we are enough, that we are beautiful and that we are loved. It may sound like a cliché, yet when we are able to hear these inner messages that are given to us in myriad ways through the natural magic and synchronicity of life, then we are truly home – wherever we are. Our sense of safety, well-being and joy comes from deep within our own sense of self-love and self-confidence rather than from any outer source of acknowledgement or success. To fully come home to ourselves is a lifetime's journey and yet one that we can commit to in every moment when we show a willingness to become our own lover.

TO FULLY COME HOME TO OURSELVES IS A LIFETIME'S JOURNEY.

There is the home we find in certain geographic places on the earth. Some of us, like me, know where these places are from the moment we are born. Others spend their lifetime searching for 'their place'. Those of us who know where home is, yet find themselves distanced from it, experience a deep sense of loss and separation. There were many times in my journey when I wished I had no home to miss, but like most narrative threads, there comes a time for this part of the story to come full circle.

Ever since I left Colorado at the age of six, I would dream of a specific place in the mountains. In my imagination, I would stand looking at the snow-capped peak of Mount Evans glinting in the sunlight and the rosy glow of the morning sun as it hit the red earth, sparkling with quartz and mica crystals, and the slow movement of the meadow grasses framed by the Ponderosa pines. This particular vision of the mountains persisted through my journey and became my iconic image of Colorado, the home I missed. It also became the inner sanctum to which I would retreat in my meditations and dreams for healing and information.

Once, I even had this vision when I was participating in a marriage ceremony inside the King's Chamber of the Great Pyramid in Egypt. At the climax of the ceremony (the very moment when I would least expect to be focusing on anything other than the ceremony in front of me), the mountains appeared in my mind's eye once again. There it was, insistent, and calling to me.

Yet despite its persistence, I had almost given up on moving back to Colorado any time soon. Euan's two children live in England and my work takes me all over the world – both facts that make settling anywhere except Europe challenging. On top of the logistics of the situation, the ache of being separated from the land I loved hadn't healed or gone away and was draining to me. It had become one of the only areas of my life that remained in dis-ease. I was ready to bring myself to a place of peace and acceptance. I was finally ready to 'let go' of the mountains and allow my soul story to take me where it would, even if this meant never going back to the beloved home of my childhood. There are some hurts that we cannot hold onto forever. For every wound there comes a time of healing, if we allow it.

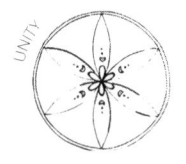

Euan and I were staying at the Sprucetree cabin and I had awoken with a clear message to do a ceremony. The ancestors had told me in my dreams that the time had come to release the pain this old story had held for me. I drew my visions of the land and the inner agony my separation from it caused me on a piece of paper and with Euan witnessing, burned it outside All Faiths' Chapel, blowing away the ashes of my old story over the top of the sundial that rests there in memory of Laurel. I let go of the pain. I cried. I hurt. I let go of the longing. I surrendered to the wisdom and imagination of the universe and let go of my old human story.

'If you love something, set it free. If it comes back to you, it's yours and if it doesn't, it was never meant to be.'[49] When I was a child, my grandmother had sent to me, in England, a small card that had these words of wisdom embossed in dark blue script. They had stayed with me ever since.

> IF YOU LOVE SOMETHING, SET IT FREE.
> IF IT COMES BACK TO YOU, IT'S YOURS AND IF IT DOESN'T,
> IT WAS NEVER MEANT TO BE.

When we can truly release something we are attached to, we free the person, place or thing from our stuck beliefs and energy that prevent it from manifesting in the right way. In burning my image on the paper, I released all my expectations, all my attachments and my story of Colorado being the only home I would ever be happy in. I let go of my first beloved, the lover I have longed for all my life and I felt at peace for the first time in decades. I was 38 years old.

A few days later Euan and I were in Evergreen having coffee. As I went out to the car to get my laptop, my gaze was drawn to the left-hand side of the small courtyard of shops. It was a real estate agents that I hadn't noticed before. Something picked up in my energy field and compelled me like a magnet to walk over to the door. Finding it open, I walked in, wondering on some level why I was here.

"*Hi, I'm Jules,*" said a warm voice from behind a desk towards the back of the room. "*Can I help you?*"

To my surprise, my legs walked over to her desk and sat down. Taking a deep breath, I started to recount the whole story of my love affair with Colorado and my visions of a specific piece of land in the mountains (even the part about being shown my vision inside the Great Pyramid). Instead of raising her eyebrows and looking at me like I was crazy, which my logical brain half expected her to do, she smiled and said, "*You know, I may have a piece of land that is really similar to that. Maybe we should take a look?*"

The following day, I stood on top of a boulder with tears rolling down my face. My eyes gazed at the meadow from my visions. Ponderosa pines stood all around me and I was transfixed by the snow-capped view of Mount Evans that for so many years I had only seen in my dreams.

"*I can't believe it's actually here!*" I said to Euan as he came over to join me. "*Do you think we are really supposed to be here, now?*" I asked him (and the universe) as we walked back towards Jules' car.

"*Anything is possible with you these days,*" he said, slinging his arm around my shoulders.

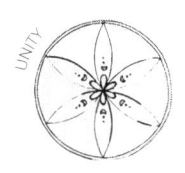

A few weeks later, I found myself in Aswan, Egypt, halfway through running a retreat and in the midst of the chaos of an Egyptian national holiday. The ping of a message chimed on my mobile phone. Hardly daring to look, my breath caught in my throat and my heart pumped in my chest like a drum. The angels nudged me encouragingly and I took my phone out.

"Your offer has been accepted – you are now officially under contract."

Nature gasped and held her breath. This was it.

A whole-body shiver of delight moved through me and I found myself enveloped in the arms of my Egyptian brothers in celebration. A large part of me couldn't quite believe that it was happening.

Shortly after this monumental message, my trip in Egypt came to an end. I returned to Colorado to sit in the Title Deeds office in Evergreen and sign my name against the piece of land that I had seen in my heart and mind ever since I was a little girl. There really are no words that can describe how I was feeling (and continue to feel today) every time I set foot on its sacred ground. No language comes close to expressing the gratitude in my heart, and yet the journey to accepting its gift has been far from easy.

As I sat in the midday sunshine, my back pressed against a large Ponderosa tree in the meadow of my dreams (and now my reality), I found myself reflecting on the journey that had brought me here. My tree friend reassured me that I was always going to make it. They had apparently been waiting for me to return for many years. I wasn't so sure. There had been many times when I had strayed off my path. So many times when I had almost let despair and distraction win.

IT IS SO HARD SOMETIMES TO FIND THE THREAD
OF OUR AUTHENTIC STORY AMONGST THE GROWING PILES
OF SOCIAL RUBBLE.

Our restory path is rarely an easy one and it takes vision, determination and courage to travel it fully. We are living in times where the old narratives are dissolving around our ears. It is so hard sometimes to find the thread of our authentic story amongst the growing piles of social rubble. Yet persevere we must if we are to create a new human mythology – one that tells the story of unity rather than separation. We must first come home to ourselves before we can come home to our place and community on earth. We must remember and return home to our deep connection with our earth family, before we can fully come home to our soul story and our unique place in the cosmology of life. I had to travel a full circuit through the narrative cycle; awakening to my spark of light, moving through my tests with courage and listening to the clues that would eventually lead me to the 'death' and metamorphosis of my old human story. I know that only then was I ready to return, receive and accept the gift of my heart's desire. I had to surrender my human story so the narrative of my soul could lead me home to unity with creation, ready to serve the greater mythology of life that moves through us all.

A friend and teacher Susan Powell[50] once said to me, 'We have two choices in this life. We can either drag our canoe against the flow of life's river, headed towards the shore that we think we need to reach. Or we can get into our boat, allowing the current to take us where it will and trusting that we will arrive at precisely the right place, at the right time.'

Having traveled my journey thus far, I now know that I will forever opt to go with the flow of life. I trust that every experience, every person and every place that I reach along the way is there for a reason and that I am able to both learn from and give to it. The greatest gift I receive is knowing that the 'story of me' is intricately a part of the greater 'story of we' and that I am one cell of light amongst countless others residing within the vast cosmic being of the universe. I am happy. I am whole and I am able to dance with the beautiful chaos of life lightly. And I know that dreams can come true.

Of course, now the journey begins again. With the spark of my soul's light leading me forwards, I walk tall towards the start of a new universal trail, never forgetting how grateful I am to live every single moment on this beautiful earth.

My home.
Our home.
Within us all, always.

UNITY JOURNEY

CAN YOU SURRENDER TO THE BIGGEST STORY THERE IS?

For one final time I ask you to find a place of silence, somewhere you won't be disturbed, and settle in. Make sure you have created an environment in which you can feel safe, comfortable and reflect.

Breathe deeply and take stock of everything around you that you have cause to be grateful for. The air moving in and out of your lungs, the light shining on your skin, your lover, your body's wisdom and health, your family, your work, your play. Acknowledge your gratitude for everything you get to experience as a living breathing human walking the earth at this time in history.

Then open your journal and start to make a list of everything in life you wish you could change in some way. These could be personal experiences or social, environmental situations that you find unacceptable. It could be a situation where you feel powerless to help or change things. Remember, as humans we are unified as much through our doubt, confusion and suffering as we are through our ambition, love and bliss.

As you write your list, notice how your physical body responds to the tension of wanting to change what is. Anything that brings up a feeling of wanting to do more, change things or fight the system: write it down.

Once complete, take a moment to go through your list and, one by one, imagine that you could let that problem or conflict 'go to Spirit'. That you can surrender and release your need to make something happen or change the unfolding of events because you completely and utterly trust that the universe is already creating the perfect outcome (whether your mind happens to agree with it or not!). Surrender your need to change the situation and imagine for a moment that the situation in question has already resolved itself perfectly in the biggest cycles of time that the universe can offer. Imagine that each thing on your list is a ripple in space/time that is simply in the process of playing out its thread in the story of evolution for all beings. Can you trust that everything holds both a lesson and a blessing?

After you have worked through your entire list you might want to do something physical to assimilate the space you have created by your surrender. Take a walk, go for a swim, make love, dance; whatever you find yourself craving in the moment. Take the time to feel the freedom and ecstasy that comes with surrender and then resolve to bring more of this practice into your life if it feels right to you.

EPILOGUE

Good morning, Deer Heart Woman. It's always good to hear your voice especially in the morning: the beginning of another day to walk on this sacred earth mother. Our dreams are very important. Wherever we go, wherever we are at certain times in our life, dreams will always come that will show us where we are. We can always choose where we want to be at a certain time because we were all given the freedom of choice, but destiny is totally opposite. Destiny is already laid out and we are here for that sole purpose: to fulfill our destiny. We all go looking for our destiny and many times we think we have found it, then all of a sudden things change. 99% of the time our destiny was right in front of us all the time but we always take off running in circles trying to find it. Like children we run off on our own, our own thinking, feeling, seeing. Some find it sooner than others, some might find it when they are older and some just keep missing it, walking right past it. Some never find it and those who don't find and fulfill will just have to come back and start all over. I was very fortunate that the grandfathers came and retrieved me from self-destruction. They brought me back and said this is why you are here. I was literally put back on track and found my destiny. It is so beautiful to know that now there is nothing else in my life but to fulfill this and then I can go home. What I am telling you is what they told me, showed and taught me, so I am telling you and sharing with you. That's all I can do. So follow your heart Deer Heart Woman and your spirit, always.

Love and prayers
Izzy

I received this beautiful email after reaching out to my uncle Izzy for advice on a series of dreams I had been having in Egypt. His wisdom reminded me of where I had traveled to in my journey and what I had to surrender to next.

When we embark on the adventure of manifesting our destiny (a process called life), we have to face the inevitable confusion, doubt, anxiety and impatience that comes with the alchemical transformations of traveling around the Restory Cycle. In the process of our adventures any shadow patterns that stand in the way of our inner liberation surface to be loved and illuminated into higher forms. The narrative path presents us with a dynamic dance between our darkness and our light and the journey is messy, intense, scary and uncertain. It's rarely glamorous and often full of fear because that's what we have to face in order to evolve. But equally what we are offered is beauty-filled, vibrant and 'alive' in the deepest sense of that word.

LEARNING HOW TO INTERACT AUTHENTICALLY RECONNECTS US TO THE GIFTS OF OUR HUMANITY.

Living in tough bliss is the path of the wounded healer. The wounds we gather along our journey ultimately make us stronger and more human. Instead of following the traditional hero's path, which is one of isolation and separation from the world, we discover that it is actually our experiences of learning how to interact authentically and unify within the system of life that reconnects us to the gifts of our humanity. Instead of running away to find adventure out in the world, we run directly into the quest of our everyday life and seek to find the treasure that lies within it. We cease seeking fame and external recognition as the source of happiness and instead give thanks for the joy that comes from living our true story. As one of my favorite authors Rob Bell[51] says, 'What we need now more than ever is courage and love to cook up new ways of being human together.' I believe this more with every day that passes.

Living like this, we straddle the polarities with every step we take. Courage and weakness, joy and pain, fear and love. Our modern mythology is changing and the side of the story which we stand on is only ever up to us. It's all too easy to get sucked into the stories of darkness and doom, yet the stories of light and hope have equal power should we choose to see them. Indeed, one could not survive without the other. When we choose to open our hearts and live in loving compassion through the joyful moments and the fearful ones, we truly rise above our human narrative and live in sync with the greater myth of the universe.

The key to having this choice is our ability to sink into the stillness that resides beyond our stories. When we realize that we are not victims of life but the writers of it, all that remains are truth, love and the boundless, timeless imagination of life continuously available to us in our moments of silence. In this space, we are able to listen to our story unfolding around us and become aware of our interconnection with the ecosystem of the planet. We begin to experience our life as a sensuous, playful dance where every experience is an opportunity to learn, grow and become more 'us'.

> SINK INTO THE STILLNESS THAT RESIDES
> BEYOND OUR STORIES.

This for me is the real meaning and manifestation of love: a word often uttered and rarely understood. It is this deeper form of ecological, universal, compassionate love that brings balance to our decisions and integrity to our actions. When we live in love, we can detach from the drama of the old stories dying around us, trusting that there is a bigger myth playing out in the grand cycles of time. We surrender our opinions and judgments, acutely aware that our own narrative lens is limited by the extent of our current beliefs and experiences. This acceptance allows us to gain a wider perspective, constantly moving beyond the edge of our mythic comfort zones. Joseph Campbell[52] reminds us: 'True myth is designed to carry us forwards in evolution rather than keep us stuck.' When we actively participate in the creation of a living mythology, we cannot help but surrender to growth.

Traveling through the narrative cycle is akin to a modern-day initiation back into the wholeness and unity of life. Each stage is necessary in order for us to fully realize and embody our unique gifts. We cannot bypass, avoid or fast track because if we did, we would not come to know who we really are at a cellular level. We cannot rush, force or control the process either. We must commit and dedicate ourselves to the journey, come what may, and accept that the journey is an eternal spiral. Once we have traveled one cycle of the wheel we naturally come back to the beginning again, yet knowing it in a different more expanded form. Our ending becomes our beginning and our death our rebirth. Our journey as a soul is continuous and evolving.

> OUR ENDING BECOMES OUR BEGINNING
> AND OUR DEATH OUR REBIRTH.

What compels us to travel through the restory spiral again and again you may ask? Our inherent human love of adventure? The natural urge for life to evolve into greater expressions of existence? Or maybe, it's the realization that 'we' are a part of a far bigger story in the universe than we can ever fully know in human form. Life breathes in and breathes out in eternal cycles. All beings must periodically die in order to be reborn. The ancient and infinite forces of evolution and involution are powerful beyond measure and will pull us ever forwards in the mythic spiral of creation and destruction – if we surrender to them of course.

As our local and global societies undergo their own journey to restory themselves, we become increasingly attuned to assisting this process in our own ways. Like an ecosystem in transformation, we are each being given the opportunity to support and be supported through the wider, bigger shifts in the planetary human story as it unfolds and transforms. The dying embers of the old fires of mechanistic separation are still clinging to life and yet their time is almost done. The dominant western narratives of the last 500–600 years that placed human logic as the central and superior force over nature and cosmos are being unpicked. As they fade, they take with them the myths that have fueled hierarchy, superiority, isolation and greed and yet from their ashes, a new more expanded ecological narrative is emerging. The fuel of our new story burns with a universal energy. It is the mythic spark that moves us collectively from a story of 'me' to a story of 'we'. We must decide how to restory and redesign our human myths, personal and collective, to lead us through these times of transition.

> THE FUEL OF OUR NEW STORY BURNS
> WITH A UNIVERSAL ENERGY.

Having come to the end of one cycle of the narrative wheel, I am now beginning another in the eternal dance of life. Perhaps our paths will cross in the future as we journey through this blissful dance of creation. I hope so. I pray so. I trust so.

I leave you now with words from my grandfather.[53] May they remind you as they remind me of the only story there is underneath it all: boundless life.

> *Take time to listen to the clear voice of spirit*
> *singing out from that world around the red rocks.*
> *To the new man rising from the old man, hearing this rare,*
> *new and always one song echoed off these rocks.*
> *Go often and see them.*
> *Don't forget this ever new and so generative voice*
> *– that came, that comes.*
> *Go often and see them – to listen for the song*
> *that you can hear. Hear this music.*
> *See it all. Go into the park and climb the path*
> *up the mountain to look.*
> *To look.*
> *To look down where the music was first sung.*
> *Hear it.*
> *See it.*
> *Whatever is eternal and universal in all religions*
> *is the mind and the heart of the true religion.*
> *The intensity of this moment.*
> *Always.*

ENDNOTES

1. Black Elk & John Neihardt, *Black Elk Speaks*, 1988
2. Maria Popova, *How to Tell a True Tale*, 2007
3. Danielle LaPorte & Linda Silversten, *Your Big Beautiful Book Plan*, 2016
4. Art Giser, Energetic NLP Lecture, 2014
5. Carl Jung, *Memories, Dreams, Reflections*, 1995 edition
6. Joseph Campbell, *The Hero with a Thousand Faces*, 1949
7. Genevieve Boast, 'The Earth Spark', 2016
8. Joseph Campbell, *The Hero with a Thousand Faces*, 1949
9. Wikipedia, Laurel Elizabeth Keyes, 2016
10. Carl Sagan, *Cosmos*, 1980
11. Koshare Indian Dances, Koshare Indian Museum, La Junta, Colorado
12. Rudolf Steiner, *Waldorf Education & Anthroposophy*, 2017
13. Joseph Campbell, *The Hero with a Thousand Faces*, 1949
14. Bill Plotkin, *Nature and the Human Soul*, 2008
15. George Lucas, *Star Wars*, 1977 onwards
16. John Conley, *Ninon de Lenclos*, 2017
17. Rudolf Steiner, *Angels*, 1996
18. Matthew Fox & Rupert Sheldrake, *The Physics of Angels*, 1996
19. Richard Rudd, *Gene Keys*, 2013
20. David Abram, *The Spell of the Sensuous*, 1996
21. Metro-Goldwyn-Mayer, *The Wizard of Oz*, 1939
22. Wikipedia, Laurel Elizabeth Keyes, 2017
23. Laurel Elizabeth Keyes, *Sundial*, 1981
24. T S Eliot, *The Four Quartets*, 1959
25. William Boast, *Masters of Change*, 1997
26. Noel Charlton, *Understanding Gregory Bateson*, 2008
27. Charles Eisenstein, *Sacred Economics*, 2011
28. The Change Foundation, formerly Cricket for Change, 2009
29. Art Giser, Energetic NLP Sessions at the Festival of Enlightenment, Colorado, 2011

30 Heyoka Merryfield, *Sundancing the Muse*, 2011
31 Susan Powell, *Medicine Wheels and More*, 2011
32 Heyoka Merryfield, The Temple of Earth and Sky, Stevensville, Montana
33 Bill Plotkin, *Soulcraft*, 2003
34 Animas Valley Institute, Colorado, 2017
35 Lawrence Bloom, The Gateway, Delhi, India, 1997
36 Barbara Marx Hubbard, *Conscious Evolution*, 1998
37 Joseph Campbell, *The Hero with a Thousand Faces*, 1949
38 Tom Kaypacha Lescher, *The New Paradigm Astrology Cooperative*, 2014
39 Rupert Sheldrake, *The Presence of the Past*, 1988
40 Hassan Ali Ahmed, Luxor Taxi, 2014
41 Ameer Kareem, The Flower of Life Guesthouse, Abydos, 2017
42 Giles Hutchins, personal email, 2016
43 Izzy Zephier, Chief Black Spotted Horse, 2015
44 Scilla Elworthy, from *Behind Every Old General*, a Soul Biographies film by Nic Askew, 2017
45 Rebekah Shaman, Ayahuasca Retreats, 2015
46 Brooke Medicine Eagle, 2016
47 Tanah Whitemore, Sacred Ground International, 2016
48 Taken from Audrey Cole, *Wings Alive*, 2016
49 Anonymous quote, rumored to be written by Richard Back who refutes it, 1985
50 Susan Powell, Personal Communication, 2012
51 Rob Bell & Pete Holmes, Live event in LA, California, April 2017
52 Joseph Campbell, *The Hero with a Thousand Faces*, 1949
53 William Boast, *Seminalia: The Omnific Journey*, 2004

BIBLIOGRAPHY

Abram, D. (1996), *The Spell of the Sensuous*, Toronto: Vintage Books

Abram, D. (2005), Storytelling and Wonder, retrieved from *http://wildethics.org/essay/storytelling-and-wonder/*

Abram, D. (2010), *Becoming Animal: An Earthly Cosmology*, Vintage Books, Random House

Abram, D. & Harding, S., (April, 2016), *Dark Ecology*, a short course at Schumacher College, *Dartington, UK*

Ali Ahmed, H. (2014), Luxor Taxi & Tours, retrieved from *www.luxortaxi.com*

Askew, N. (2017): Scilla Elworthy, Behind Every Old General, retrieved from *http://nicaskew.com/collection/behind-every-old-general/*

Bell, R. (Director), *Everything is Spiritual,* (2007), Video/DVD, Zondervan

Bell, R. H., & Holmes, P. (2017), *Live event at the Largo, Los Angeles*

Berry, T. (1999), *The Great Work: Our way into the future*, Bell Tower, New York

Black Elk & Neihardt, J. (1988), *Black Elk Speaks: Being the life story of a holy man of the Oglala Sioux,* University of Nebraska Press

Bloom, L. (1997), *The Gateway,* Delhi, India

Boast, G. Beyond Human Stories, retrieved from *http://www.beyondhumanstories.com/*

Boast, G. (2016), *The Earth Spark,* unpublished manuscript

Boast, K. (2017), Earthkind Education, retrieved from *https://www.facebook.com/earthkindeducation/*

Boast, W. (2004), *Seminalia: The Omnific Journey,* InstantPublisher

Boast, W. & Martin, B. (1997), *Masters of Change: How great leaders thrived in turbulent times,* Executive Excellence Publishing

Bushere, B. (1999), Koshare Indian Museum, retrieved from *http://www.kosharehistory.org/*

Campbell, J. (1949), *The Hero with a Thousand Faces,* Princeton University Press

Campbell, J. (2004), *Pathways to Bliss: Mythology and personal transformation,* New World Library

Charlton, N. (2008), *Understanding Gregory Bateson: Mind, Beauty and the Sacred Earth,* State University of New York Press

Cole, A., Wings Alive, retrieved from *http://wingsalive.com/*

Conley, J. (2017), Ninon de Lenclos: 1620-1705, retrieved from *http://www.iep.utm.edu/lenclos/*

Dellinger, D. (2011), *Love Letter to the Milky Way* (Fourth ed.), White Cloud Press

Eisenstein, C. (2011), *Sacred Economics: Money, Gift, and Society in the Age of Transition,* Evolver Editions

Eisenstein, C. (2013), Synchronicity, myth, and the new world order, retrieved from *http://charleseisenstein.net/synchronicity-myth-and-the-new-world-order/*

Eliot, T. S. (1959), *The Four Quartets,* Harcourt

Ferrini, P. (1996), *The Silence of the Heart: Reflections of the Christ Mind,* Heartways Press

Metro-Goldwyn-Mayer (Producer), & Fleming, V. (Director), (1939), *The Wizard of Oz,* [Motion Picture]

Fox, M. (1999), *Sins of the Spirit, Blessings of the Flesh,* Gateway

Fox, M. & Sheldrake, R. (1996), *The Physics of Angels,* Harper Collins

Gafni, M. (2002), *Soul Prints: Your Path to Fulfillment,* Fireside

Gafni, M. (2006), *The Erotic and the Holy*, Sounds TrueGiser, A. (2014), Energetic NLP, retrieved from *http://energeticnlp.com/*

Harding, S. (2013), *Animate Earth: Science, Intuition and Gaia* (Second ed.), Green Books

Houston, J. (1995), *The Passion of Isis and Osiris: A Gateway into Transcendent Love,* The Ballantine Publishing Group

Hutchins, G. (2012), *The Nature of Business: Redesigning for Resilience,* Green Books

Hutchins, G. (2016), *Future Fit,* The Write Factor

Isaacs, W. (1999), *Dialogue and the Art of Thinking Together: A Pioneering Approach to Communicating in Business and Life*, Bantam Doubleday Dell Publishing Group

Jung, C. G. (1995), *Memories, Dreams, Reflections*, Fontana Press

Kareem, A. (2017), The Flower of Life Guesthouse, Abydos, retrieved from *http://www.guesthouse-floweroflife.com/*

Keyes, L. E. (1981), *Sundial: I Count the Sunny Hours*, Gentle Living Publications

(Aug, 2016), Laurel Elizabeth Keyes, Gentle Living Publications, retrieved from *https://en.wikipedia.org/wiki/Laurel_Elizabeth_Keyes*

LaPorte, D. & Silversten, L., (2016), Your Big Beautiful Book Plan, retrieved from *http://yourbigbeautifulbookplan.com/*

Lescher, T. (2014), The New Paradigm Astrology Cooperative | Brought to you by Kaypacha!, retrieved from *http://newparadigmastrology.com/*

Lucas Film (Producer), & Lucas, G. (Director), (1977), *Star Wars: A New Hope,* [Motion Picture]

Macy, J. (1991), *World as Lover, World as Self,* Parallax Press

Macy, J. & Brown, M., (2014), *Coming Back to Life*, New Society Publishers

Marx Hubbard, B. (1998), *Conscious Evolution: Awakening the Power of our Social Potential*, New World Library

Marx Hubbard, B. (2001), *Emergence: The Shift from Ego to Essence*, Hampton Roads Publishing

Medicine Eagle, B. (1991), *Buffalo Woman Comes Singing*, Ballantine Books

Montana PBS (Producer) & Merryfield, H. (Director), (2011), *Sundancing the Muse*, [Video/DVD]

Merryfield, H. (2017), Heyoka Art Studio: The Temple of Earth and Sky, retrieved from *http://www.heyoka-art.com/*

Midgley, M. (2004), *The Myths We Live By*, Routledge

Plotkin, B. (2003), *Soulcraft: Crossing Into the Mysteries of Nature and Psyche*, New World Library

Plotkin, B. (2008), *Nature and the Human Soul: Cultivating Wholeness and Community in a Fragmented World*, New World Library

Popova, M. (2017), How to Tell a True Tale, retrieved from *http://tinyurl.com/ybehm6x9*

Powell, S. (2011), Medicine Wheels and More, retrieved from *http://medicinewheelsandmore.com/*

Puhakka, K. (1995), *Restoring Connectedness in the Kosmos: A Healing Tale of Deeper Order, The Human Psychologist, 23* (Autumn)

Reason, P. & Hawkins, P., (1988), Storytelling as Inquiry; in P. Reason (Ed.), *Human Inquiry in Action: Developments in New Paradigm Research* (pp. 79-101), Sage Publications

Richardson, J. (2005), Writing: A Method of Inquiry, in N. K. Denzin, & Y. S. Lincoln (Eds.), *The SAGE Handbook of Qualitative Research* (3rd ed., pp. 959) Sage

Rudd, R. (2013), *Gene Keys: Unlocking Your Higher Purpose*, Watkins

Sagan, C. (1980), *Cosmos*, Random House

Sams, J. (1999), *Dancing the Dream: The Seven Sacred Paths of Human Transformation,* Harper Collins

Sams, J. & Carson D. (1988), *Animal Medicine Cards,* St Martin's Press

Seeley, C. & Thornhill, E. (March 2014), *Artful Organisation,* Ashridge Business School

Seeley, C. The Fool and the Great Turning [PDF], retrieved from *http://www.wildmargins.com/Wild_Margins/Artful_Knowing_files/TheFoolAndTheGreatTurning.pdf*

Seeley, C. & Reason, P. (2008), Expressions of Energy: An Epistemology of Presentational Knowing, in Liamputtong, P. & Rumbold, J. (Ed.), *Knowing Differently: Arts-Based & Collaborative Research*, Nova Science Publishers

Shaman, R. (2004), *The Shaman's Last Apprentice,* Self-Published

Shaman, R. (2017), Living Shamanically, retrieved from *https://rebekahshaman.com/*

Sheldrake, R. (1988), *The Presence of the Past: Morphic Resonance and the Habits of Nature,* Icon Books

Sinclair, A. (2007), *Leadership for the Disillusioned: Moving Beyond Myths and Heroes to Leading That Liberates,* Allen & Unwin

Steiner, R., Waldorf Education & Anthroposophy [PDF], retrieved from *https://www.rsarchive.org/Download/Waldorf_Education_and_Anthroposophy_1-Rudolf_Steiner-304.pdf*

Steiner, R. (1996), *Angels,* Rudolf Steiner Press

Whitemore, T., Sacred Ground International, retrieved from *http://www.sacredgroundintl.org/*

Zephier, I. (2015), Izzy Zephier, Chief Black Spotted Horse, retrieved from *https://www.facebook.com/profile.php?id=100014580344873*

Zimmerman, J. & Coyle, V. (2009), *The Way of Council,* Bramble Books

INDEX

A

Abundance xiv, 186–187, 194, 241
Adventure v, 6–8, 12, 18, 26, 48, 52, 64, 76, 80, 93, 98, 111, 142, 148, 151, 173, 218, 231, 253, 262, 278, 304, 306
Agency 246, 248
Alchemy 10, 12, 249–252, 256
All Faith's Chapel
Amazon 278
Ancestors viii, 33, 94, 184, 219, 221, 235, 266, 286–287, 290, 296
Ancestral 7, 34, 185, 263
Angels 80, 137, 140–142, 144, 147, 152, 163, 167, 189, 191, 199–200, 203, 239, 242, 280, 282, 286, 288, 298, 310, 313, 315

B

Beauty xiv, xvi, 23, 26, 28, 35, 80, 91, 98, 101, 143–144, 147, 152, 173, 175, 185, 198, 208, 223, 226, 228, 231, 238, 267, 269, 281, 284, 304, 310
Beyond Human Stories 38, 309
Bliss 70, 79, 111, 123, 131, 154, 157, 177, 223, 229–230, 236, 259, 282–284, 292–293, 300, 304, 310
Brooke Medicine Eagle vii, xvi, 285, 316
Business 29, 102, 112, 114, 116, 131, 143, 150, 155, 165, 186, 191, 193–194, 196, 286, 311, 313
Butterfly xv, 127, 136, 156, 171, 180, 218

C

Cambridge 36, 46
Caterpillar 127, 130, 179, 280
Ceremonial 212, 214, 262, 267, 290
Chaos 138, 241, 249, 257, 259, 264, 297, 299
Chief Black Spotted Horse 261–262, 284, 313, 316
Clues xv, 8, 10, 76–78, 86, 94, 108, 111, 116–117, 121–123, 127, 183, 220, 249–250, 258, 299
Cocoon xv, 127, 129–130, 136–137, 179–180, 183–184, 202, 280
Colorado 20, 22, 26, 28, 35, 48, 144, 219–220, 260, 295–298, 315–316
Comfort zone challenges 10, 70
Comfort zones 6, 13, 75, 251, 285, 305
Communion 7, 104, 154, 176, 219, 248–249, 293
Community 13, 25, 32, 107, 160, 166, 184–186, 207, 214, 223, 234, 250, 299, 312
Connected xiii, xvi, 17–18, 24, 37, 65, 70, 147, 162, 184, 230, 254, 261, 271
Consciousness 5, 78, 85, 90, 106, 131, 139, 142, 184, 197–198, 202, 230, 249, 252, 255, 257, 259, 271, 278, 284, 293
Contemplate 8, 22, 285
Cosmology 195, 228, 299, 309
Courage xv, 4, 29, 44, 77, 90, 94, 100, 111, 114, 116, 133, 136, 138, 149, 151, 155, 157, 159, 167, 228, 250, 252, 260, 298–299, 304
Creator xiv, 11, 207, 264–265, 282, 285–290, 292
Crisis xiii, 129, 133, 137

317

D

Dark 23, 26, 31, 39, 44, 46–47, 49, 54–55, 57–59, 81–82, 84–85, 87–89, 97–98, 105, 109–110, 113–115, 123, 129, 131, 135, 137–138, 144–145, 154, 176–177, 197, 203, 212, 215, 218, 220–221, 227, 249, 259–260, 274–275, 279–281, 292, 296, 309

Dark night of the soul 129, 137–138, 260

Death xiii, 50–51, 53, 59–60, 76, 110, 128–130, 134, 160, 175, 183, 225–227, 232, 246, 258, 263, 269–270, 274–275, 281, 299, 306

Deer 23, 172, 262, 284–285, 291–292, 303

Deer heart woman 284–285, 291–292, 303

Destiny 7, 19, 77, 115, 137, 155, 227, 240, 246, 253, 259, 277, 303–304

Discernment 78, 206–207

Dreams xiii, 6, 48, 52, 59, 76, 85, 96, 108, 114, 117–118, 132, 144, 167, 187, 227, 254, 257–259, 273, 277, 295–299, 303, 311, 315

E

Eagle vii, xvi, 27, 210, 213, 215–216, 262–263, 283, 285, 290, 312, 316

Earth viii, x, xiii–xvi, 11, 13–14, 17, 19–20, 24, 28–29, 32, 34–36, 50–51, 60–61, 65, 80, 96–97, 106, 110, 133, 135, 173, 176, 184–185, 189, 198, 213–215, 217–219, 221–223, 228–230, 232, 238, 250, 254–255, 263–266, 273, 275, 277–279, 283–284, 286, 288–289, 292–295, 299–300, 303, 309–312, 315–316

Ecosystem 5, 184, 186, 224, 278, 305–306

Ecstatic 51, 86, 131, 187, 248

Ego 31, 63, 65, 68–69, 83, 88–90, 104, 113, 120, 146, 151, 155, 161, 164, 167, 196, 222, 248, 251, 262, 291, 312

Egypt 251–256, 258–260, 295, 297–298, 303

Emergency Happiness 187, 193

England 36, 46–51, 56, 58, 92, 112, 144, 158, 188, 211, 239, 269, 295–296

Evolve 9, 18, 128–129, 194, 232, 250, 304, 306

F

Family viii, 11, 14, 17, 20, 22, 24–27, 30, 32, 34–36, 52, 56–57, 62, 86, 90, 95, 101, 117, 122, 132–133, 155, 158–160, 166, 168, 173, 194, 196, 219, 227, 230, 239, 241, 252–253, 255, 257–258, 260–261, 267, 274, 283–284, 299–300

Fear 6–7, 26–27, 35, 57–59, 61, 81–82, 87–91, 107, 110–111, 114, 120, 136, 143, 157–158, 164, 191–193, 200, 203, 205, 218, 226–227, 232–233, 236, 259–261, 271, 273–276, 279–280, 292, 304

Flow 3–4, 18, 70, 78, 100, 155, 163–164, 185, 187, 192, 194, 218, 251, 259, 278, 287, 290, 299

Freedom 28, 54, 87, 93, 101–102, 104, 118, 120, 136, 148, 178–179, 186, 218, 251, 301, 303

G

Genius 7, 18–19, 22, 37, 135, 183

Gifts xv–xvi, 6, 8–10, 19, 22, 25–27, 30, 45, 61, 70–71, 97, 101, 116, 128, 142, 167, 171–172, 178, 180, 183–187, 193–195, 205, 207, 217–218, 220, 227–228, 233, 241–242, 248–249, 256–257, 266, 278, 288, 304–305

Gnosis 5, 142

God 84, 174, 247, 249, 289

Grace 21, 105, 128, 135, 142, 185–186, 286, 290
Great Spirit 288
Gratitude vii–viii, 38, 85–87, 93, 99, 145, 147, 173, 208, 219, 222–223, 227, 239, 268–269, 276, 298, 300

H
Healing xv, 11, 13, 49, 56, 76, 97, 106, 138, 142, 160, 183, 235, 239, 272, 276, 278, 295, 312
Heart xiii–xv, 3, 5, 17–19, 22–23, 28, 33, 51–53, 59, 82, 84, 88, 91–92, 97, 101, 117, 121–122, 138, 147, 153, 160–162, 164, 166, 169, 173, 176, 178–179, 196, 199–201, 221–222, 224, 228, 231, 233–234, 236, 238, 240, 259, 264, 267, 269, 273–274, 278–279, 281, 284–286, 290–292, 298–299, 303, 307, 310
Hero xv, 8, 10, 13, 18, 185, 232, 246, 304, 310, 315–316
Hero's journey 8, 10, 18, 185
Heyoka Merryfield 210, 316
Home 18, 23–24, 30, 32, 35, 37, 48, 50–51, 55, 59, 75–76, 88–89, 101, 103, 105, 109, 111, 114, 118–119, 123, 133, 136, 138, 141, 144, 149, 158, 172–173, 175, 183, 219–220, 224, 226, 230, 235, 239, 250, 258, 260–261, 269, 273, 286–287, 292–296, 299, 303
Human journey 8, 13, 214
Human story viii, 5–6, 10, 18, 43, 61, 129, 177, 233, 247, 255, 296, 299, 306

I
Identity 6, 30, 77, 127, 136–137, 148, 183, 218, 280
Illusion 82, 85, 106, 254
Imaginal cells 127, 129, 161, 179–180, 249

Imagination 22, 25–26, 28, 39, 47, 58–59, 62, 77, 79, 81–82, 96–97, 99, 103, 112, 123, 143, 161, 176, 187, 195, 295–296, 305
Indigenous 10, 27, 221, 250, 257, 263, 278
Initiation 6–7, 10, 14, 44, 60, 128, 137, 158, 176, 305
Instinct 189–190, 210, 226, 247
Integrity 44, 62, 78, 93, 95, 111, 116, 149–150, 158, 161, 185, 233, 305
Interconnection 5, 14, 100, 185, 246, 249, 263, 276, 293, 305
Intimacy 151, 232, 258
Intuition 30, 49, 65, 94, 97, 101–102, 109, 120, 138, 155, 158, 162, 176, 196, 200, 202, 221, 229, 241, 247, 272, 311
Izzy Zephier 262, 284, 313, 316

J
Jesus 205, 274
Journey xv, 5–8, 10–13, 18–19, 25, 37, 43, 46, 50, 70, 85, 123, 127, 129, 131, 136, 140, 155, 159, 165–166, 172, 174, 179, 183–186, 193, 207, 209, 212–214, 216–217, 219–220, 223, 226, 229–233, 235, 241–242, 246, 249–253, 255–256, 260, 266, 268, 270–271, 278, 283–285, 288, 292, 294–295, 298–300, 304, 306–307, 309, 316
Joy xvi, 35–37, 50–51, 53, 98, 101, 104, 106, 111, 119, 145–146, 166, 172, 174, 176–177, 183, 186, 203, 205, 215, 229, 257, 275, 283–284, 291–292, 294, 304

K
Kiva 33–34, 221, 227, 275

L
Lawrence Bloom x, 316
Laurel Elizabeth Keyes 173, 311, 315

Leadership 112–113, 185, 190, 313
Life vii, ix, xiii, xv–xvi, 3, 5–14, 17–19, 21–22, 24, 27–30, 32–34, 36–39, 43–46, 48–51, 53–54, 56, 60–61, 63, 68–71, 75–78, 82, 84–88, 91–93, 96, 98–103, 105–108, 110–113, 115–116, 118–121, 123, 127–131, 133–144, 146–149, 152–153, 155, 158, 160–161, 163–164, 166–167, 169, 171, 174, 176–180, 183–190, 194, 202–203, 206–207, 209, 211, 214–215, 217–219, 222, 225–228, 230–232, 236–238, 241–242, 245–251, 255, 257–259, 261, 265–267, 269–270, 274–277, 280, 282–283, 285–289, 291–292, 294–296, 299–301, 303–307, 309, 311, 316
Light viii, xv, 13, 18, 20, 23, 30–31, 35, 39, 44–45, 50, 71, 75, 78, 85, 98, 110, 123, 130–131, 139, 147, 150–152, 154–155, 160, 177–178, 183, 195, 198–203, 205–206, 208–209, 215, 221, 227, 229, 231, 237, 249, 251, 253, 255–256, 281–284, 289, 292, 299–300, 304–305
Love xiv–xv, 17, 22, 25, 27–28, 30, 32–36, 48, 51, 53, 58, 62–63, 65–69, 80, 83–86, 96, 101–102, 105–106, 122, 127, 132, 136, 138, 144–145, 147–148, 151, 154–155, 157–158, 163–167, 174, 177–179, 185, 188, 190, 195–196, 202–207, 227, 229–230, 232–233, 235–239, 241, 248–249, 251, 253, 257–258, 260, 263, 266, 268–269, 275–276, 278, 282–285, 288, 292–294, 296–297, 300–301, 303–306, 310–311
Love for nothing 257
Lover 23, 63, 85, 101, 155, 175, 294, 296, 300, 311

M

Magic 7, 11, 13, 18, 22–23, 35, 37, 39, 77–79, 99–100, 111, 123, 141, 144, 146, 149, 166, 184, 186, 217, 223, 233, 236, 238, 242, 248, 250, 257, 259, 276–277, 294
Manifesting 7, 254, 296, 304
Mask 5, 44, 84, 88–89, 96, 105, 112, 117, 127, 131, 144, 155, 294
Memories 5, 9, 19, 22, 25, 34, 38, 46, 48, 56–57, 61, 109, 138, 141, 231, 250, 255–256, 266, 280, 311, 315
Metamorphosis 10, 128–131, 136, 149, 160, 179, 183–184, 246, 249–250, 299
Modern mythology 10, 13, 246, 263, 304
More than human 215, 232, 250
Mystery 23, 65, 85, 114, 285
Myth 5, 10, 14, 36, 49, 52–53, 69, 213, 246, 252, 258, 305, 310

N

Narratives 4, 6–7, 11, 13, 19, 43–44, 75, 86, 94, 100, 129, 142, 184, 232, 246, 254, 259, 263, 298, 306
Natural magic 123, 223, 294
Nature 10, 17, 29–30, 39, 46–47, 61, 63, 65, 75–76, 78, 82, 109, 118, 132, 136–137, 140, 145–147, 151, 155, 157, 173, 176, 184–185, 191, 195, 198, 208, 212, 219, 221, 245, 249, 252, 254, 277–278, 286–288, 291, 293, 298, 306, 311–313, 315
Numb 5, 18, 132

O

Old Story 129–130, 166, 184, 225, 241, 271, 296
One vii, xiii, xvi, 4, 6–11, 13–14, 17–21, 23–24, 26, 28–31, 34–35, 37, 43, 48–58, 60, 62–65, 67–71, 77–78, 81, 83–85, 87–88, 90, 93–98, 100,

102–110, 113–115, 118–119, 127–129, 131, 133, 136, 139–140, 142, 144, 147, 149–151, 154–158, 160–161, 163–166, 171–172, 174, 176–178, 183–186, 188–189, 192–193, 195–197, 199, 201, 203, 205, 207, 209–210, 212–213, 215–220, 222–224, 226–228, 231–232, 234, 237–238, 245, 247, 249–252, 257–262, 265, 268–270, 272–273, 276–277, 280, 282–283, 285–286, 289–290, 292–295, 298–300, 304–307

Oneness xiv, 34, 147

Orion 24, 225

P

Pain 18, 31–32, 35–36, 45–46, 50–53, 55–57, 59, 63, 68–69, 81–82, 92, 130–131, 142, 150, 157–158, 177, 232, 259, 263, 271–274, 276, 279, 282, 284, 292, 296, 304

Paradox 10, 12

Patience 162

Pele 232, 235, 237–239

Purpose xv, 5, 8, 18, 37, 45, 87–88, 99–101, 104, 106, 127, 130–131, 133, 148, 174, 176, 179, 186–187, 258, 303, 312

Q

Quest 36, 44, 75, 80, 82, 174, 217, 219–220, 225, 232, 240, 285, 304

R

Re-story 8

Rebekah Shaman 278, 316

Rebel 44, 54, 64–65, 67, 105, 113, 130, 155, 192

Reborn 13, 127, 136, 227, 229, 283–284, 306

Reconnection xv, 6, 173, 184, 222

Reimagining 6

Remember 7, 21–22, 25–27, 29–31, 34–37, 46, 50, 52, 65, 82, 84–85, 89, 101–102, 108, 115, 117, 119–120, 123, 128, 137, 147, 155, 157, 160, 190, 194, 222, 240–241, 264, 266, 277, 293, 299–300

Responsibility 6–7, 11, 14, 45, 93, 96, 100–101, 132, 162, 166, 183, 206, 246–247, 259, 263, 285

Restore 6, 240

Rocky Mountains 22, 35, 209

S

Sacred xvi, 23, 33–34, 60, 70, 83, 85, 173–174, 176, 179, 186, 213, 217, 221, 224, 231–235, 237, 259, 261, 264–265, 284–287, 289, 291, 298, 303, 310, 313, 315–316

Sacred ground 286, 291, 298, 313, 316

Seed of life 10, 18

Senses 45, 80, 138, 144, 157, 188–189, 220, 229, 241, 254

Sensual 63, 78–79, 155

Separation 5, 36, 44, 46, 52, 63, 68–69, 172, 177, 241, 246, 249, 282, 292, 295–296, 298, 304, 306

Sex 62–66, 83, 85, 99, 119, 257

Silence ix, 17, 33, 37, 47, 57, 68–69, 84, 92, 102, 115, 120–121, 132, 151, 155, 158, 173–175, 190, 211, 213, 216, 219, 235–237, 239, 258–260, 264, 268, 274, 280, 286, 288, 290, 292, 300, 305, 310

Socialization 6–7, 43

Soul viii, 7–8, 18–19, 22–23, 30, 33, 35, 37, 48, 50, 53, 61, 63, 70, 76, 78, 82, 84–85, 87, 91, 100, 112, 118, 123, 129, 131, 134, 137–138, 147–149, 154–155, 163–164, 172–173, 176, 179, 187, 202, 206, 228–229, 238, 241, 249–250, 252, 259–262, 279, 282, 284, 286–288, 290, 295, 299, 306, 310, 312, 315–316

Spark vii, xv, 7–8, 10, 17–19, 25, 37–39, 128, 172, 178, 183, 187, 202–203, 220, 234, 246, 249–250, 281–282, 294, 299, 307, 309, 315
Spirit 18, 60, 100, 107, 111, 116, 123, 131, 141, 147, 151, 163, 174, 188, 195–196, 214, 220, 222, 249, 259, 264, 267, 274, 288, 300, 303, 307, 310
Sprucetree 172–176, 178, 207, 212, 214, 231, 296
Star seed 222, 228
Star Wars 23, 50–51, 170–171, 311, 315
Stars 17, 19, 21–25, 34, 79, 109, 153–154, 180, 198, 220, 229–231, 241, 264, 266, 275, 283
Stories vii, xiii, 4–9, 12–13, 18–19, 21–22, 30–31, 38–39, 49, 57, 84, 86, 91, 94, 100, 105, 110, 113, 116, 122, 130, 143, 147–150, 155, 157–160, 178, 183–184, 186, 213, 222, 227–228, 232–233, 242, 251–253, 260–261, 263, 270–271, 304–305, 309
Story of me 6, 299
Story of we 299
Story-making 8, 10, 277
Surrender 129–130, 228, 232, 245–247, 250, 255, 263, 266, 273, 280, 282, 284, 299–301, 304–306
Synchronicity 4, 13, 18, 100, 123, 135, 163, 224, 247, 294, 310

T

Tests xv, 10, 43–45, 53, 57, 61, 70, 76, 123, 141, 249–250, 294, 299
Tough Bliss 123, 131, 284, 304
Transformation xv, 11–12, 21, 45, 129, 131, 137, 159–160, 166, 226, 251, 257, 289–290, 306, 310, 313
Trust ix, 18, 86, 98, 114, 158–159, 169, 188–190, 194, 218, 245–247, 260, 276, 289, 292, 299–300, 307

U

Unconscious 12, 22, 25, 49, 61, 67, 116–117, 130, 160
Unity xiv, xvi, 5, 10, 24, 63, 147, 154, 241, 245–246, 248–251, 261, 265–266, 277, 284, 287, 292–293, 298–300, 305
Universal servant 227
Universe 7, 10, 14, 20, 24, 37, 53–54, 75, 77, 80, 84, 87, 103, 108, 110–111, 117, 123, 127–128, 142, 147, 151, 155, 160, 163, 165–167, 175, 184, 187, 198, 205, 207, 211, 214–215, 218, 220, 224, 228, 231, 238–240, 242, 245–248, 250, 254, 256, 259–260, 276–279, 283, 285, 288, 292–293, 296–297, 299–300, 305–306

V

Vanity 6–7
Vibration 33, 70, 80, 92, 138–139, 153, 199, 205, 214, 265
Victim 90, 115, 129, 246
Vision Quest 217, 219, 225, 232, 240, 285
Vocation 218
Vows 121–122, 234, 236–238
Vulnerability 6–7, 110, 226

W

Walking our talk 11, 116
Wandering 29, 60, 183, 201, 218
Warrior 47, 107, 208, 263, 269, 291
White Buffalo Woman xvi, 290
Wilderness 19, 47, 219, 223
Wisdom xv, 10, 18, 20, 29, 44, 51–52, 96, 121, 142, 144, 171, 173, 175, 178, 184–185, 198, 214, 250, 260, 284, 286, 289, 296, 300, 303

Made in the USA
Columbia, SC
19 January 2018